Cognitive Behaviour Therapy for Obsessive-Compulsive Disorder

Also published by Oxford University Press

Oxford Guide to Low Intensity CBT Interventions
Bennett-Levy, Richards, Farrand, Christensen, Griffiths, Kavangh, Klein, Lau, Proudfoot, Ritterband, Williams, and White

Oxford Guide to Surviving as a CBT Therapist
Mueller, Kennerley, McManus, and Westbrook

Oxford Guide to Metaphors in CBT
Stott, Mansell, Salkovskis, Lavender, and Cartwright-Hatton

Oxford Guide to CBT for People with Cancer, 2e
Moorey and Greer

Oxford Guide to the Treatment of Mental Contamination
Rachman, Coughtrey, Shafran, and Radomsky

Oxford Guide to Behavioural Experiments in Cognitive Therapy
Bennett-Levy, Butler, Fennell, Hackmann, Mueller, and Westbrook

Cognitive Behaviour Therapy for Obsessive-Compulsive Disorder

Victoria Bream

Clinical Psychologist, Centre for Anxiety Disorders and Trauma, South London and Maudsley NHS Foundation Trust, UK

Fiona Challacombe

Clinical Psychologist, Centre for Anxiety Disorders and Trauma, South London and Maudsley NHS Foundation Trust, UK

Asmita Palmer

Clinical Psychologist, Independent Practitioner

Paul Salkovskis

Professor of Clinical Psychology and Applied Science, University of Bath, UK

OXFORD
UNIVERSITY PRESS

OXFORD
UNIVERSITY PRESS

Great Clarendon Street, Oxford, OX2 6DP,
United Kingdom

Oxford University Press is a department of the University of Oxford.
It furthers the University's objective of excellence in research, scholarship,
and education by publishing worldwide. Oxford is a registered trade mark of
Oxford University Press in the UK and in certain other countries

Published in the United States of America by Oxford University Press
198 Madison Avenue, New York, NY 10016, United States of America

British Library Cataloguing in Publication Data
Data available

Library of Congress Control Number: 2017935039

ISBN 978-0-19-870326-6

Oxford University Press makes no representation, express or implied, that the
drug dosages in this book are correct. Readers must therefore always check
the product information and clinical procedures with the most up-to-date
published product information and data sheets provided by the manufacturers
and the most recent codes of conduct and safety regulations. The authors and
the publishers do not accept responsibility or legal liability for any errors in the
text or for the misuse or misapplication of material in this work. Except where
otherwise stated, drug dosages and recommendations are for the non-pregnant
adult who is not breast-feeding

Links to third party websites are provided by Oxford in good faith and
for information only. Oxford disclaims any responsibility for the materials
contained in any third party website referenced in this work.

To Seraphina, Bert, Shackleton, Isabella, Martha, Nikhita, Cora, and Duncan.

Foreword

In the nineteen-fifties psychologists interested in abnormal behaviour began studying obsessive-compulsive problems. In the early stages, attention was focussed on intense repetitive handwashing, which the affected people felt compelled to carry out to remove feelings of contamination. This evidently irrational, abnormal behaviour became the most notable manifestation of a psychological disorder. In succeeding years interest expanded to include compulsive checking and repetitive doubting.

During this period the prevailing 'school' of psychology was Behaviourism, in which exclusive attention was paid to observable behaviour. Compulsive handwashing was certainly that, and psychologists made reasonable progress in developing a technique for reducing this observable problem. It was found that repeated prolonged exposure to the stimuli (contaminants) that set off the washing steadily decreased the compulsive urges providing that the patient was prevented from executing the washing. However, obsessions— recurrent, disturbing intrusive thoughts and images—were outside the scope of a behaviourist approach.

In the nineteen-eighties cognitive ideas were infused into abnormal psychology, and in 1985 Paul Salkovskis presented a cognitive analysis of obsessive-compulsive disorder (OCD) that transformed our understanding of the disorder. It laid the basis for a significant improvement in therapy— behaviour therapy for OCD grew into cognitive behaviour therapy (CBT for OCD). Among other advances, it prepared the ground for an understanding of obsessions—not observable behaviours. In addition, Salkovskis drew attention to the seriously inflated sense of responsibility that afflicts so many patients with OCD.

Unlike most of the other anxiety disorders, there are several different manifestations of OCD. A valuable component of the book is the rich supply of clinical material, and it includes five cases that illustrate some of the varying forms of the disorder: compulsive checking, contamination fears, ruminations, 'not just-right' feelings, and religious obsessions. Mental contamination is a recent addition and includes some surprising variations, such as a fear of morphing, visual contamination, and self-contamination.

Several of the techniques for treating OCDs that are described and explained in this book were devised by Professor Salkovskis, who combines his basic research with an active clinical practice. He is an eminent authority on OCD and other anxiety disorders. The book consists of four sections: a comprehensive account of the disorder, assessment, treatment, and outlook. Given the imprimatur of Paul Salkovskis, it is authoritative, insightful, and comprehensive.

S. J. Rachman

Preface

OCD can have a devastating impact on people's lives—daily struggles with anxiety, an ever-contracting world in terms of freedom, opportunity, and ambition. Effective treatment for OCD can be energizing, radical, and life-changing.

One of the key skills in becoming a competent therapist is 'pattern recognition'—spotting OCD in all its many guises and being able to decipher the relationship between intrusive thoughts, beliefs about and meanings of these intrusions, and maintaining factors such as safety-seeking behaviours. The examples given in this volume are a broad representation of people with OCD with different features in terms of the content of thoughts and behaviours. The disparate examples also reveal the common themes in OCD—appraising thoughts as signalling threat, an inflated sense of responsibility linked to that, related beliefs in the over-importance of thoughts, and the subsequent 'logical' responses to this belief—behaviours intended to reduce the potential for harm; attention and reasoning biases that reinforce the meaning; and automatic responses of anxiety, dread, or guilt. As treatment unfolds for each individual described, the careful application of empirically grounded techniques starts with empathic engagement and continues with skilful interweaving of discussion of past experience, metaphor, and guided discovery related to both past and new experiences alongside a genuine belief that this problem can be overcome.

Core therapeutic competencies for OCD have been identified (Roth and Pilling, 2007), albeit mainly derived from exposure and response prevention (ERP). The theoretical model and treatment approach described in this volume is the version of cognitive behavioural treatment incorporating ERP devised and adapted by Paul Salkovskis with input from an array of colleagues, including the coauthors of this book. These and other competences and metacompetences are addressed within this version of the cognitive behavioural model and the treatment directly derived from it.

Reference

Roth, A. D. & Pilling, S. (2007). *The Competences Required to Deliver Effective Cognitive and Behavioural Therapy for People with Depression and with Anxiety Disorders*. London: Department of Health.

Acknowledgements

Our greatest thanks go to those inspirational and courageous people we have met who have stood up to OCD and undertaken the treatment described.

Many thanks to our past and present colleagues from the Centre for Anxiety Disorders and Trauma at the Maudsley Hospital, Bath University, Oxford University, and elsewhere. To name but a few: Linda Atkinson, David M Clark, Alicia Deale, Liz Forrester, Mark Freeston, James Gregory, Nick Grey, Brynjar Halldórsson, Alice Kerr, Osamu Kobori, Claire Lomax, Olivia Gordon, Hjalti Jónsson, Joy Mcguire, Jack Rachman, Alison Roberts, Roz Shafran, Blake Stobie, Tracey Taylor, David Veale, and Abi Wroe.

We are indebted to Alison Roberts, Chris Irons, and Joe Poole for their feedback.

Table of contents

Chapter 1

Before you meet someone with obsessive-compulsive disorder: understanding the problem

Helping people who suffer from obsessive-compulsive disorder (OCD) is a complicated and rewarding task. To be able to really help, it is crucial for the therapist to be able to think clearly about the problem and how it affects the person, and then, through careful and active listening, begin to reach an understanding of his or her experience. The aim of such understanding is not only for the therapist to be able to make sense of what is happening, but also to help the person feel understood in a way that can evolve into the shared understanding that forms the basis of treatment itself, grounded in mutual trust and respect. In the sections that follow, we summarize key aspects of such understanding from psychological and other perspectives, including selected research evidence, which can and should be usefully shared with those with OCD.

1.1 What is OCD … and what does it look like?

'Did I leave the gas on?'   'Image of sex with my boss'

'Stabbing a baby'   'This doesn't feel right'   'Did I lock it?'

'I'm going to say "fuck" in church'   'I might catch AIDS'

The current diagnostic criteria for OCD listed in ICD-10 (*International Statistical Classification of Diseases and Related Health Problems*, the diagnostic manual of the World Health Organization; WHO, 2014) state that:

'the essential feature is recurrent obsessional thoughts or compulsive acts. Obsessional thoughts are ideas, images or impulses that enter the patient's mind again and again in a stereotyped form. They are almost invariably distressing and the patient often tries, unsuccessfully to resist them. They are however, recognized as his or her own thoughts even though they are involuntarily and often repugnant. Compulsive acts or rituals are stereotyped behaviors that are repeated again and again. They are not inherently enjoyable, nor do they result in the completion of inherently useful tasks. Their function is to prevent some objectively unlikely event, often involving harm to or caused by the patient, which he or she fears might not otherwise occur. Usually this behavior is recognised as pointless or ineffectual and repeated attempts are made to resist. Anxiety is almost invariably present.'

DSM-V (*Diagnostic and Statistical Manual of Mental Disorders*, fifth edition), the manual of the American Psychiatric Association (2013), provides a broadly similar definition.

Although this way of describing OCD can be helpful as an 'operational definition' and generally orienting to the phenomenology, it has some shortcomings in terms of helping us to understand the lived experience of OCD and the mechanisms involved. An alternative way of understanding obsessional problems is to take a more directly phenomenological view—how is OCD experienced by the person and his or her loved ones? Towards this end, we introduce five case descriptions that represent common presentations of OCD; we will use these examples to illustrate key points and then, in the rest of this book, follow them through treatment:

WALTER: 'It all started with the newspaper reports of these police investigations into abuse. It disgusts me to think of these childhood heroes and what they were up to all along. Then there've been a few cases of people being accused and it turning out that they were innocent. Now that's scary! That's how this problem started. I'm terrified that maybe I've done something in the past that I didn't mean to or didn't realize it was abuse. I'm worried that one of my old pupils is going to come out of the woodwork and tell the police about something I've done. It got me thinking "what if I was accused?" I can't bear it—it feels like my life is over. It's only a matter of time before the police come knocking on the door. Sometimes I wonder whether it would be better to end it all before that happens. At least I'd spare my family the shame and humiliation.' (OCD characterized by rumination.)

LYDIA: 'I think people would be really surprised to know I have a problem. I'm quite outgoing and confident, except when the problem is really bothering me. I have lived with it for such a long time that it's really a part of who I am. I guess I've got used to the fact it can take a few hours of my time each day. I have got my checking routine down to an art—I need to check things in groups of threes, sometimes 3×3×3. I focus as much as I can on what I'm doing and count aloud to keep track of where I am in the sequence. I get really annoyed with my husband Mike if he interrupts me when I'm trying to do my checks as then it takes much longer. I suppose it's not his fault, although it is very upsetting when I'm in the middle of it.' (OCD characterized by checking.)

SAUL: 'I've always been one for having things "just so" and liking things ordered and tidy. I remember as a child there was no way that I would wear odd socks, and I never liked being messy. I can always remember having the feeling that if I didn't do things the right way that something bad would happen but it used to be just a passing feeling of anxiety. Once I left home and started having more responsibilities, I noticed more and more that I had to do things in a particular way. My family and friends know that I have "my ways" and they don't say much; I feel so guilty as I know that they are worried about me as I'm always so stressed and tired. I don't think I'll lose my job as most of the time I do it really well, but I worry that if I got another more demanding job I'd get more stressed and I wouldn't be able to do it. I'd really like to study and become a fitness instructor, but I feel quite stuck. I don't even get the chance to go to the gym as I'm too exhausted; also, I started having to do things in a "just-so" way there and I feel too embarrassed to go back.' (OCD characterized by 'not just-right experiences'.)

JESSIE: 'My husband tells me I'm paranoid about germs but I'm just doing everything I can to protect our baby. It was such a struggle to get pregnant after lots of IVF treatment that I can't allow anything to go wrong. He doesn't seem to understand that, while I'm pregnant, it's down to me to make sure the baby is okay. I had no idea of all the things that you have to be careful about. I'd never heard of toxoplasmosis until one of the mums at my antenatal group told me about it. Since then I'm extra careful around cats. I won't visit my sister any more because she has a cat. I had a blazing row with my husband yesterday for leaving the kitchen window open—I just don't understand how he can be so careless when he knows the neighbors have a cat and it could easily get in.' (OCD characterized by contamination fears.)

JANE: 'I've always been quite observant of my faith, but over the years it has just intensified. I am now attending church every day and sometimes twice a day if possible. But I can't do anything without a thought popping up that I'm not doing things in the right way. It's really getting me down. It's hard to be present in the moment, even when I'm with my children and husband. But if I let myself focus on it, the panic rises that I may be damned. I've had this problem for a really long time and have had so many therapists. I really don't know what to do anymore.' (OCD characterized by religious obsessions and compulsions.)

Despite the variety in their experiences, Walter, Lydia, Saul, Jessie, and Jane all suffer from common forms of OCD. Two sets of factors unite their experience. The first is experiential factors; that is, the distress, disability, and human cost resulting from their experiences and the difficulty they have in dismissing their thoughts or changing the behaviours which interfere with their day-to-day functioning. The second is the mechanisms that underpin and maintain the obsessional problems in terms of perception of threat and responsibility for harm and directly related attempts to seek safety; we will identify these later. Keeping these descriptions of both the form and perceived function of obsessions and compulsions in mind will help make the problem begin to feel understandable within a cognitive-behavioural framework. On this basis, we can define obsessions and compulsions thus:

> Obsessions: recurrent thoughts, images, impulses, or doubts that create awareness of the potential for danger which the person can cause or prevent.

> Compulsions: actions or reactions that are intended by the person experiencing obsessions both to prevent the danger of which the obsession has created awareness and to diminish responsibility for its occurrence, or to undo or neutralize things which may have already happened.

As OCD develops, the focus of compulsions may become increasingly directed towards achieving 'just-right' feelings; such feelings are sought as a means of achieving certainty regarding both threat and responsibility. Reducing anxiety is often a secondary intention, but only where this does not interfere with the overriding intention of preventing a feared outcome for which the person regards himself or herself as responsible. It is not unusual for the performance of compulsive behaviours to be accompanied by *increased* anxiety or other feelings of discomfort.

Distress: obsessions that create an awareness of potential danger typically provoke discomfort and distress, which can take several forms depending on the focus of threat; most typically, but not invariably, this is experienced as anxiety. If the threat is perceived as being in the future anxiety is most likely, whereas worries concerning both recent and more distant past events tend to elicit depression, guilt, and shame. Although seldom mentioned, anger can also be an emotional response, often to the horror of the person experiencing it.

Although compulsions are not usually perceived as the primary source of distress, because they increasingly interfere with the person's life and relationships they often begin to cause a range of emotions, particularly depression, self-criticism, shame, and anger directed towards the self or others. In fact, it is the attempts to deal with fears (washing, checking, and neutralizing) that typically cause the most interference in the person's life. As described in Section 3.2, what happens is that, for the affected person, the solution becomes the problem.

1.2 Normal phenomena related to OCD

Before seeking to understand OCD as a clinical problem, we consider it important to place it in the context of normal experiences and psychological processes. This is not merely an academic exercise, but an integral part of both generating a shared understanding and formulating the subsequent treatment. The thoughts at the beginning of the chapter were reported by a sample of people who *did not have OCD*. An absolutely crucial study by Rachman and de Silva (Rachman and de Silva, 1978) asked a community sample about the occurrence of unwanted and unacceptable intrusions. They found that 79.9% of non-clinical participants reported obsessions, and that, in terms of content, these could not be distinguished from obsessional thoughts reported by a parallel clinical sample. This finding was subsequently replicated by Salkovskis and Harrison in 1984, who found that 88.2% of their non-clinical sample experienced obsessions. Salkovskis (personal communication) sought to interview those who reported not experiencing intrusions but none agreed to be interviewed, suggesting that social desirability factors may be operating. Certainly a rate of 99% was reported in a student sample by Freeston *et al.*, 1991. Therefore we can say with confidence that intrusive thoughts of *all types,* including those that often characterize OCD, occur in the vast majority of people and probably in all. However, it is also obvious that most people do not have OCD and therefore are likely to be reacting differently in terms of their emotional and behavioural responses. This notion is central to the cognitive understanding of OCD described by Salkovskis (1985), and is developed more fully in Section 1.8 as underpinning cognitive-behavioural therapy (CBT) treatment.

1.3 How common is clinical OCD and what are the main types?

Some early epidemiological studies suggested that OCD may be common in the general population, but this was almost certainly a consequence of screening measures prone to false positives. A particularly well conducted UK-based study (Torres *et al.*, 2006) found relatively low rates of OCD of around 1.2%, matching a similar figure of 1.1% from a large and robust US study (Ruscio *et al.*, 2010; Torres *et al.*, 2006). One of the lessons from this apparent disparity with early studies is that OCD is not a qualitatively distinct syndrome, with its diagnosis almost certainly more dependent on the level of disability and interference required rather than the pattern of symptomatology. On this basis, the lifetime prevalence of OCD (according to DSM-IV criteria, revised in 1994) has been estimated at between 0.5% and 3.5%. OCD is slightly more prevalent overall in women than men (1.44:1) (Torres *et al.*, 2006). Women seem to be about one-and-a-half to two times more likely than men to meet criteria for OCD in their lifetime (Angst *et al.*, 2004; Karno *et al.*, 1988). However, these ratios appear to be age-dependent, with there being evidence that males may account for more cases occurring before the age of 10 (Ruscio *et al.*, 2010). Later peaks of incidence have been found in females (Nestadt *et al.*, 1998).

Although cross-cultural comparisons have been made showing OCD to have a consistent prevalence across cultures (Weissman *et al.*, 1994), OCD appears to be less common in minority groups within a particular culture, although this may be a matter of stigma in reporting symptoms (Karno *et al.*, 1988).

Within the broader category of diagnosis, the form and content of obsessions and compulsions are many and varied, and OCD is often regarded as a very heterogeneous disorder. This has led researchers to examine whether there are meaningful subtypes of the disorder, which may enable a better understanding of its causes and consequences. Factor analytic approaches using large surveys of reported symptoms have led to the proposal of broad categories or subtypes of symptoms that may have different implications for causation and treatment. For example, Mataix-Cols and colleagues reviewed factor analytic studies of OCD dimensions and outlined four symptom dimensions (symmetry/ordering, hoarding, contamination/cleaning, and obsessions/checking). They argued that these subtypes were associated with distinct patterns of comorbidity, genetic transmission, neural substrates, and treatment response (Mataix-Cols *et al.*, 2005). Obsessional hoarding is the only subgroup related to OCD that the evidence strongly suggests is different from other presentations.

Until recently considered as a part of OCD (Pertusa *et al.*, 2010; Seaman *et al.*, 2010), in general hoarding has been found to differ on a number of phenomenological and outcome variables, leading to its new status as a stand-alone disorder in DSM-V (American Psychiatric Association, 2013; Mataix-Cols *et al.*, 2010). It will not be discussed extensively in this volume (for information on threat-related hoarding see Section 4.1). Otherwise, for OCD subtypes the similarities in terms of underpinning psychological processes (rather than symptom 'constellations') are greater than the differences.

Although, according to current diagnostic definitions, it is possible to be troubled by obsessions or compulsions alone (Torres *et al.*, 2006), the vast majority of people with OCD appear to experience both (Foa and Kozak, 1995). We consider that, in OCD, obsessions and compulsions always coexist, but that assessors may fail to identify the 'missing' aspect of OCD (for example, not identifying the difference between intrusive thoughts (obsessions) and subsequent rumination related to the appraisal of the thoughts (compulsions) (see Salkovskis and Westbrook, 1989). Similarly, some people present with compulsions seemingly in the absence of intrusions and negative meanings, which may be teased out in the process of assessment and formulation; as described in Section 2, this is particularly likely in more chronic cases with very frequent and demanding compulsive behaviour. In addition, for many individuals the co-occurrence of symptoms in a number of different categories is not uncommon, and categorization into distinct groups may be difficult. Of participants in a recent study, 26% could not be readily classified into one of the subgroups described by Mataix-Cols *et al.* (Matsunaga *et al.*, 2010). The disorder can therefore present with a wide variety of symptoms, even within the individual at a single timepoint. However, although this might seem bewildering for the treating therapist, it appears that there is a common phenomenology across OCD 'subtypes' which corresponds to shared psychological processes. Understanding this will help you and the person with OCD to deal with what is essentially the same problem in all its different guises.

1.4 **Common presentations of OCD**

1.4.1 **Contamination fears**

Contamination-focussed OCD is one of the most well known forms of OCD, owing to its high prevalence (about 25–50% of people with OCD) (Ruscio *et al.*, 2010; Rasmussen and Eisen, 1990; Rasmussen and Eisen, 1992) and the obvious behavioural impact of the problem in the form of extensive washing, cleaning, and avoidance. 'Contamination' can encompass a wide range of specific fears, which may be culturally, situationally, or historically influenced, such as the fear of contact with and/or the risk of passing on germs and disease, typically those that are the focus of fears at any given historical moment. This can be non-specific ('harmful germs') or a range of diseases which represent the current invisible menace, such as HIV, swine flu, toxoplasmosis, or Ebola. Poisons and toxins that are hard to detect can also form the focus of fears; examples would be asbestos, bleach, and carcinogens. Recently, the idea of 'mental contamination' (contamination without physical contact with, or transmission of, substances) has been highlighted; that is, the possibility of being contaminated by or absorbing negative characteristics of particular people or types of people (see Section 4.3). In contamination OCD, contamination is perceived as dangerous, contagious, and possessing an intensity which does not decay even over very long periods of time.

Emotional responses to perceived contaminants include both fear and disgust, with the latter increasingly recognized as an important component. Experimental research has indicated that disgust may take longer to decay than anxiety responses (McKay, 2006). Both disgust and fear can contribute to emotional reasoning that reinforces the fear (Verwoerd *et al.*, 2013; Rachman *et al.*, 2015); that is, the experience of the negative emotions is seen as proof that something bad really is happening (see Section 1.8.1). This remains controversial, however, with there being evidence that anxiety may increase disgust, but that disgust may not substantially increase anxiety (Edwards & Salkovskis, 2006), suggesting that disgust may not be a primary factor in contamination fears, but rather a complication that needs to be considered.

Contamination OCD is sometimes thought to have the greatest effect on families and people living with sufferers (Albert *et al.*, 2010a; Stewart *et al.*, 2008), probably because of its pervasiveness. Others are often required to strive for and follow the same standards of cleanliness as the sufferer, although the lack of shared beliefs driving contamination fears inevitably leads to failure and frequently leads to conflict or stress.

1.4.2 Checking and other forms of verification

The function of checking is to make sure that something did or did not happen, or that particular things are a certain way (verification). For some people it is a particularly prominent behaviour, and OCD revolving around harm avoidance/checking has been suggested as characterizing a distinct subtype (Mataix-Cols *et al.*, 2005). Epidemiological data suggests that checking is the most common form of compulsion (Rasmussen and Eisen, 1992; Ruscio *et al.*, 2010). Checking can take an extremely wide range of forms, including but not confined to simply looking to see the state of an object, repeating actions, mental rehearsal, seeking reassurance, and so on.

1.4.3 Rumination

OCD featuring 'only' thoughts without overt compulsions is common, and has been labelled by some people with OCD as a particular subtype (pure 'O'). However, both intrusive thoughts themselves and the responses to intrusive thoughts are probably invariably present (Salkovskis *et al.*, 1997), and include mental rituals and checking, mental argument, neutralizing 'bad' thoughts with 'good' ones (e.g. use of prayer to counter religious contraventions)—so it is likely that 'pure O is seldom so'. The content of intrusive thoughts or doubts that provoke subsequent rumination can be anything that is taboo or otherwise runs contrary to the values of the individual, such as sexual, violent, or blasphemous thoughts, or perceived carelessness/irresponsibility in those who regard these as unacceptable.

Religious OCD (also known as scrupulosity) often falls under the broader category of rumination type OCD, and may have been the most pervasive form of OCD historically (Rachman and Hodgson, 1980); for example, the problems experienced by Martin Luther in the sixteenth century. The construct of scrupulosity, whilst being one of the earliest recognized forms of OCD, is not clearly defined and can include only obsessions and compulsions unique to specific religious doctrine (e.g. eternal damnation, violation of ritual purity laws) or be much broader to include a more general fear of the moral consequences of actions (Nelson *et al.*, 2006). The core fear across religions within scrupulosity is related to a fear of sinning, often revolving around the observance of religious rituals or applying religious laws in other contexts of life. The specifics are indicated by the particular religion and/or moral stance of the person. There is some evidence that this type of OCD may be particularly common in societies in which religious beliefs and values (rather than overt observance) are particularly strong (Radomsky *et al.*, 2014).

1.4.4 **Symmetry and ordering**

Symmetry and ordering are well recognized features of OCD (e.g. Pietrefesa and Coles, 2009). In addition to physically lining up items or performing actions in a certain order, ordering can manifest in mental rituals; for example, having silently to count the corners of all the windows in a room. As with other presentations of OCD, these urges to do things in a certain way are conceptualized as unwanted intrusions, particularly in terms of doubt, that are appraised in a negative/threat-related way, generating anxiety and safety-seeking behaviours (SSBs). What can be distinctive about ordering compulsions is that the desired outcome is a 'just-right' feeling (Coles *et al.*, 2003). As discussed in Section 1.8.7, this can be conceptualized in terms of seeking certainty (Wahl *et al.*, 2008). Ordering can also be driven by 'magical thinking' (e.g. Einstein and Menzies, 2004), i.e. the idea that, if items are not ordered, something bad will happen as a result; 'magical thinking' may well not differ from worrying about highly improbable concerns, as occurs across obsessional symptoms. Symmetry and ordering have been associated with earlier onset and therefore greater chronicity in those with adult OCD (Kichuk *et al.*, 2013). Sometimes this has been referred to as 'not just-right' feelings; we consider it to be the striving for (and failing to achieve) 'just-right' feelings. This is most likely a consequence of operating 'elevated evidence requirements'. That is, because the person with OCD fears being responsible for serious harm to themselves or others, they strive to be *completely certain* that things are safe/complete/clean. The feeling of things being 'just right' or a positive mood are striven for as a marker that this is so. However, the endless effort to achieve such feelings is counterproductive, leading to endless striving and compulsions.

1.5 **The impact of OCD**

OCD can be a particularly severe and disabling problem. Studies examining the impact on individuals have frequently found a severe impact on quality of life in individuals with OCD (Albert *et al.*, 2010b; Bobes *et al.*, 2001; Subramaniam *et al.*, 2012), although unfortunately all anxiety disorders can have a significant impact on quality of life, particularly in mental health and social functioning (Olatunji *et al.*, 2007). Torres *et al.* (2006) noted some specific impairments in OCD relative to people diagnosed as having other anxiety disorders. People with OCD were less likely to be married, more likely to be unemployed, were more likely to subsist on very low incomes, and were more likely to have low occupational status. They were also more likely to report impaired social and occupational functioning (Torres *et al.*, 2006). Torres *et al.* (2006) describe OCD as 'a rare yet severe mental disorder … an atypical neurosis', 'sometimes reaching a level of impairment comparable to that seen in psychotic disorders' (Torres and Prince, 2006). Subramaniam *et al.* (2012) found that, overall, 'patients with OCD scored better on quality of life domains than people with major depressive disorder; however, they show no difference or score worse than patients with schizophrenia'. Some studies have found that self-rated impairments in some domains of quality of life (psychological wellbeing and social relationships) were worse than in a group of people with schizophrenia and depression (Bobes *et al.*, 2001; Stengler-Wenzke *et al.*, 2006b). Torres *et al.* (2006) found that OCD is associated with more comorbidity and more marked social and occupational impairment than the common mental disorders with which it is often grouped.

Unsurprisingly, greater symptom severity has been associated with poorer quality of life in OCD (Eisen *et al.*, 2006; Fontenelle *et al.*, 2010; Rosa *et al.*, 2012). Eisen *et al.* (2006) suggest that a Yale–Brown Obsessive Compulsive Scale (YBOCS; a clinical scale used in many treatment trials) score of at least 20 was associated with significant decline in quality of life compared with those with lower scores still over the clinical threshold (a YBOCS score of 8 or above). A longer duration of the illness has also been related to a greater impact on quality of life (Dell'Osso *et al.*, 2013).

Another marker of the severity of the illness is the finding that 25.7% of those with OCD in the British comorbidity survey had attempted suicide, while 63.3% had experienced suicidal thoughts (Torres *et al.*, 2006). Similarly, Torres *et al.* (2011) reported that 36% of their sample had experienced lifetime suicidal thoughts, 20% had made plans, and 10% had made attempts. However, this level of suicidality has not been found in all studies (Alonso *et al.*, 2010).

Unfortunately the impairments in quality of life can outlast symptom reduction in OCD (Srivastava *et al.*, 2011). Although treatment improved quality of life, those in remission had scores falling between those of people with current OCD and healthy controls (Huppert *et al.*, 2009), not differing significantly from the comparison groups. This will be discussed in Section 1.9, but probably represents 'collateral damage', where the extent of the person's OCD, typically reaching high levels of severity in the late teens and early 20s, interferes with crucial aspects of personal development such as education, employment, and relationships in ways which persist beyond the symptoms of OCD.

OCD is thus known to curtail the life trajectory of individuals and prevent them trying to achieve their goals, sometimes because of direct interference from the disorder but also because of the impact of beliefs associated with the disorder, such as lack of self-efficacy. These beliefs and general sequelae may persist beyond treatment; simply speaking, the damage caused by a prolonged period of OCD may not be fully reversible, e.g. employment, education, relationships, childbearing. Further, even the experience of having been a sufferer can have an ongoing influence on self-perception, and fears of relapse can persist. The symptoms may cause irreparable damage that continues to reverberate for some time, such as the impact from divorce or separation owing to the demands of the problem (Goodwin *et al.*, 2002; Subramaniam *et al.*, 2012), or consequences of the decision not to have children because of OCD when biologically able (Neziroglu *et al.*, 1992). In treatment this needs to be acknowledged, especially when it is experienced as feelings of grief for the loss.

1.6 **Impact on families**

OCD affects not only the person with OCD but those around them and, given the pervasive nature of the problem across situations, the impact on family members is often great (Albert *et al.*, 2007; Angermeyer *et al.*, 2006; Black *et al.*, 1998; Cicek *et al.*, 2013; Grover and Dutt, 2011; Laidlaw *et al.*, 1999; Stengler-Wenzke *et al.*, 2006a). The impact on family members can be indirect (for example, developing psychological problems as a result of worrying about their loved one) or direct by involvement in the symptoms (for example, by giving reassurance or following obsessional rules). More detail about some of the specific issues that affect families and how to work with them is provided in Section 4.4.

1.7 **What causes OCD?**

As a therapist working with OCD you *will* get asked this question. It is understandable that people want to know the reasons why they are experiencing something that causes them distress and disability; in many cases this may help us solve the problem. However, as with all psychological disorders, there are no simple answers and still plenty of questions, and the correct answer is simply 'no-one knows'. Furthermore, understanding the causes of a problem such as OCD, even if possible, may do little to advance our understanding of how to deal with it when someone has developed the problem. The main areas of influence thought to impact on the development of OCD are biological/genetic influences, learned behaviours and beliefs, social context, and triggering incidents. In terms of treatment, there are really only two evidence-based options, which are pharmacotherapy and CBT, with pharmacotherapy being at best weakly based in biological theory and CBT being more firmly rooted in behavioural and cognitive-behavioural theory. Given the focus of this book, we will briefly review biological approaches before turning to a more detailed examination of the cognitive behavioural understanding.

The theoretical approaches developed in three main areas: genetics, neuroanatomy, and neuropharmacology. Each is discussed in the next sections.

1.7.1 Biology: genetics

Most biological approaches to the understanding of OCD are based on the assumption that it is a neuropsychiatric disease, something which is very much in doubt. Overall, genetic studies indicate a largely non-specific heritability for anxiety disorders, with a high degree of comorbidity between anxiety disorders and with other mood disorders (Kendler *et al.*, 1995; Middeldorp *et al.*, 2005; Trzaskowski *et al.*, 2012; van Grootheest *et al.*, 2007). In other words, there may be some tendency towards anxiety that runs in families, although this is probably only slight.

The raised familial prevalence of OCD in many studies has led to a search to identify specific genetic factors that may be involved; note, however, that there are conditions which may lead clinicians to place too much weight on such factors to the detriment of their patients (Rimes and Salkovskis, 1998). Studies have reported a high heritability for OCD-related behaviours in children (Bolton *et al.*, 2007; Eley *et al.*, 2003) compared with, for example, a 73% heritability estimate for separation anxiety disorder in children (Bolton *et al.*, 2006). However, it has been difficult to determine a specific heritability or genetic locus for OCD, possibly owing to varied methodological approaches (lack of standardized diagnostic criteria, small sample sizes, lack of blind assessments, assessment of obsessional symptoms rather than diagnosed OCD), and the complexity and heterogeneity of the illness itself (Pauls and Alsobrook, 1999). In addition, the picture is also complicated by a high level of comorbidity, particularly with other anxiety and mood disorders in people with OCD, and the finding that relatives also display a higher number of a range of other psychiatric disorders. Put differently, the failure to identify an appropriate and reliable phenotype means that there is little chance of identifying a genotype even if it exists.

Despite a proliferation of studies, genetic approaches have not so far identified consistent candidate genes in OCD (Liu *et al.*, 2013; Pauls, 2010; Stewart *et al.*, 2013; Taylor, 2013). Over 80 candidate genes have been identified, with none so far reaching genome-wide significance and only one being replicated. Genes related to serotonin regulation have been more consistently implicated, although mechanisms remain unclear and this is unlikely to be specific to OCD (Lin, 2007; Taylor, 2013). Genetics are likely to be involved in a complex interplay with other genes, epigenetic effects, and environmental factors (Iervolino *et al.*, 2011; Pauls, 2010; Taylor, 2011).

Some researchers have proposed that some 'subtypes' of OCD are more influenced by genetic factors, in particular 'early-onset' OCD, with both obsessive compulsive behaviours and OCD under strong genetic influence (Bolton *et al.*, 2007). Conversely, later onset OCD may be more accountable to environmental stress (Millet *et al.*, 2004; Rea *et al.*, 2011). However, such results may have more to do with the preconceptions of those conducting the studies than any real effect. OCD is a heterogeneous entity and it may be that particular symptom presentations such as ordering are more influenced by genetic factors (Hanna *et al.*, 2005). Other types of symptoms, such as checking, washing, and obsessional symptoms, may be more related to belief domains, which could be more environmentally influenced (Rea *et al.*, 2011). Moreover, those with early or later onset of symptoms have been shown to have no differences in response to psychological treatment (Lomax *et al.*, 2009).

It should also be noted that most OCD is sporadic; that is, it occurs in people who do not have first-degree relatives who suffer from the condition. The identification of people in the extended family with OCD or 'OCD traits', as is often done, is massively prone to confirmatory bias. Leaving aside the negative impact of labelling psychiatric problems as 'biological' (Lam and Salkovskis, 2007), there is no obvious value in offering biological explanations to those who suffer from OCD.

1.7.2 Memory and neuropsychological deficit theories

Various suggestions have been made regarding the role of memory in OCD. In terms of face validity, the 'specific and direct memory deficit' account is the most obvious. According to this view, those who check have deficits in memory manifest as impaired verbal and visual recall, and recall of actions. Compulsive checking can thus be accounted for by an understandable effort to compensate for poor memory (Ecker and Engelkamp, 1995; Sher *et al.*, 1983). If you really have poor memory and are aware of it, then it would be reasonable to seek to counteract this by repeating and/or checking. The 'non-specific and indirect memory' account suggests that memory deficits are rather like brain scan results: they are neuropsychological markers of brain lesions (Savage *et al.*, 1996), and the memory problems are not directly involved in OCD symptoms such as checking.

Thus far, there has been an almost complete failure to identify any actual neuropsychological impairment (Constans *et al.*, 1995; Cougle *et al.*, 2007; Hermans *et al.*, 2003; Moritz *et al.*, 2009a; Tolin *et al.*, 2001). Radomsky and Rachman (1999) found people with OCD to have significantly *better* memory in OCD-relevant situations. In addition, poor confidence in memory has been consistently found in OCD patients relative to both healthy and anxious controls (Constans *et al.*, 1995; Cougle *et al.*, 2007; Ecker and Engelkamp, 1995; Hermans *et al.*, 2003; McNally and Kohlbeck, 1993) and non-action visual memory tasks (MacDonald *et al.*, 1997; Tallis *et al.*, 1999; Tolin *et al.*, 2001). Woods *et al.* (2002) note that poor memory confidence is a particularly robust finding amongst people with OCD who check, and carries larger effect sizes across studies than the effect sizes among studies of memory deficits.

There is a third alternative, which is that people with OCD mistakenly believe themselves to have poor memory, leading to checking and repeating (Cougle *et al.*, 2007). *Perceived* memory deficits would operate by leading the person with OCD to use counterproductive 'compensatory' strategies, which actually have the effect of maintaining or further decreasing the illusion of poor memory. This links to cognitive theory because appraisal of intrusive thoughts in terms of responsibility for harm has the effect of making the person with OCD particularly fearful of the consequence of memory failure, leading them to 'try too hard' to be sure that an action has been completed, which leads to lowered confidence in memory. People with OCD may mentally rehearse previous actions, seeking a vivid recollection; this type of checking is likely to progressively reduce confidence in their recollections. We conclude that memory is relevant to the understanding and treatment of OCD, but not in terms of any structural abnormality, more in terms of the adverse effects of 'trying too hard' and the way this impacts on confidence in memory.

1.7.3 Neuropharmacology: the myth of the biochemical imbalance

It is common to see and hear mental health professionals describing the cause of OCD in terms of a 'biochemical imbalance'. It is worth noting that the term itself makes no sense in terms of either psychology or brain science (Lilienfeld *et al.*, 2015), but tends to be used to suggest some abnormality of neurotransmitter regulation. These approaches have focussed on one particular neurotransmitter, serotonin (5-hydroxytryptamine; 5-HT), not for a priori theoretical reasons but because of a pragmatic finding from Fernandez and Lopez-Ibor (1967), which was taken up later by Rapoport (Rapoport *et al.*, 1989), who noted the effectiveness of the serotonin active tricyclic antidepressant, clomipramine, relative to tricyclics, which did not substantially impact on serotonin. This led to the so-called serotonin hypothesis; initially, it was suggested that there was a gross deficit in serotonin; when this was not identified, increasingly subtle abnormalities were suggested, with the evidence overall remaining implausible at best. Because serotonin is somewhat important in the orbital frontal cortex and the basal ganglia, this view has become linked to theories suggesting structural abnormalities. Pharmacological challenge studies have failed to find any consistent abnormalities. Gross *et al.* (1998) argue that the most robust evidence for the serotonin hypothesis is the specificity of Serotonin reuptake inhibitors (SRI) and selective serotonin reuptake inhibitor (SSRI) medication. However, given that this effect was the observation that generated the hypothesis, it cannot reasonably be considered as evidence for it. The fact that serotonin-active medication is also effective across the range of anxiety disorders, depression, eating disorders, and so on suggests that there is little, if any, specificity. One of the more interesting psychopharmacological findings is the rapid and substantial relapse associated with the tapering and discontinuation of SRIs and SSRIs; this seems to be greater than in other disorders treated by this class of drugs. It is unclear why this should be so. Overall, there is a place for SRIs and SSRIs in the treatment of more severe OCD (Skapinakis *et al.*, 2016) provided that evidence is shared as part of informed patient choice. Combination treatments may be slightly helpful for some people with OCD, although discontinuation issues have yet to be fully addressed.

1.7.4 Brain lesion theories: the magic of the brain image

There have been a number of suggestions regarding structural brain problems; one of the most widely adopted is the orbitofrontal–subcortical hypothesis, which suggests that obsessional symptoms are associated with abnormalities in information processing related to neural networks in the orbitofrontal cortex and basal ganglia and thalamus, the orbitofrontal–subcortical circuit. These areas are believed to be involved in the control of thought and action. Although very inconsistent, brain imaging studies sometimes detect abnormalities, both structurally and functionally, in these areas. The most consistent findings concern abnormalities in the brain activity in the frontal lobe (Cottraux and Gerard, 1998). Swedo *et al.* (1992) used positron emission tomography (PET) to assess bloodflow in patients with OCD before and after they received drug treatment, and again 1 year later, noting that improvement in obsessional symptoms was correlated with a reduction in the activity of the orbitofrontal cortex. Despite very extensive research on structural and functional brain imaging, there have been no consistent findings that illuminate OCD. We conclude that, given the volume of research over several decades, it is unlikely that there are any gross abnormalities of brain structure. We also believe that, to propagate such theories as anything other than speculation, is potentially harmful as there is evidence that both those who suffer mental health problems and the public are negatively affected by biological accounts of psychiatric problems (Lam and Salkovskis, 2007; Lam *et al.*, 2005).

1.7.5 **Schizophrenia: 'mad ideas'**

From time to time, a link between OCD and schizophrenia has been proposed, starting with the Freudian view that OCD symptoms were a defence mechanism against 'weak ego boundaries', with the suggestion that to remove such symptoms would result in the contents of the id spilling over into the ego in an uncontrolled way, producing psychosis. In particular, compulsions were regarded as important in this respect, leading to historical advice not to interrupt or discourage them. The fact that exposure and response prevention (ERP) is so very effective without psychosis breaking out is, in our view, conclusive evidence that this view is mistaken. However, the general notion that psychosis and OCD were linked has persisted, even in the face of epidemiological evidence to the contrary (Salkovskis, 1996). Enright (1996) and others have argued that OCD is best understood as an aspect of schizotypal personality thus:

> 'If OCD is not diagnostically related to schizophrenia, it is nevertheless possible that there may be common ground at a functional level … OCD patients may experience greater numbers of unwanted thoughts because of a failure to inhibit intrusions associated with the spreading semantic activation from environmental stimuli … OCD subjects retain integrated and rational thought processes outside of their obsessional focus. In these subjects, therefore, the failure of inhibition appears to become especially focused to produce OCD symptoms.'
>
> (Enright, 1996)

Salkovskis (1996), however, suggested that there are major problems with the use of schizotypy scales in the assessment of OCD, in particular the issue of criterion contamination.

In conclusion, inevitably biology plays a role in the development of any characteristic or problem, as the brain is clearly the organ of the mind, but it is not deterministic and the current status of our knowledge about it offers no appropriate targets for intervention.

We note that biological and related approaches have been used as a rationale to continue the entirely discredited and morally questionable practice of psychosurgery, either in the form of operating on the brain or inserting electrodes as part of 'deep brain stimulation'. Given the long and dishonourable heritage such approaches have, and the lack of evidence for their efficacy, it seems to us to reflect a combination of the understandable desperation of those suffering from OCD and the profound failure of understanding of those clinicians who advocate this abusive approach. We do not rule out the possibility that a 'brain' basis for understanding may emerge and inform better treatment. However, we consider that this is unlikely to be a simple 'disease' model. The future may bring some better understanding to the brain/environment complexity, which could further the understanding and treatment of OCD. However, there is little sign of this happening at present.

1.7.6 Behavioural theory: Meyer, Rachman, and exposure and response prevention

Meyer (1966), probably drawing somewhat on the work of Wolpe (1958), reported the successful behavioural treatment of two cases of chronic obsessional neurosis, followed by a series of successful case reports. Meyer's work heralded the application of psychological models to obsessions and the development of effective behavioural treatments. He took as his starting point animal models of compulsive behaviour (see, for example, Metzner, 1963), which proposed that ritualistic behaviours were a form of learned avoidance. Behaviour therapy for phobias, based on similar models, had proved successful in the treatment of phobic avoidance through desensitization, but attempts to generalize these methods to compulsions had been unsuccessful. Meyer argued that it was necessary to tackle avoidance behaviour directly by ensuring that compulsions did not take place within or between treatment sessions. His thinking anticipated cognitive approaches in that he emphasized the role of the expectations of harm in obsessions and the importance of invalidating these expectations during treatment, but this was subsequently regarded as peripheral to the major task of preventing compulsions.

At around the same period, Rachman, Hodgson, and Marks (1971) developed treatment methods in which exposure to feared situations was the central feature. These differing approaches were subsequently incorporated into a highly effective programme of behavioural treatment incorporating the principles of exposure with response prevention. Support for the use of this method came from a series of experiments in which it was demonstrated that, when a ritual is provoked, discomfort and the urge to ritualize spontaneously decay when no ritualizing takes place. In addition, subsequent provocation then results in progressively less discomfort being evoked.

Rachman (1971) clearly and elegantly specified the behavioural theory of OCD, derived from Mowrer's two-process model (Mowrer, 1951). Behavioural treatment of OCD is based on the hypothesis that obsessional thoughts have, through conditioning, become associated with anxiety that has failed to extinguish. Sufferers have developed escape and avoidance behaviours (such as obsessional checking and washing), which prevent the extinction of anxiety. This leads directly to the behavioural treatment known as ERP, in which the person is: (a) exposed to stimuli that provoke the obsessional response, and (b) helped to prevent avoidance and escape (compulsive) responses, which would otherwise 'switch off' the provoking stimuli (Salkovskis and Kirk, 1989; Steketee and Foa, 1985). An important contribution to the development of ERP was the observation that the occurrence of obsessions leads to an increase in anxiety, and that the compulsions lead to its subsequent attenuation. When the compulsions were delayed or prevented, people with OCD experienced a spontaneous decay in anxiety and the urges to perform compulsions. Continued practice led to the extinction of anxiety (e.g. Rachman and Hodgson, 1980). The 'spontaneous decay experiments' that demonstrated this were crucial both for therapists and patients to be confident that, if they confronted their fears, anxiety and discomfort would diminish and ultimately disappear (see Figures 3.8, 3.9, and 3.10, page 123–124).

These early behavioural theories and experiments set the stage for later cognitive-behavioural theory and treatment.

1.8 Cognitive theory and its implications

The phenomenology of OCD is particularly well accounted for by cognitive-behavioural models. The cognitive-behavioural theory developed following a focus on the meaning attributed to (internal or external) events—the cornerstone of cognitive theories of psychopathology (Beck, 1976). The cognitive-behavioural theory builds on behavioural theory as it begins with an identical proposition that obsessional thinking has its origins in normal intrusive cognitions. However, in the cognitive theory the difference between normal intrusive cognitions and obsessional intrusive cognitions lies not in the occurrence or even the (un)controllability of the intrusions themselves, but rather in the interpretation made by people with OCD about the occurrence and/or content of the intrusions. If the appraisal is focussed upon harm or danger, then the emotional reaction is likely to be anxiety. Such evaluations of intrusive cognitions and consequent mood changes may become part of a mood-appraisal negative spiral but would not be expected to result in compulsive behaviour. Cognitive-behavioural models therefore propose that normal obsessions become problematic when either their occurrence or content are interpreted as personally meaningful and threatening (Rachman, 1997; Salkovskis, 1985, 1997), and it is this *interpretation* which mediates the distress caused (Barrera and Norton, 2011; Purdon, 2001).

Thus, according to the cognitive hypothesis, OCD would occur if intrusive cognitions were interpreted as an indication that the person may be, may have been, or may come to be, responsible for harm or its prevention (Rachman, 1997, 1998; Salkovskis, 1985, 1989, 1997). Central to how threatening this appraisal is the idea of not only how likely the outcome is, but how 'awful' this is to the individual. Furthermore, this is set against the individual's sense of how they might cope in these circumstances.

According to cognitive models, the interpretation of an intrusive thought results in a number of voluntary and involuntary reactions which each in their turn can have an impact on the strength of belief in the original interpretation. Negative appraisals can therefore act as both *causal* and *maintenance* agents in OCD. The cognitive model of OCD is drawn out fully in Figure 1.1.

This model has been supported by studies that show that obsessions are likely to be troubling when the content goes against personally held values or a sense of self (Rowa *et al.*, 2005). Clinical and analogue research has also shown that compulsive behaviours such as checking, thought suppression, and avoidance

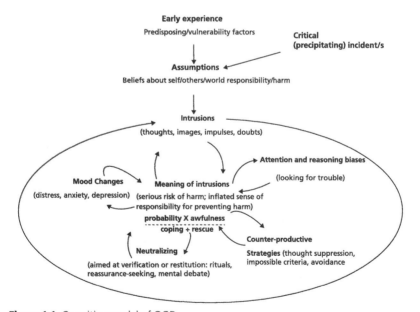

Figure 1.1 Cognitive model of OCD.
Data from Paul M. Salkovskis, Obsessional-compulsive problems: A cognitive-behavioural analysis, *Behaviour Research and Therapy, 23*(5), 571–83, doi:10.1016/0005-7967(85)90105-6, 1985, Elsevier Ltd.

serve to increase a sense of danger or doubt and increase the frequency of obsessional thoughts (Freeston *et al.*, 1991; Giele *et al.*, 2012; Marcks and Woods, 2007; Markowitz and Purdon, 2008) and increased preoccupation with the intrusive thought (Tolin *et al.*, 2002).

Theoretically, the occurrence or content of the obsessional intrusion activates or interacts with background beliefs, such as assumptions about responsibility, e.g. 'it is better to be safe than sorry' (Salkovskis *et al.*, 2000) to make the problematic interpretation more likely. Experimental manipulations of responsibility have also been shown to increase obsessional-like behaviours on some tasks, e.g. making the participant responsible for turning off a stove (see Section 3.2; Arntz *et al.*, 2007; Ladouceur *et al.*, 1995).

Responsibility-related interpretations produce a number of responses, which in turn have the effect of: (a) increasing or preventing the reduction of responsibility beliefs, and (b) triggering further intrusions.

The key elements are:

Intrusions that are interpreted in terms of responsibility for harm: these interpretations provoke discomfort, anxiety, and depression, which in turn increase the frequency of intrusions and make negative interpretations yet more likely.

Increased attention is focussed on the intrusions and/or stimuli that trigger them: this usually leads the person to become more preoccupied with the intrusions, thus increasing their occurrence and making them seem more out of control and threatening.

Responsibility interpretations that lead the person to use counterproductive strategies intended to reduce threat and responsibility: these can include attempts to reduce the occurrence of the thoughts (such as thought suppression) and the adoption of unusual and sometimes unattainable criteria for completion of actions (for example, judging an action to be safely completed only when a particular mood state is achieved).

Safety-seeking behaviours (Salkovskis, 1991), such as neutralizing or checking, that strengthen the idea that harm would otherwise have occurred, increasing the perception of responsibility. Avoidance of difficult situations and seeking reassurance (having the effect of displacing, diluting, or sharing responsibility) further contribute to the maintenance of negative beliefs and can also increase the likelihood of further intrusion, doubt, and preoccupation.

Figure 1.2 illustrates the model using the example of OCD focussed on checking and preventing harm.

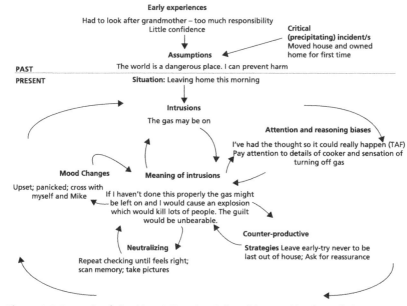

Figure 1.2 Example of checking OCD using Salkovskis' cognitive formulation.

Figure 1.3 illustrates the model using the example of contamination-focussed OCD.

Recognizing and understanding safety-seeking behaviours is crucial to developing an idiosyncratic formulation. Box 1.1 describes how the concept was first identified.

The cognitive-behavioural conceptualization of OCD mirrors the cognitive approach to other types of anxiety disorder in that a particular non-threatening situation becomes the focus of concern as a result of beliefs concerning danger or threat. In cognitive terms, OCD results from the way in which the person interprets not only the *content* but also the *occurrence* of intrusive thoughts, images, impulses, and doubts.

1.8.1 Maintaining factors in OCD

Once the interpretation has been activated, the person's responses then serve to maintain this belief in a potentially endless variety of specific but functionally equivalent ways. These responses and reactions vary in the degree to which they are directly controllable by the person. They may also differ in the degree to which the person is aware of them. However, for any given individual a constellation of responses will be present, in each case resulting from, but also

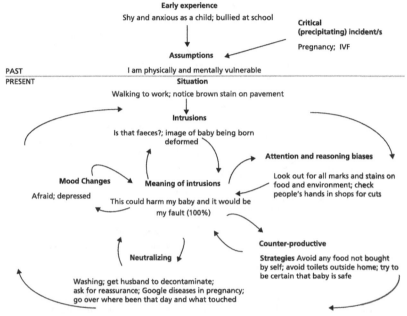

Figure 1.3 Example of contamination OCD using Salkovskis' cognitive formulation.

Box 1.1 Safety-seeking behaviours

There is a central paradox in anxiety disorders: why do people fail to learn from their own repeated experiences that a threatening situation is not in fact unsafe? In a theoretical paper, Paul Salkovskis first described the concept of safety-seeking behaviour (SSB) in anxiety disorders which helps to explain this problem. In the face of perceived danger the particular SSB arises from and is logically linked to the threat. Examples would be controlling breathing in a panic attack where the feared outcome was suffocation or stepping back from the platform edge for a person who worries they may jump or push another off. Such behaviour may be anticipatory (avoidant) or consequent (escape). These responses to perceived threat are particularly potent maintaining factors as they prevent disconfirmation of the feared outcome.

Key reference: Salkovskis P. (1991). The importance of behaviour in the maintenance of anxiety and panic: a cognitive account. *Behavioural and Cognitive Psychotherapy*, **19**, 6–19.

fuelling the problematic interpretation. This series of vicious circles constitutes the 'petals' of the vicious flower of an idiosyncratic OCD formulation (see Figure 1.1). Once present, these factors also increase the sensitivity to triggers and the likelihood of further obsessive episodes. Further links could be made between the maintaining factors, which often interact with and reinforce each other and sometimes overlap (e.g. anxiety and ex-consequentia reasoning). There follows a brief description of the most common maintaining factors.

1.8.1.1 Emotion

The predominant emotional response in OCD is anxiety. The activation of stress systems focusses attention and thinking on threat (Toates, 1995), which can include both external and internal threat. Threat brings the amygdala online, which choreographs information-searching from the environment and primes defensive systems (the 'fight–flight mechanism'). In essence, the emotion of anxiety functions to make signals of threat more salient, apparent, and believable. Anxiety can be very aversive to experience, particularly if coupled with beliefs that it will continue to increase and will persist indefinitely. Therefore responses which curtail anxiety are very reinforcing.

Other emotions can be present in OCD, such as disgust, anger, shame, and sadness. It is important to establish whether these are present at the time the person is engaged in symptoms or whether these are secondary emotions.

1.8.1.2 Ex-consequentia (emotional) reasoning

The presence of anxiety in OCD, and across anxiety disorders, can trigger secondary appraisals, such as 'this must be dangerous *because* I am anxious' (Arntz *et al.*, 1995). This information is incorporated into the evaluation of threat, and therefore maintains the belief that there is a danger. The physical symptoms of anxiety can also cause ambiguous sensations that can be seen as evidence for the original interpretation, particularly in those seeking physical signs that they are going mad/sexually aroused/on the verge of acting on their thoughts. It is possible to experience unwanted physiological sexual arousal in the context of anxiety, which can further reinforce negative beliefs (Warwick and Salkovskis, 1990).

1.8.1.3 Counterproductive safety-seeking behaviours

This is a broad heading including a large range of compulsions that are triggered by and meaningfully related to the interpretation of particular thoughts or sensations. SSBs in OCD include washing, cleaning, and checking, but can be wide-ranging and idiosyncratic. SSBs can be aimed at reducing threat, anxiety, or responsibility. SSBs can be roughly classified into those aimed at restitution (putting right, e.g. cleaning) and those aimed at verification (e.g. checking). They can be overt (physical) or covert (mental).

The reason that SSBs are counterproductive is that they prevent disconfirmation of the fear and they can themselves increase uncertainty and doubt. For example, given a perception of serious threat (e.g. I could make my baby seriously ill if this bottle is contaminated), the level of certainty of non-contamination/cleanliness required is very high. If things are done in this way and the baby is safe it can reinforce the perception that this level of cleanliness is necessary. However, increased washing and vigilance can lead to persistent doubt that the task has been performed correctly. Interruptions or becoming aware that one is distracted during a wash or check can lead to repetition of the behaviour, which becomes increasingly easily triggered.

Neutralizing is a form of SSB aimed at restitution and may take the form of engaging in rituals such as doing things a set amount of times or replacing 'bad' thoughts with 'good' thoughts. This can feel anxiety-relieving and is thus reinforcing.

1.8.1.4 Reassurance-seeking

Excessive reassurance-seeking should be considered to be an SSB (Kobori and Salkovskis, 2013; Parrish and Radomsky, 2006, 2010, 2011; Salkovskis and Kobori, 2015), taking the form of an interpersonally focussed checking. What differentiates excessive reassurance-seeking from other SSBs is that it not only deals with the perception of threat but can also transfer perceived responsibility to another person (Kobori and Salkovskis, 2013; Salkovskis, 1996, 1999). It can take the form of searching for authoritative information, questioning others, or self-reassurance. Given the need for certainty driving the behaviour in the first place, the effectiveness of reassurance is often shortlived, as consequent doubt quickly follows. Ambiguous responses or information also fuel doubt and a sense of threat (Parrish and Radomsky, 2011). Recent research has identified the presence of excessive reassurance-seeking across the range of anxiety disorders, with specific differences being noted in OCD in relation to the degree of care exercised in seeking reassurance (Kobori and Salkovskis, 2013).

1.8.1.5 Attention and reasoning biases

It has long been known that attention biases play a role in the maintenance of anxiety disorders. These biases are related to the particular concerns of the individual rather than being a more general characteristic. The bias has the features both of hypervigilance towards and increased difficulty disengaging from threat cues (da Victoria et al., 2012; Moritz et al., 2009b). Such biases increase the availability of triggers for the problem, which becomes more generalized, and can seem to provide evidence for the problematic interpretation; for example, noticing unpleasant thoughts or scanning the environment for people who look unwell. In therapy, it is sometimes discussed as a way of 'looking for trouble'—if you look for trouble, you find it.

These biases can lead people to overestimate the probability of threat, which is furthermore magnified by the personal sense of 'awfulness' of the outcome.

1.8.1.6 Internally referenced criteria

People with OCD often seek a feeling of being 'just right' when engaging in rituals and compulsions to determine when to stop (Wahl *et al.*, 2008). In doing so, they become aware of their internal states and the discrepancy between a current and a desired state. Furthermore, importance becomes attached to resolving this gap. In the context of an anxiety problem, internal states are altered, making 'just-right' feelings hard to attain and maintain. There may be an additional threat belief or beliefs concerning the tolerability of not feeling just right (Coles *et al.*, 2005). There has been increasing research interest into the related concept of 'not just-right experiences' (NJREs), which has been conceptualized as a general trait that could confer vulnerability to OCD, and has been linked with perfectionism and intolerance of uncertainty (Coles *et al.*, 2003).

1.8.1.7 Thought–action fusion

Thought–action fusion is: (a) the belief that thinking about an unacceptable or disturbing event makes it more likely to happen, and (b) the belief that having an unacceptable thought is the moral equivalent of carrying out the unacceptable or disturbing action (Shafran *et al.*, 1996). As such, it is a very specific type of responsibility appraisal; what goes on in your mind can cause dangerous things to happen. Although relevant to many disorders, high belief in these concepts has a particular role to play in explaining the maintenance of OCD, in which both the content and occurrence of intrusive thoughts can be interpreted as signalling danger.

1.8.1.8 Thought suppression

A common reaction to the experience of unwanted intrusive thoughts is to try to push them away, use distraction, or otherwise block the thought out. This can lead to an increase in frequency of feared thoughts owing to the 'rebound effect'. This describes the effect whereby such thoughts tend to occur more frequently if suppression is used. Research findings are somewhat inconsistent on this effect in OCD; additionally, people with OCD tend to appraise the recurrence of thoughts that they have tried to suppress negatively, which also affects mood (Markowitz and Purdon, 2008; Purdon et al., 2005).

1.8.1.9 Rumination and 'mental argument'

Rumination as a response to obsessive fears can take many forms. This may be scanning memories of the past for anything that may be consistent with the fear, pondering 'why' questions or 'what if' scenarios or trying to convince oneself why the fear or trigger may be safe or unsafe. Rumination in each of these forms involves engaging with ambiguous information that is likely to increase anxiety and doubt and gives further importance to the threat interpretation. Mental argument can be a type of neutralizing/putting right, and can therefore be important as a covert compulsive behaviour (Salkovskis and Westbrook, 1989).

1.8.1.10 Avoidance

Avoidance of situations, tasks, people, sensations, and thoughts are all commonly present in OCD, and pervasive avoidance is associated with high levels of interference in functioning. Avoidance functions as a maintenance factor by preventing disconfirmation of the initial interpretation and thus reinforces it, particularly as anxiety diminishes. The implicit conclusion is that a bad outcome has been averted as a result of this avoidance, rather than being unrelated. Avoidance can be subtle; for example, delegating particular tasks to confer responsibiliy on to another person. In treatment it is best conceptualized as an SSB that needs to be either eliminated or, preferably, reversed to become 'anti-OCD behaviour' (see Section 3.7.6).

In some severe cases the compulsions are so prolonged when triggered that avoidance becomes the only means left of moderating the demands of OCD. For example, some people with contamination fears paradoxically avoid washing for as long as they can because of the knowledge that embarking on a wash will take many hours.

Table 1.1 gives examples of how these maintaining factors might operate in specific forms of OCD.

1.8.2 Belief domains and other evidence

The interest in belief domains has followed from the development of cognitive approaches (Salkovskis, 1985). A range of belief domains has been associated with OCD in a number of cross-sectional studies. The Obsessive Compulsive Cognitions Working Group pragmatically identified six domains of belief as important in OCD: inflated responsibility (Salkovskis et al., 2000), threat overestimation,

Table 1.1 Examples of maintaining factors in different OCD presentations

Maintaining factor	How it maintains OCD	Examples
Anxiety	Reinforces beliefs that interpretation was correct	Walter feeling anxious when near his students and believing they will notice him looking weird
Neutralizing	Prevents disconfirmation of belief	Jessie washing Jane praying
Checking	Increases doubt and lowers confidence	Lydia checking the taps a set number of times Jessie 'tracking' contamination in her mind
Seeking reassurance	A form of checking; increases doubt and lowers confidence	Jane consulting the Bible
Attention biases	Enhances perception of threat	Jessie googling information on infections during pregnancy
Internally referenced criteria	Keeps internal focus	Saul repeating actions until they 'feel right' Jessie washing until she 'feels clean'
Thought–action fusion	Fuels belief that thoughts are important and dangerous	Jane's mind wandering in church
Thought suppression	Does not work completely; may lead to further thoughts and further misinterpretations about the meaning of the recurrence	Walter pushing sexual images out of his mind
Rumination	Increases doubt; lowers mood	Walter scanning his memory for any evidence of being a bad person, dwelling on any ambiguity and comparing himself to known sex offenders
Avoidance	Prevents disconfirmation of belief; lowers confidence; safety-seeking behaviour	Lydia never being the last to leave work

perfectionism, need for certainty (Tolin *et al.*, 2003), over-importance of thoughts, and control of thoughts (Rachman, 1997). Other overlapping concepts, such as thought–action fusion and metacognitions, have also been identified as relevant (Myers *et al.*, 2009; Shafran *et al.*, 1996). Measured by the obsesssive beliefs questionnaire (OBQ), these condense into three factors (Steketee, 2005): responsibility/ threat estimation, perfectionism/intolerance of uncertainty, and importance/control of thoughts. Participants with clinical OCD have been found to be higher than healthy control participants in these domains (Steketee *et al.*, 2003).

The particular expression of symptoms has been related to specific belief domains. Research with clinical samples has shown that responsibility/threat estimation has been linked with rumination and obsessive thoughts (Julien *et al.*, 2006), and consistently with contamination/washing and neutralizing (Calleo *et al.*, 2010; Tolin *et al.*, 2008; Wheaton *et al.*, 2010), but not invariably (Brakoulias *et al.*, 2013).

Perfectionism/intolerance of uncertainty has been linked with checking (Julien *et al.*, 2006), obsessions (Tolin *et al.*, 2008), and symmetry (Calleo *et al.*, 2010; Wheaton *et al.*, 2010). The importance and control of thoughts has been more consistently linked with impulse anxiety (Julien *et al.*, 2006) and obsessions (Tolin *et al.*, 2008; Wheaton *et al.*, 2010).

Interestingly, no interaction effects were found between belief domains on symptoms in a study by Taylor *et al.* (2005), suggesting that they are distinct contributory factors. Clinically this suggests each is worth investigating in its own right.

Although all these belief domains have been found to be associated with obsessional symptoms, few are specific to OCD, particularly when compared with other anxiety disorders, although people with OCD have been found to score more highly (Steketee *et al.*, 1998; Tolin *et al.*, 2006). Only beliefs about the need to control thoughts were found to distinguish OCD from other anxiety disorders, after controlling for trait anxiety and depression (Tolin *et al.*, 2006).

In addition, also with the exception of the relationship between obsessions and thought control, a significant subsection of people with other forms of obsessional symptoms do not score highly on these belief domains (Taylor *et al.*, 2006). This highlights the heterogeneity of the disorder and the limitations of existing models in generating predictors for the development of all obsessive-compulsive symptoms.

Salkovskis and colleagues propose a solution to these apparently confusing and potentially contradictory observations. They suggest: (i) that many of the belief domains identified are special cases of responsibility (e.g. over-importance of thoughts, thought–action fusion), and (ii) that some beliefs are relevant but not specific to OCD; e.g. perception of threat and perfectionism, inter alia. We consider that intrusive thoughts that are appraised as threatening, but where the appraisal does not involve responsibility, will not lead to compulsions/neutralizing. Responsibility appraisals, together with values that generate concern about being responsible for causing or preventing harm, form the bridge between intrusions and the motivation for compulsive behaviour (Salkovskis *et al.*, 2000).

1.8.3 Formation of beliefs—the example of responsibility

Another means by which early experience may influence vulnerability to OCD is the impact on the formation of relevant beliefs. Beck (1976) proposed that early life experiences give rise to core beliefs, which function as the basis for the interpretation of subsequent experiences, including internal stimuli such as thoughts and feelings.

Inflated responsibility beliefs are a prominent concept in the cognitive model of OCD (Salkovskis *et al.*, 2000). The specific definition of responsibility in this model is:

> 'The belief that one has power which is pivotal to bring about or prevent subjectively crucial negative outcomes. These outcomes are perceived as essential to prevent. They may be actual, that is, having consequences in the real world and/or at a moral level.'
>
> (Salkovskis, 1996)

In a theoretical paper discussing routes to the development of increased responsibility beliefs, P. Salkovskis *et al.* (1999) speculated that one pathway for this to occur could be an early developed and broad sense of responsibility that is deliberately or implicitly encouraged during childhood. This may develop if the child has to assume actual responsibility within the home, but may also arise if the child is scapegoated for events outside his or her control. A second possible parental influence on the development of inflated responsibility could also be that rigid and extreme codes of conduct and duty are imposed on the child. A third possible mechanism may be excessively anxious parents explicitly or implicitly withholding responsibility from the child. Such parents may convey the sense that problems and threat are constantly present and that outside is an unpredictable and threatening place, without developing a sense in the child that they are competent to deal with such difficulties. Finally, a child may perceive they were responsible for harm, or may in fact have been responsible for harm. Inflated responsibility could therefore be attributable to parental influence, other childhood experiences, or a combination of the two.

General support for the influence of early experience on responsibility beliefs has been found in that recalled overprotective and authoritarian parenting styles have been associated with responsibility appraisals (as well as other belief domains). These appraisals partially mediated the relationship between parenting and obsessive-compulsive symptoms (Timpano *et al.*, 2010).

1.8.4 Phenomenology and natural history in cognitive-behavioural terms

If beliefs and/or genetic vulnerabilities are part of the diathesis for the development of a disorder, it is likely that they interact with subjectively stressful environmental events to make the development of the problem more likely. Few studies have examined the transition from subclinical symptoms to full-blown disorder. In one study to look at this, Coles *et al.* (2012) found that individuals that eventually developed full-blown OCD retrospectively reported that generalized anxiety, perfectionism, impaired work or school performance, social isolation, preoccupation with details, and intolerance of uncertainty frequently emerged after their initial OC symptoms but before full criteria for OCD were met. Increases in stress level, the desire for things to feel 'just right', and the amount of attention paid to thoughts were perceived as having played an important role in the transition to OCD. Prospective results from a large cohort study also showed that social isolation, negative emotionality as well as lower IQ all predicted subsequent presentation of OCD and obsessive-compulsive symptoms in adulthood (as assessed at age 26 or 36) (Grisham *et al.*, 2011).

The context in which a disorder begins is important in terms of understanding the problem on the level of individual experience as well as the aetiology of the disorder more broadly. However, the relationship between the onset of a disorder and a particular event can be complex. Distal events may influence proximal factors that then play a role in the development of OCD. For example, a case series by Arnold (1999) noted that six out of their sample of seven women with postpartum onset OCD had experienced sexual abuse which may only have become 'online' as a factor in the context of pregnancy and childbirth. It may be the interaction of more and less recent experiences (amongst other factors) that can then lead to the development of difficulties.

The only study to demonstrate specificity of type of life event and the onset of disorder is Finlay-Jones and Brown (1981), who demonstrated that loss events were linked with depression whilst dangerous events were linked with anxiety. Those who experienced both types of events were most likely to develop mixed depression and anxiety. Stressful life events and trauma have been implicated in the development of OCD (de Silva and Marks, 1999), particularly in those with an onset in adolescence or adulthood (Millet *et al.*, 2004). When comparing lifetime rates of severe traumatic events in people with and without OCD, no differences were found by Grabe *et al.* (2008), suggesting that, for most people, traumatic events are not the main trigger for obsessional difficulties. By comparison, rates of OCD of 40% in people with post-traumatic stress disorder (PTSD) have been reported (Nacasch et al., 2011).

A study by Rosso et al. (2012) found that 60.9% of their sample of 329 people with OCD had experienced at least one stressful life event in the 12 months prior to onset of significant OCD symptomatology, with 24.9% experiencing a very stressful life event. Women were more likely to develop OCD following a stressful life event, and the likelihood increased further if they had experienced a 'very stressful life event'. This finding may have been influenced by the inclusion of gender-specific (or gender-weighted) events such as miscarriage and unwanted pregnancy in the list of life events shown to respondents. The presence of stressful life events prior to onset was also related to a more sudden onset and the development of somatic obsessions. Importantly, the study did not enquire about significant *positive* life events such as getting a new job, which may have caused stress in oblique ways, such as via the increase in responsibility.

It can be helpful to understand the influences of past experiences on the development of and vulnerability to the problem. This is likely to aid engagement, promotion of the point that the problem is understandable, and may also suggest specific targets for intervention and reappraisal.

1.9 Evidence for the effectiveness of behavioural and cognitive behavioural therapy for OCD

Since Meyer first described ERP for OCD in 1966 (Meyer, 1966), evidence has been accruing for the efficacy of behavioural and cognitive-behavioural approaches. Exposure and response prevention, usually based on habituation as the mechanism for change, has been demonstrated as having large effect sizes (mean $d = 1.18$) compared with other active treatments such as relaxation training (McKay et al., 2015). In vivo, therapist-guided ERP, enhanced with imaginal exposure to catastrophic outcomes, is associated with the largest effect sizes (Abramowitz, 1996; McKay et al., 2015). ERP can also have a disconfirmatory rationale; symptom reduction using ERP has been associated with belief change in the dimensions described earlier (Whittal et al., 2005). ERP is the predominant approach in the US and several studies have demonstrated its efficacy. It is equivalent or superior to clomipramine or combined therapy (e.g. Franklin et al., 2002; McKay et al., 2015).

CBT for OCD evolved from ERP. CBT includes both targeted cognitive and behavioural elements, including exposure and response prevention, and therefore overlaps to some extent with ERP. However, CBT is distinguished by the central focus on interpretations and beliefs. CBT has been found to achieve slightly better improvement and recovery rates than ERP (Whittal *et al.*, 2005), although a recent meta-analysis found that there was no significant difference between ERP and cognitive therapy (Ost *et al.*, 2015).

Unlike medication, CBT is a treatment involving active participation. CBT requires the person with OCD to attend sessions regularly and complete experiments and homework tasks between sessions (Abramowitz *et al.*, 2002). CBT completion has been shown to lead to better outcomes and lower relapse rates (Simpson *et al.*, 2012; Whittal *et al.*, 2008), but in routine practice few may receive the input of 12 weekly sessions described in most trials (Mancebo *et al.*, 2006). Moreover, dropout rates for ERP/CBT may be high, reported at 51% in one study (Santana *et al.*, 2013), but are likely to be at about 15% on average (Ost *et al.*, 2015).

CBT has become one of the main lines of treatment for OCD. It is has been shown to be effective in a number of studies (Nakatani *et al.*, 2005; Olatunji *et al.*, 2013; Simpson *et al.*, 2013), with meta-analysis estimating post-treatment effect sizes of 1.39 (Hedges' g) and follow-up of 0.4 (Hedges' g) (Olatunji *et al.*, 2013).

A recent systematic review and meta-analysis of CBT for OCD showed that CBT yielded very large effect sizes compared to wait list and placebo (1.31 and 1.33, respectively [Hedges'g]; Ost *et al.*, 2015). It is recommended in the UK by The National Institute for Health and Care Excellence (NICE) as an effective treatment for OCD (NICE guideline CG31, 2005). Finally, gains with ERP/CBT seem to be durable at 1–2-year follow-up (McKay *et al.*, 2015).

The treatment described in this book has been evaluated in a randomized controlled trial, comparing CBT (including ERP presented as behavioural experiments), ERP presented with a habituation/extinction rationale without explicit reappraisal and a waitlist (Salkovskis *et al.*, in preparation). Results indicate that both active treatments are better than the waitlist condition, and that, on the primary outcome measure, observer-rated YBOCS, CBT was superior to ERP both at the end of treatment and at the 1-year follow-up point. There was a significant group × measure × time interaction, which was accounted for by the CBT group doing better than the ERP group both on the YBOCS obsessions and compulsions scales, with the difference being greater for the obsessions subscale. Other measures followed the same pattern, showing both treatments doing well, but CBT being superior.

1.9.1 **What are the predictors of change in CBT?**

CBT has been found to be effective for all presentations of OCD, with some variations according to symptom dimension. Those with obsessions related to responsibility for harm in particular may do well with CBT, with hoarding being the least amenable to standard treatment (Abramowitz *et al.*, 2003; Eisen *et al.*, 2013; Mataix-Cols *et al.*, 2002). A positive development is that hoarding is no longer defined as part of OCD under DSM-V and tailored treatment protocols are now being used. One study has found that, for those with violent obsessions, engaging with or approaching treatment may be particularly difficult and this symptom dimension has been associated with treatment refusal (Santana *et al.*, 2013). However, evidence for effects of subtype are not consistent across the literature (Knopp *et al.*, 2013). There has been a suggestion that the presence of secondary hoarding might be a negative indication for the treatment of OCD; however, a recent study found that this was very clearly not so (Seaman *et al.*, 2010).

CBT is appropriate for use with all symptom types—in some trials those with sexual/religious obsessions have demonstrated worse outcomes than other subtypes (Keeley *et al.*, 2008). Earlier onset has been associated with poorer outcomes in some studies (Jakubovski *et al.*, 2013; Keeley *et al.*, 2008). A notable exception is a study by Lomax *et al.* (2009), who found an equivalent outcome using CBT based on Salkovskis' model of OCD. The authors suggest that some additional sessions may be required for more longstanding presentations. Greater symptom severity has been associated with worse treatment outcome, although the inflexibility of most trial protocols precludes the possibility that more sessions or more intensive delivery may enhance treatment (Keeley *et al.*, 2008).

Comorbid depression, particularly severe depression meeting criteria for major depressive disorder, may decrease treatment response (Keeley *et al.*, 2008). Much less is known about the effect of other patterns of comorbidity on outcome.

High levels of family accommodation, whereby family members are involved in compulsions and avoidance, has been associated with poorer outcome; by the same token, treatments involving families have obtained improved results (Thompson-Hollands *et al.*, 2014).

Treatment adherence may include attending all planned sessions, as well as engagement in sessions and doing agreed homework tasks. Homework completion has been shown to relate to better outcomes in CBT (Kazantzis *et al.*, 2016). Unsurprisingly, adherence appears to be related to better outcomes (Whittal *et al.*, 2005). People with OCD may have a range of fears and obstacles which prevent them either participating fully in, or maintaining treatment (Mancebo *et al.*, 2011). More research is needed on improving adherence (McKay *et al.*, 2015).

1.9.2 'Treatment resistance' in OCD

There is no exact consensus on the definition of 'treatment resistance' in OCD, despite widespread use of the term. However, at its core is that the person has not responded to several attempts at evidence-based psychological or pharmacological treatments. A recent study in a paediatric group defined as 'treatment-resistant' determined that previous treatment was inadequate in 95% of cases, primarily because of insufficient use of exposure techniques (Krebs *et al.*, 2015). Similarly, Stobie and colleagues investigated previous experiences of therapy in 57 people with 'treatment-refractory' OCD. Of these, only 40% reported having CBT, with 60% of those having inadequate CBT, defined as lack of exposure techniques, lack of homework, or spending the sessions talking about childhood (Stobie *et al.*, 2007). These studies indicate that considerable caution should be used in labelling a person 'treatment-resistant'. This is particularly important given the potentially enabling role of positive beliefs and therapeutic optimism, both in people seeking treatment and therapists. If someone with OCD realizes that his or her therapist is pessimistic about the likelihood of him or her being able to change, we believe that, to a considerable extent, this will be transmitted to the person and will become a self-fulfilling prophecy.

1.9.3 Medication and CBT

SSRIs are recommended in the UK by NICE as an effective treatment for OCD (NICE guideline CG31, 2005). SSRIs work by increasing the amount of the neurotransmitter serotonin available in the system and are used to treat a range of disorders, including depression and other anxiety problems. In some studies SSRIs have been found to produce comparable symptom reduction to cognitive therapy and exposure therapy (Abramowitz, 1997), although at least 50–60% of people do not respond (Goodman *et al.*, 1989) and relapse rates upon discontinuation are relatively high (Fineberg *et al.*, 2013). In a recent meta-analysis, CBT was significantly better than antidepressants, and the addition of antidepressants did not potentiate the effect of CBT (Ost *et al.*, 2015). SSRIs typically take 2–4 weeks to take effect; people with moderate to severe OCD will need to continue for at least 12 months (http://www.nhs.uk/Conditions/Obsessive-compulsive-disorder/Pages/Treatment.aspx; accessed 19 July 2015). There are currently six SSRIs prescribed in the UK:

Citalopram (Cipramil)

Escitalopram (Cipralex)

Fluoxetine (Prozac or Oxactin)

Fluvoxamine (Faverin)

Paroxetine (Seroxat)

Sertraline (Lustral)

Antipsychotic augmentation has been recommended for treatment-refractory OCD (defined as non-response to medication and CBT), although the efficacy of this is far from clear, particularly when compared with CBT (Matsunaga *et al.*, 2009; Simpson *et al.*, 2013), with the latter well-conducted study showing no difference from placebo, and CBT having a very large effect size. Recently Veale *et al.* conducted a meta-analysis of augmentation studies in OCD. They found weak evidence for the short-term efficacy of low doses of risperidone and aripiprazole, which they suggest should be monitored for efficacy at 4 weeks. They did not find evidence for the effectiveness of any other antipsychotics (Veale *et al.*, 2014).

1.9.4 **Help-seeking in OCD**

Rates of help-seeking in OCD appear to be low, for both psychological and pharmacological interventions. Only 28% of respondents in one UK study had ever sought help (Pollard *et al.*, 1989). People with severe symptoms (30.9%) were more likely to have received treatment than people with moderate symptoms (2.9%) in the last year. A recent review of help-seeking patterns in OCD found lifetime help-seeking rates of 0–41% (Schwartz *et al.*, 2013). A report by the WHO investigated studies from 37 countries and found the median treatment gap for OCD was 57.3%, meaning this number did not receive treatment. Globally the figure is likely to be higher as data were not available from developing countries, where treatment services are more likely to be lacking (Kohn *et al.*, 2004).

Researchers have consistently found that help-seeking in OCD is often delayed by a number of years, from onset, the average ranging across studies from 8 to 17 (Pigott, 2004; Stobie *et al.*, 2007). However, a recent study identified a mean delay of 3.28 years (standard deviation 4.25 years) (Belloch *et al.*, 2009), suggesting that the lag from onset to help-seeking may be improving. Although younger people are more likely to seek help (Cullen *et al.*, 2008; Goodwin *et al.*, 2002; Levy *et al.*, 2013), those with earlier onset OCD may seek help later (Stengler *et al.*, 2013), perhaps because the problem is seen more as part of their core personality, rather than as a separate difficulty that juxtaposes with other factors.

A further likely reason for delay is that sufferers and those around them may not recognize their symptoms as part of a problem until the symptoms have progressed significantly (Coles and Coleman, 2010). The person's own appraisal of thoughts as meaning they are 'bad' or 'mad' can lead people to conceal symptoms for fear of judgement or reprisal (Belloch *et al.*, 2009; Newth and Rachman, 2001).

There can be further delays from appropriate diagnosis to appropriate treatment (Stobie *et al.*, 2007; Torres *et al.*, 2006). Wahl *et al.* (2010) found that only 28% of an outpatient sample the researchers screened and confirmed as having

OCD had also been given that diagnosis by their consultant. A vignette study suggested that professional misidentification of OCD may be common (Glazier *et al.*, 2013). Torres reported that only 5% of their community sample with OCD were receiving CBT (Torres *et al.*, 2006).

A recent qualitative study (Robinson *et al.*, 2016) using in-depth individual semi-structured interviews was conducted by a researcher with personal experience of OCD and its treatment using CBT thematic analysis to identify enablers and barriers. Barriers identified were stigma, 'internal/cognitive' factors, not knowing what their problem was, factors relating to their GP or treatment, and fear of criminalization. Positive enablers identified were being supported to seek help, information and personal accounts of OCD in the media, and confidence in their GP. Negative enablers, which were more important than the positives, were reaching a crisis point and for some participants (whose intrusive thoughts were about harming children) feeling driven to seek treatment because of the nature of the thoughts; that is, seeking help to prevent the 'harm' they feared they were capable of doing.

1.10 **Key points for clinical practice**

Intrusive thoughts of all descriptions are normal

Appraisal of the occurrence and content of thoughts is what drives the emotional and behavioural reactions found in OCD

Beliefs regarding responsibility and threat perception act as vulnerability factors

CBT can work for all forms of OCD

'Treatment resistance' may reflect inadequate treatment—more or better sessions may be required

Involving families can help in treatment outcome.

References

Abramowitz, J. S. (1996). Variants of exposure and response prevention in the treatment of obsessive-compulsive disorder: A meta-analysis. *Behavior Therapy*, 27(4), 583–600. doi: http://dx.doi.org/10.1016/S0005-7894(96)80045-1

Abramowitz, J. S. (1997). Effectiveness of psychological and pharmacological treatments for obsessive-compulsive disorder: A quantitative review. *Journal of Consulting and Clinical Psychology*, 65(1), 44–52.

Abramowitz, J. S., Franklin, M. E., Schwartz, S. A., & Furr, J. M. (2003). Symptom presentation and outcome of cognitive-behavioral therapy for obsessive-compulsive disorder. *Journal of Consulting and Clinical Psychology*, 71(6), 1049–57.

Abramowitz, J. S., Franklin, M. E., Zoellner, L. A., & DiBernardo, C. L. (2002). Treatment compliance and outcome in obsessive-compulsive disorder. *Behavior Modification*, *26*(4), 447–63.

Albert, U., Bogetto, F., Maina, G., Saracco, P., Brunatto, C., & Mataix-Cols, D. (2010a). Family accommodation in obsessive-compulsive disorder: Relation to symptom dimensions, clinical and family characteristics. *Psychiatry Research*, *179*(2), 204–11. doi: http://dx.doi.org/10.1016/j.psychres.2009.06.008

Albert, U., Maina, G., Bogetto, F., Chiarle, A., & Mataix-Cols, D. (2010b). Clinical predictors of health-related quality of life in obsessive-compulsive disorder. *Comprehensive Psychiatry*, *51*(2), 193–200. doi: http://dx.doi.org/10.1016/j.comppsych.2009.03.004

Albert, U., Salvi, V., Saracco, P., Bogetto, F., & Maina, G. (2007). Health-related quality of life among first-degree relatives of patients with obsessive-compulsive disorder in Italy. *Psychiatric Services*, *58*(7), 970–6. doi: http://dx.doi.org/10.1176/appi.ps.58.7.970

Alonso, P., Segalas, C., Real, E., *et al.* (2010). Suicide in patients treated for obsessive-compulsive disorder: A prospective follow-up study. *Journal of Affective Disorders*, *124*(3), 300–8. doi: http://dx.doi.org/10.1016/j.jad.2009.12.001

American Psychiatric Association. (2013). *Diagnostic and Statistical Manual of Mental Disorders* (5th ed.). Washington, DC: American Psychiatric Association.

Angermeyer, M. C., Kilian, R., Wilms, H.-U., & Wittmund, B. (2006). Quality of life of spouses of mentally ill people. *International Journal of Social Psychiatry*, *52*(3), 278–85. doi: http://dx.doi.org/10.1177/0020764006067186

Angst, J., Gamma, A., Endrass, J., *et al.* (2004). Obsessive-compulsive severity spectrum in the community: Prevalence, comorbidity, and course. *European Archives of Psychiatry and Clinical Neuroscience*, *254*(3), 156–64. doi: http://dx.doi.org/10.1007/s00406-004-0459-4

Arnold, L. M. (1999). A case series of women with postpartum-onset obsessive-compulsive disorder. *Primary Care Companion Journal of Clinical Psychiatry*, *1*(4), 103–8.

Arntz, A., Rauner, M., & van den Hout, M. (1995). 'If I feel anxious, there must be danger': Ex-consequentia reasoning in inferring danger in anxiety disorders. *Behaviour Research and Therapy*, *33*(8), 917–25. doi: http://dx.doi.org/10.1016/0005-7967%2895%2900032-S

Arntz, A., Voncken, M., & Goosen, A. C. (2007). Responsibility and obsessive-compulsive disorder: An experimental test. *Behaviour Research and Therapy*, *45*(3), 425–35. doi: http://dx.doi.org/10.1016/j.brat.2006.03.016

Barrera, T. L., & Norton, P. J. (2011). The appraisal of intrusive thoughts in relation to obsessional-compulsive symptoms. *Cognitive Behaviour Therapy*, *40*(2), 98–110. doi: http://dx.doi.org/10.1080/16506073.2010.545072

Beck, A. T. (1976). *Cognitive Therapy and the Emotional Disorders*. New York, Penguin, p. 356.

Belloch, A., del Valle, G., Morillo, C., Carrio, C., & Cabedo, E. (2009). To seek advice or not to seek advice about the problem: The help-seeking dilemma for obsessive-compulsive disorder. *Social Psychiatry and Psychiatric Epidemiology*, *44*(4), 257–64. doi: http://dx.doi.org/10.1007/s00127-008-0423-0

Black, D. W., Gaffney, G., Schlosser, S., & Gabel, J. (1998). The impact of obsessive-compulsive disorder on the family: Preliminary findings. *Journal of Nervous and Mental Disease*, *186*(7), 440–2.

Bobes, J., González, M. P., Bascarán, M. T., Arango, C., Sáiz, P. A., & Bousoño, M. (2001). Quality of life and disability in patients with obsessive-compulsive disorder. *European Psychiatry, 16*(4), 239–45. doi: http://dx.doi.org/10.1016/S0924-9338(01)00571-5

Bolton, D., Eley, T. C., O'Connor, T. G., et al. (2006). Prevalence and genetic and environmental influences on anxiety disorders in 6-year-old twins. *Psychological Medicine, 36*(3), 335–44.

Bolton, D., Rijsdijk, F., O'Connor, T. G., Perrin, S., & Eley, T. C. (2007). Obsessive-compulsive disorder, tics and anxiety in 6-year old twins. *Psychological Medicine, 37*(1), 39–48.

Brakoulias, V., Starcevic, V., Berle, D., Milicevic, D., Hannan, A., & Martin, A. (2013). The relationships between obsessive-compulsive symptom dimensions and cognitions in obsessive-compulsive disorder. *Psychiatric Quarterly, 85*, 133–5. doi: http://dx.doi.org/10.1007/s11126-013-9278-y

Calleo, J. S., Hart, J., Bjorgvinsson, T., & Stanley, M. A. (2010). Obsessions and worry beliefs in an inpatient OCD population. *Journal of Anxiety Disorders, 24*(8), 903–8. doi: http://dx.doi.org/10.1016/j.janxdis.2010.06.015

Cicek, E., Cicek, I. E., Kayhan, F., Uguz, F., & Kaya, N. (2013). Quality of life, family burden and associated factors in relatives with obsessive-compulsive disorder. *General Hospital Psychiatry, 35*(3), 253–8. doi: http://dx.doi.org/10.1016/j.genhosppsych.2013.01.004

Coles, M. E., & Coleman, S. L. (2010). Barriers to treatment seeking for anxiety disorders: Initial data on the role of mental health literacy. *Depression and Anxiety, 27*(1), 63–71. doi: http://dx.doi.org/10.1002/da.20620

Coles, M. E., Frost, R. O., Heimberg, R. G., & Rheaume, J. (2003). 'Not just right experiences': Perfectionism, obsessive-compulsive features and general psychopathology. *Behaviour Research and Therapy, 41*(6), 681–700. doi: http://dx.doi.org/10.1016/S0005-7967%2802%2900044-X

Coles, M. E., Hart, A. S., & Schofield, C. A. (2012). Initial data characterizing the progression from obsessions and compulsions to full-blown obsessive compulsive disorder. *Cognitive Therapy and Research, 36*(6), 685–93. doi: http://dx.doi.org/10.1007/s10608-011-9404-9

Coles, M. E., Heimberg, R. G., Frost, R. O., & Steketee, G. (2005). Not just right experiences and obsessive-compulsive features: Experimental and self-monitoring perspectives. *Behaviour Research and Therapy, 43*(2), 153–67. doi: http://dx.doi.org/10.1016/j.brat.2004.01.002

Constans, J. I., Foa, E. B., Franklin, M. E., & Mathews, A. (1995). Memory for actual and imagined events in OC checkers. *Behaviour Research and Therapy, 33*(6), 665–71. doi: http://dx.doi.org/10.1016/0005-7967%2894%2900095-2

Cottraux, J., & Gerard, D. (1998). Neuroimaging and neuroanatomical issues in obsessive-compulsive disorder: Toward an integrative model—perceived impulsivity. In R. P. Swinson, M. M. Antony, S. Rachman & M. A. Richter (eds.), *Obsessive-compulsive Disorder: Theory, research, and treatment.* (pp. 154–80).

Cougle, J. R., Salkovskis, P. M., & Wahl, K. (2007). Perception of memory ability and confidence in recollections in obsessive-compulsive checking. *Journal of Anxiety Disorders, 21*(1), 118–30. doi: http://dx.doi.org/10.1016/j.janxdis.2006.03.015

Cullen, B., Samuels, J. F., Pinto, A., et al. (2008). Demographic and clinical characteristics associated with treatment status in family members with obsessive-compulsive disorder. *Depression and Anxiety, 25*(3), 218–24. doi: http://dx.doi.org/10.1002/da.20293

da Victoria, M. S., Nascimento, A. L., & Fontenelle, L. F. (2012). Symptom-specific attentional bias to threatening stimuli in obsessive-compulsive disorder. *Comprehensive Psychiatry, 53*(6), 783–8. doi: http://dx.doi.org/10.1016/j.comppsych.2011.12.005

de Silva, P., & Marks, M. (1999). The role of traumatic experiences in the genesis of obsessive-compulsive disorder. *Behaviour Research and Therapy, 37*(10), 941–51. doi: http://dx.doi.org/10.1016/S0005-7967%2898%2900185-5

Dell'Osso, B., Benatti, B., Buoli, M., *et al.* (2013). The influence of age at onset and duration of illness on long-term outcome in patients with obsessive-compulsive disorder: A report from the International College of Obsessive Compulsive Spectrum Disorders (ICOCS). *European Neuropsychopharmacology, 23*(8), 865–71. doi: http://dx.doi.org/10.1016/j.euroneuro.2013.05.004

Ecker, W., & Engelkamp, J. (1995). Memory for actions in obsessive-compulsive disorder. *Behavioural and Cognitive Psychotherapy, 23*(4), 349–71. doi: http://dx.doi.org/10.1017/S1352465800016477

Edwards, S., & Salkovskis, P. M. (2006). An experimental demonstration that fear, but not disgust, is associated with return of fear in phobias. *Journal of Anxiety Disorders, 20*(1), 58–71. doi: http://dx.doi.org/10.1016/j.janxdis.2004.11.007

Einstein, D. A., & Menzies, R. G. (2004). Role of magical thinking in obsessive-compulsive symptoms in an undergraduate sample. *Depression and Anxiety, 19*(3), 174–9. doi: http://dx.doi.org/10.1002/da.20005

Eisen, J. L., Mancebo, M. A., Pinto, A., *et al.* (2006). Impact of obsessive-compulsive disorder on quality of life. *Comprehensive Psychiatry, 47*(4), 270–5. doi: http://dx.doi.org/10.1016/j.comppsych.2005.11.006

Eisen, J. L., Sibrava, N. J., Boisseau, C. L., *et al.* (2013). Five-year course of obsessive-compulsive disorder: Predictors of remission and relapse. *Journal of Clinical Psychiatry, 74*(3), 233–9. doi: http://dx.doi.org/10.4088/JCP.12m07657

Eley, T. C., Bolton, D., O'Connor, T. G., Perrin, S., Smith, P., & Plomin, R. (2003). A twin study of anxiety-related behaviours in pre-school children. *Journal of Child Psychology and Psychiatry, 44*(7), 945–60.

Enright, S. (1996). Obsessive compulsive disorder as a schizotype. In R. Rapee (Ed.), *Controversies in the Anxiety Disorders.* New York: Guilford.

Fernandez, C. E., & López-Ibor, A. J. (1967). [Use of monochlorimipramine in psychiatric patients who are resistant to other therapy]. *Actas Luso-Espanolas de Neurologia y Psiquiatria, 26*(2), 119–47.

Fineberg, N. A., Reghunandanan, S., Brown, A., & Pampaloni, I. (2013). Pharmacotherapy of obsessive-compulsive disorder: Evidence-based treatment and beyond. *Australian and New Zealand Journal of Psychiatry, 47*(2), 121–41. doi: http://dx.doi.org/10.1177/0004867412461958

Finlay-Jones, R., & Brown, G. W. (1981). Types of stressful life event and the onset of anxiety and depressive disorders. *Psychological Medicine, 11*(4), 803–15.

Foa, E. B., & Kozak, M. J. (1995). DSM-IV field trial: Obsessive-compulsive disorder. *The American Journal of Psychiatry, 152*(1), 90–6.

Fontenelle, I. S., Fontenelle, L. F., Borges, M. C., *et al.* (2010). Quality of life and symptom dimensions of patients with obsessive-compulsive disorder. *Psychiatry Research, 179*(2), 198–203. doi: http://dx.doi.org/10.1016/j.psychres.2009.04.005

Franklin, M. E., Abramowitz, J. S., Bux, D. A., Jr., Zoellner, L. A., & Feeny, N. C. (2002). Cognitive-behavioral therapy with and without medication in the treatment of obsessive-compulsive disorder. *Professional Psychology: Research and Practice, 33*(2), 162–8.

Freeston, M. H., Ladouceur, R., Thibodeau, N., & Gagnon, F. (1991). Cognitive intrusions in a non-clinical population: I. Response style, subjective experience, and appraisal. *Behaviour Research and Therapy, 29*(6), 585–97. doi: http://dx.doi.org/10.1016/0005-7967%2891%2990008-Q

Giele, C. L., van den Hout, M. A., Engelhard, I. M., Dek, E. C., & Hofmeijer, F. K. (2012). Obsessive-compulsive-like reasoning makes an unlikely catastrophe more credible. *Journal of Behavior Therapy and Experimental Psychiatry, 42*(3), 293–7. doi: http://dx.doi.org/10.1016/j.jbtep.2010.12.012

Glazier, K., Calixte, R. M., Rothschild, R., & Pinto, A. (2013). High rates of OCD symptom misidentification by mental health professionals. *Annals of Clinical Psychiatry, 25*(3), 201–9.

Goodman, W. K., Price, L. H., Rasmussen, S. A., Delgado, P. L., Heninger, G. R., & Charney, D. S. (1989). Efficacy of fluvoxamine in obsessive-compulsive disorder: A double-blind comparison with placebo. *Archives of General Psychiatry, 46*(1), 36–44. doi: http://dx.doi.org/10.1001/archpsyc.1989.01810010038006

Goodwin, R., Koenen, K. C., Hellman, F., Guardino, M., & Struening, E. (2002). Helpseeking and access to mental health treatment for obsessive-compulsive disorder. *Acta Psychiatrica Scandinavica, 106*(2), 143–9. doi: http://dx.doi.org/10.1034/j.1600-0447.2002.01221.x

Grabe, H. J., Ruhrmann, S., Spitzer, C., *et al.* (2008). Obsessive-compulsive disorder and posttraumatic stress disorder. *Psychopathology, 41*(2), 129–34. doi: http://dx.doi.org/10.1159/000112029

Grisham, J. R., Fullana, M. A., Mataix-Cols, D., Moffitt, T. E., Caspi, A., & Poulton, R. (2011). Risk factors prospectively associated with adult obsessive-compulsive symptom dimensions and obsessive-compulsive disorder. *Psychol Med, 41*, 2495–2506. doi: 10.1017/S0033291711000894

Gross, R., Sasson, Y., Chorpa, M., & Zohar, J. (1998). Biological models of obsessive-compulsive disorder. In: R. Swinson, M. Antony, S. Rachman and M. Richter (eds). *Obsessive-compulsive Disorder: Theory, research, and treatment.* New York, Guilford (pp. 141–53).

Grover, S., & Dutt, A. (2011). Perceived burden and quality of life of caregivers in obsessive-compulsive disorder. *Psychiatry and Clinical Neurosciences, 65*(5), 416–22. doi: http://dx.doi.org/10.1111/j.1440-1819.2011.02240.x

Hanna, G. L., Fischer, D. J., Chadha, K. R., Himle, J. A., & Van Etten, M. (2005). Familial and sporadic subtypes of early-onset obsessive-compulsive disorder. *Biological Psychiatry, 57*(8), 895–900. doi: http://dx.doi.org/10.1016/j.biopsych.2004.12.022

Hermans, D., Martens, K., De Cort, K., Pieters, G., & Eelen, P. (2003). Reality monitoring and metacognitive beliefs related to cognitive confidence in obsessive-compulsive disorder. *Behaviour Research and Therapy, 41*(4), 383–401. doi: http://dx.doi.org/10.1016/S0005-7967%2802%2900015-3

Huppert, J. D., Simpson, H., Nissenson, K. J., Liebowitz, M. R., & Foa, E. B. (2009). Quality of life and functional impairment in obsessive-compulsive disorder: A comparison of patients with and without comorbidity, patients in remission, and healthy controls. *Depression and Anxiety, 26*(1), 39–45. doi: http://dx.doi.org/10.1002/da.20506

Iervolino, A. C., Rijsdijk, F. V., Cherkas, L., Fullana, M. A., & Mataix-Cols, D. (2011). A multivariate twin study of obsessive-compulsive symptom dimensions. *Archives of General Psychiatry, 68*(6), 637–44. doi: http://dx.doi.org/10.1001/archgenpsychiatry.2011.54

Jakubovski, E., Diniz, J. B., Valerio, C., *et al.* (2013). Clinical predictors of long-term outcome in obsessive-compulsive disorder. *Depression and Anxiety, 30*(8), 763–72. doi: http://dx.doi.org/10.1002/da.22013

Julien, D., O'Connor, K. P., Aardema, F., & Todorov, C. (2006). The specificity of belief domains in obsessive-compulsive symptom subtypes. *Personality and Individual Differences, 41*(7), 1205–16. doi: http://dx.doi.org/10.1016/j.paid.2006.04.019

Karno, M., Golding, J. M., Sorenson, S. B., & Burnam, M. (1988). The epidemiology of obsessive-compulsive disorder in five US communities. *Archives of General Psychiatry, 45*(12), 1094–9. doi: http://dx.doi.org/10.1001/archpsyc.1988.01800360042006

Kazantzis, N., Whittington, C., Zelencich, L., Kyrios, M., Norton, P. J., & Hofmann, S. G. (2016). Quantity and quality of homework compliance: A meta-analysis of relations with outcome in cognitive behavior therapy. *Behavior Therapy, 45*, 755–72. doi: http://dx.doi.org/10.1016/j.beth.2016.05.002

Keeley, M. L., Storch, E. A., Merlo, L. J., & Geffken, G. R. (2008). Clinical predictors of response to cognitive-behavioral therapy for obsessive-compulsive disorder. *Clinical Psychology Review, 28*(1), 118–30. doi: http://dx.doi.org/10.1016/j.cpr.2007.04.003

Kendler, K. S., Walters, E. E., Neale, M. C., *et al.* (1995). The structure of the genetic and environmental risk factors for six major psychiatric disorders in women: Phobia, generalized anxiety disorder, panic disorder, bulimia, major depression, and alcoholism. *Archives of General Psychiatry, 52*(5), 374–83.

Kichuk, S. A., Torres, A. R., Fontenelle, L. F., *et al.* (2013). Symptom dimensions are associated with age of onset and clinical course of obsessive-compulsive disorder. *Progress in Neuro-Psychopharmacology & Biological Psychiatry, 44*, 233–9. doi: http://dx.doi.org/10.1016/j.pnpbp.2013.02.003

Knopp, J., Knowles, S., Bee, P., Lovell, K., & Bower, P. (2013). A systematic review of predictors and moderators of response to psychological therapies in OCD: Do we have enough empirical evidence to target treatment? *Clinical Psychology Review, 33*(8), 1067–81. doi: http://dx.doi.org/10.1016/j.cpr.2013.08.008

Kobori, O., & Salkovskis, P. M. (2013). Patterns of reassurance seeking and reassurance-related behaviours in OCD and anxiety disorders. *Behavioural and Cognitive Psychotherapy, 41*(1), 1–21. doi: http://dx.doi.org/10.1017/S1352465812000665

Kohn, R., Saxena, S., Levav, I., & Saraceno, B. (2004). The treatment gap in mental health care. *Bulletin of the World Health Organization, 82*(11), 858–66.

Krebs, G., Isomura, K., Lang, K., *et al.* (2015). How resistant is 'treatment-resistant' obsessive-compulsive disorder in youth? *British Journal of Clinical Psychology, 54*(1), 63–75. doi: http://dx.doi.org/10.1111/bjc.12061

Ladouceur, R., Rheaume, J., Freeston, M. H., *et al.* (1995). Experimental manipulations of responsibility: An analogue test for models of obsessive-compulsive disorder. *Behaviour Research and Therapy, 33*(8), 937–46. doi: http://dx.doi.org/10.1016/0005-7967%2895%2900024-R

Laidlaw, T. M., Falloon, I. R., Barnfather, D., & Coverdale, J. H. (1999). The stress of caring for people with obsessive compulsive disorders. *Community Mental Health Journal, 35*(5), 443–50. doi: http://dx.doi.org/10.1023/A:1018734528606

Lam, D. C. K., & Salkovskis, P. M. (2007). An experimental investigation of the impact of biological and psychological causal explanations on anxious and depressed patients' perception of a person with panic disorder. *Behaviour Research and Therapy, 45*(2), 405–11.

Lam, D. C. K., Salkovskis, P. M., & Warwick, H. M. C. (2005). An experimental investigation of the impact of biological versus psychological explanations of the cause of 'mental illness'. *Journal of Mental Health, 14*(5), 453–64.

Levy, H. C., McLean, C. P., Yadin, E., & Foa, E. B. (2013). Characteristics of individuals seeking treatment for obsessive-compulsive disorder. *Behavior Therapy, 44*(3), 408–16. doi: http://dx.doi.org/10.1016/j.beth.2013.03.007

Lilienfeld, S. O., Sauvigné, K. C., Lynn, S. J., Cautin, R. L., Latzman, R. D., & Waldman, I. D. (2015). Fifty psychological and psychiatric terms to avoid: A list of inaccurate, misleading, misused, ambiguous, and logically confused words and phrases. *Frontiers in Psychology, 6*, 1–15.

Lin, P.-Y. (2007). Meta-analysis of the association of serotonin transporter gene polymorphism with obsessive–compulsive disorder. *Progress in Neuro-Psychopharmacology and Biological Psychiatry, 31*(3), 683–9. doi: http://dx.doi.org/10.1016/j.pnpbp.2006.12.024

Liu, S., Yin, Y., Wang, Z., Zhang, X., & Ma, X. (2013). Association study between MAO-A gene promoter VNTR polymorphisms and obsessive–compulsive disorder. *Journal of Anxiety Disorders, 27*(4), 435–7. doi: http://dx.doi.org/10.1016/j.janxdis.2013.04.005

Lomax, C. L., Oldfield, V. B., & Salkovskis, P. M. (2009). Clinical and treatment comparisons between adults with early- and late-onset obsessive-compulsive disorder. *Behaviour Research and Therapy, 47*(2), 99–104. doi: http://dx.doi.org/10.1016/j.brat.2008.10.015

MacDonald, P. A., Antony, M. M., MacLeod, C. M., & Richter, M. A. (1997). Memory and confidence in memory judgments among individuals with obsessive compulsive disorder and non-clinical controls. *Behaviour Research and Therapy, 35*(6), 497–505. doi: http://dx.doi.org/10.1016/S0005-7967%2897%2900013-2

Mancebo, M. C., Eisen, J. L., Pinto, A., Greenberg, B. D., Dyck, I. R., & Rasmussen, S. A. (2006). The Brown Longitudinal Obsessive Compulsive Study: Treatments received and patient impressions of improvement. *Journal of Clinical Psychiatry, 67*(11), 1713–20. doi: http://dx.doi.org/10.4088/JCP.v67n1107

Mancebo, M. C., Eisen, J. L., Sibrava, N. J., Dyck, I. R., & Rasmussen, S. A. (2011). Patient utilization of cognitive-behavioral therapy for OCD. *Behavior Therapy, 42*(3), 399–412. doi: http://dx.doi.org/10.1016/j.beth.2010.10.002

Marcks, B. A., & Woods, D. W. (2007). Role of thought-related beliefs and coping strategies in the escalation of intrusive thoughts: An analog to obsessive-compulsive disorder. *Behaviour Research and Therapy, 45*(11), 2640–51. doi: http://dx.doi.org/10.1016/j.brat.2007.06.012

Markowitz, L. J., & Purdon, C. (2008). Predictors and consequences of suppressing obsessional thoughts. *Behavioural and Cognitive Psychotherapy, 36*(2), 179–92. doi: http://dx.doi.org/10.1017/S1352465807003992

Mataix-Cols, D., do Rosario-Campos, M. C., & Leckman, J. F. (2005). A multidimensional model of obsessive-compulsive disorder. *The American Journal of Psychiatry, 162*(2), 228–38. doi: http://dx.doi.org/10.1176/appi.ajp.162.2.228

Mataix-Cols, D., Frost, R. O., Pertusa, A., *et al.* (2010). Hoarding disorder: A new diagnosis for DSM-V? *Depression and Anxiety, 27*(6), 556–72. doi: http://dx.doi.org/10.1002/da.20693

Mataix-Cols, D., Marks, I. M., Greist, J. H., Kobak, K. A., & Baer, L. (2002). Obsessive-compulsive symptom dimensions as predictors of compliance with and response to behaviour therapy: Results from a controlled trial. *Psychotherapy and Psychosomatics, 71*(5), 255–62. doi: http://dx.doi.org/10.1159/000064812

Matsunaga, H., Hayashida, K., Kiriike, N., Maebayashi, K., & Stein, D. J. (2010). The clinical utility of symptom dimensions in obsessive-compulsive disorder. *Psychiatry Research, 180*(1), 25–9. doi: http://dx.doi.org/10.1016/j.psychres.2009.09.005

Matsunaga, H., Nagata, T., Hayashida, K., Ohya, K., Kiriike, N., & Stein, D. J. (2009). A long-term trial of the effectiveness and safety of atypical antipsychotic agents in augmenting SSRI-refractory obsessive-compulsive disorder. *Journal of Clinical Psychiatry, 70*(6), 863–8. doi: http://dx.doi.org/10.4088/JCP.08m04369

McKay, D. (2006). Treating disgust reactions in contamination-based obsessive-compulsive disorder. *Journal of Behavior Therapy and Experimental Psychiatry, 37*(1), 53–9. doi: http://dx.doi.org/10.1016/j.jbtep.2005.09.005

McKay, D., Sookman, D., Neziroglu, F., *et al.* (2015). Efficacy of cognitive-behavioral therapy for obsessive-compulsive disorder. *Psychiatry Research, 225*(3), 236–46. doi: http://dx.doi.org/10.1016/j.psychres.2014.11.058

McNally, R. J., & Kohlbeck, P. A. (1993). Reality monitoring in obsessive-compulsive disorder. *Behaviour Research and Therapy, 31*(3), 249–53. doi: http://dx.doi.org/10.1016/0005-7967%2893%2990023-N

Metzner, R. (1963). Some experimental analogues of obsession. *Behaviour Research and Therapy, 1*, 231–6.

Meyer, V. (1966). Modification of expectations in cases with obsessional rituals. *Behaviour Research and Therapy, 4*(1–2), 273–80. doi: http://dx.doi.org/10.1016/0005-7967(66)90083-0

Middeldorp, C., Cath, D., Van Dyck, R., & Boomsma, D. (2005). The co-morbidity of anxiety and depression in the perspective of genetic epidemiology: A review of twin and family studies. *Psychological Medicine, 35*(5), 611–24. doi: http://dx.doi.org/10.1017/S003329170400412X

Millet, B., Kochman, F., Gallarda, T., *et al.* (2004). Phenomenological and comorbid features associated in obsessive–compulsive disorder: Influence of age of onset. *Journal of Affective Disorders, 79*(1–3), 241–6. doi: http://dx.doi.org/10.1016/S0165-0327(02)00351-8

Moritz, S., Ruhe, C., Jelinek, L., & Naber, D. (2009). No deficits in nonverbal memory, metamemory and internal as well as external source memory in obsessive-compulsive disorder (OCD). *Behaviour Research and Therapy, 47*(4), 308–15. doi: http://dx.doi.org/10.1016/j.brat.2009.01.004

Moritz, S., Von Muhlenen, A., Randjbar, S., Fricke, S., & Jelinek, L. (2009). Evidence for an attentional bias for washing- and checking-relevant stimuli in obsessive-compulsive disorder. *Journal of the International Neuropsychological Society, 15*(3), 365–71. doi: http://dx.doi.org/10.1017/S1355617709090511

Mowrer, O. H. (1951). Two-factor learning theory: Summary and comment. *Psychological Review, 58*, 350–4.

Myers, S. G., Fisher, P. L., & Wells, A. (2009). Metacognition and cognition as predictors of obsessive-compulsive symptoms: A prospective study. *International Journal of Cognitive Therapy, 2*(2), 132–42. doi: http://dx.doi.org/10.1521/ijct.2009.2.2.132

Nacasch, N., Fostick, L., & Zohar, J. (2011). High prevalence of obsessive-compulsive disorder among posttraumatic stress disorder patients. *European Neuropsychopharmacology, 21*(12), 876–9. doi: http://dx.doi.org/10.1016/j.euroneuro.2011.03.007

Nakatani, E., Nakagawa, A., Nakoa, T., *et al.* (2005). A randomized controlled trial of Japanese patients with obsessive-compulsive disorder: Effectiveness of behavior therapy and fluvoxamine. *Psychotherapy and Psychosomatics, 74*(5), 269–76. doi: http://dx.doi.org/10.1159/000086317

Nelson, E. A., Abramowitz, J. S., Whiteside, S. P., & Deacon, B. J. (2006). Scrupulosity in patients with obsessive-compulsive disorder: Relationship to clinical and cognitive phenomena. *Journal of Anxiety Disorders, 20*(8), 1071–86.

Nestadt, G., Bienvenu, O., Cai, G., Samuels, J., & Eaton, W. W. (1998). Incidence of obsessive-compulsive disorder in adults. *Journal of Nervous and Mental Disease, 186*(7), 401–6. doi: http://dx.doi.org/10.1097/00005053-199807000-00003

Newth, S., & Rachman, S. (2001). The concealment of obsessions. *Behaviour Research and Therapy, 39*(4), 457–64. doi: http://dx.doi.org/10.1016/S0005-7967%2800%2900006-1

Neziroglu, F., Anemone, R., & Yaryura-Tobias, J. A. (1992). Onset of obsessive-compulsive disorder in pregnancy. *American Journal of Psychiatry, 149*(7), 947–50.

Olatunji, B. O., Cisler, J. M., & Tolin, D. F. (2007). Quality of life in the anxiety disorders: A meta-analytic review. *Clinical Psychology Review, 27*(5), 572–81.

Olatunji, B. O., Davis, M. L., Powers, M. B., & Smits, J. A. (2013). Cognitive-behavioral therapy for obsessive-compulsive disorder: A meta-analysis of treatment outcome and moderators. *Journal of Psychiatric Research, 47*(1), 33–41. doi: http://dx.doi.org/10.1016/j.jpsychires.2012.08.020

Ost, L. G., Havnun, A., Hansen, B., & Kvale, G. (2015). Cognitive behavioral treatments of obsessive-compulsive disorder. A systematic review and meta-analysis of studies published 1993–2014. *Clinical Psychology Review, 40*, 156–69. doi: http://dx.doi.org/10.1016/j.cpr.2015.06.003

Parrish, C. L., & Radomsky, A. S. (2006). An experimental investigation of responsibility and reassurance: Relationships with compulsive checking. *International Journal of Behavioral Consultation and Therapy, 2*(2), 174–91. doi: http://dx.doi.org/10.1037/h0100775

Parrish, C. L., & Radomsky, A. S. (2010). Why do people seek reassurance and check repeatedly? An investigation of factors involved in compulsive behavior in OCD and depression. *Journal of Anxiety Disorders, 24*(2), 211–22. doi: http://dx.doi.org/10.1016/j.janxdis.2009.10.010

Parrish, C. L., & Radomsky, A. S. (2011). An experimental investigation of factors involved in excessive reassurance seeking: The effects of perceived threat, responsibility and ambiguity on compulsive urges and anxiety. *Journal of Experimental Psychopathology, 2*(1), 44–62. doi: http://dx.doi.org/10.5127/jep.011110

Pauls, D. L. (2010). The genetics of obsessive-compulsive disorder: A review. *Dialogues in Clinical Neuroscience, 12*(2), 149–63.

Pauls, D. L., & Alsobrook, J. P. (1999). The inheritance of obsessive-compulsive disorder. *Child and Adolescent Psychiatric Clinics of North America*, 8(3), 481–96.

Pertusa, A., Frost, R. O., & Mataix-Cols, D. (2010). When hoarding is a symptom of OCD: A case series and implications for DSM-V. *Behaviour Research and Therapy*, 48(10), 1012–20. doi: http://dx.doi.org/10.1016/j.brat.2010.07.003

Pietrefesa, A. S., & Coles, M. E. (2009). Moving beyond an exclusive focus on harm avoidance in obsessive-compulsive disorder: Behavioral validation for the separability of harm avoidance and incompleteness. *Behavior Therapy*, 40(3), 251–9. doi: http://dx.doi.org/10.1016/j.beth.2008.06.003

Pigott, T. A. (2004). OCD. *CNS Spectrums*, 9(9), 14–16.

Pollard, C., Henderson, J., Frank, M., & Margolis, R. B. (1989). Help-seeking patterns of anxiety-disordered individuals in the general population. *Journal of Anxiety Disorders*, 3(3), 131–8. doi: http://dx.doi.org/10.1016/0887-6185%2889%2990007-8

Purdon, C. (2001). Appraisal of obsessional thought recurrences: Impact on anxiety and mood state. *Behavior Therapy*, 32(1), 47–64. doi: http://dx.doi.org/10.1016/S0005-7894%2801%2980043-5

Purdon, C., Rowa, K., & Antony, M. M. (2005). Thought suppression and its effects on thought frequency, appraisal and mood state in individuals with obsessive-compulsive disorder. *Behaviour Research and Therapy*, 43(1), 93–108. doi: http://dx.doi.org/10.1016/j.brat.2003.11.007

Rachman, S. (1971). Obsessional ruminations. *Behaviour Research and Therapy*, 9(3), 229–35. doi: http://dx.doi.org/10.1016/0005-7967%2871%2990008-8

Rachman, S. (1997). A cognitive theory of obsessions. *Behaviour Research and Therapy*, 35(9), 793–802. doi: http://dx.doi.org/10.1016/S0005-7967%2897%2900040-5

Rachman, S. (1998). A cognitive theory of obsessions: Elaborations. *Behaviour Research and Therapy*, 36(4), 385–401. doi: http://dx.doi.org/10.1016/S0005-7967%2897%2910041-9

Rachman, S., & de Silva, P. (1978). Abnormal and normal obsessions. *Behaviour Research and Therapy*, 16(4), 233–48. doi: http://dx.doi.org/10.1016/0005-7967%2878%2990022-0

Rachman, S., Coughtrey, A., Shafran, R., & Radomsky, A. (2015). *Oxford Guide to the Treatment of Mental Contamination*. New York, NY: Oxford University Press.

Rachman, S., Hodgson, R., & Marks, I. (1971). The treatment of chronic obsessive-compulsive neurosis. *Behaviour Research and Therapy*, 9(3), 237–47. doi: http://dx.doi.org/10.1016/0005-7967%2871%2990009-X

Rachman, S.J & Hodgson, R.J. (1980). *Obsessions and Compulsions*. Englewood Cliffs, NJ: Prentice-Hall.

Radomsky, A. S., & Rachman, S. (1999). Memory bias in obsessive-compulsive disorder (OCD). *Behaviour Research and Therapy*, 37(7), 605–18. doi: http://dx.doi.org/10.1016/S0005-7967%2898%2900151-X

Radomsky, A. S., Alcolado, G. M., Abramowitz, J. S., *et al.* (2014). Part 1—You can run but you can't hide: Intrusive thoughts on six continents. *Journal of Obsessive-Compulsive and Related Disorders*, 3(3), 269–79. doi: http://dx.doi.org/10.1016/j.jocrd.2013.09.002

Rapoport JL, Shaw P. (2008). Obsessive-compulsive disorder. In: Rutter M, Taylor E, Bishop D, *et al.* (eds.) *Rutter's Child and Adolescent Psychiatry*, 5th edn. Oxford, Blackwell Publishing, pp. 841–57.

Rasmussen, S. A., & Eisen, J. L. (1990). Epidemiology of obsessive compulsive disorder. *Journal of Clinical Psychiatry*, *51*(2, Suppl), 10–13.

Rasmussen, S. A., & Eisen, J. L. (1992). The epidemiology and clinical features of obsessive compulsive disorder. *Psychiatric Clinics of North America*, *15*(4), 743–58.

Rea, E., Labad, J., Alonso, P., *et al*. (2011). Stressful life events at onset of obsessive-compulsive disorder are associated with a distinct clinical pattern. *Depression and Anxiety*, *28*(5), 367–76. doi: http://dx.doi.org/10.1002/da.20792

Rimes, K. A., & Salkovskis, P. M. (1998). Psychological effects of genetic testing for psychological disorders. *Behavioural and Cognitive Psychotherapy*, *26*(1), 29–42.

Robinson, K. J., Rose, D., Salkovskis, P. M. (2016). Seeking help for obsessive compulsive disorder (OCD): A qualitative study of the enablers and barriers conducted by a researchers with personal experience of OCD. *Psychology and Psychotherapy: Theory Research and Practice*, 2017. doi: 10.1111/papt.12090

Rosa, A. C., Diniz, J. B., Fossaluza, V., *et al*. (2012). Clinical correlates of social adjustment in patients with obsessive-compulsive disorder. *Journal of Psychiatric Research*, *46*(10), 1286–92. doi: http://dx.doi.org/10.1016/j.jpsychires.2012.05.019

Rosso, G., Albert, U., Asinari, G. F., Bogetto, F., & Maina, G. (2012). Stressful life events and obsessive-compulsive disorder: Clinical features and symptom dimensions. *Psychiatry Research*, *197*(3), 259–64. doi: http://dx.doi.org/10.1016/j.psychres.2011.10.005

Rowa, K., Purdon, C., Summerfeldt, L. J., & Antony, M. M. (2005). Why are some obsessions more upsetting than others? *Behaviour Research and Therapy*, *43*(11), 1453–5. doi:http://dx.doi.org/10.1016/j.brat.2004.11.003

Ruscio, A., Stein, D., Chiu, W., & Kessler, R. (2010). The epidemiology of obsessive-compulsive disorder in the National Comorbidity Survey Replication. *Molecular Psychiatry*, *15*(1), 53–63. doi: http://dx.doi.org/10.1038/mp.2008.94

Salkovskis, P., Shafran, R., Rachman, S., & Freeston, M. H. (1999). Multiple pathways to inflated responsibility beliefs in obsessional problems: Possible origins and implications for therapy and research. *Behaviour Research and Therapy*, *37*(11), 1055–72.

Salkovskis, P. M. (1985). Obsessional-compulsive problems: A cognitive-behavioural analysis. *Behaviour Research and Therapy*, *23*(5), 571–83.

Salkovskis, P. M. (1989). Cognitive-behavioural factors and the persistence of intrusive thoughts in obsessional problems [comment/reply]. *Behaviour Research and Therapy*, *27*(6), 677–82.

Salkovskis, P. M. (1991). The importance of behaviour in the maintenance of anxiety and panic: A cognitive account. *Behavioural Psychotherapy*, *19*(1), 6–19.

Salkovskis, P. M. (1997). Obsessional-compulsive problems: A cognitive-behavioral analysis. In S. Rachman (Ed.), *Best of Behavior Research and Therapy* (pp. 29–41). Amsterdam, Netherlands: Pergamon/Elsevier Science Inc.

Salkovskis, P. M. (1999). Understanding and treating obsessive-compulsive disorder. *Behaviour Research and Therapy*, *37*(Suppl 1), S29–S52.

Salkovskis, P. M. (Ed.). (1996). *Frontiers of Cognitive Therapy*. New York, NY: Guilford Press.

Salkovskis, P. M., & Harrison, J. (1984). Abnormal and normal obsessions: A replication. *Behaviour Research and Therapy*, *22*(5), 549–52.

Salkovskis, P. M., & Kirk, J. (1989). Obsessional disorders. In K. Hawton, P. M. Salkovskis, J. Kirk & D. M. Clark (Eds.), *Cognitive Behaviour Therapy for Psychiatric Problems: A practical guide* (pp. 129–68). New York, NY: Oxford University Press.

Salkovskis, P. M., & Kobori, O. (2015). Reassuringly calm? Self-reported patterns of responses to reassurance seeking in obsessive compulsive disorder. *Journal of Behavior Therapy and Experimental Psychiatry, 49*(Part B), 203–8. doi: http://dx.doi.org/10.1016/j.jbtep.2015.09.002

Salkovskis, P. M., & Westbrook, D. (1989). Behaviour therapy and obsessional ruminations: Can failure be turned into success? *Behaviour Research and Therapy, 27*(2), 149–60.

Salkovskis, P. M., Westbrook, D., Davis, J., *et al.* (1997). Effects of neutralizing on intrusive thoughts: An experiment investigating the etiology of obsessive-compulsive disorder. *Behaviour Research and Therapy, 35*(3), 211–19.

Salkovskis, P. M., Wroe, A. L., Gledhill, A., *et al.* (2000). Responsibility attitudes and interpretations are characteristic of obsessive compulsive disorder. *Behaviour Research and Therapy, 38*(4), 347–72.

Salkovskis, P.M., Wahl, K., Millar J., & Gregory, J. (2017). The termination of checking and the role of just right feelings: A study of obsessional checkers compared with anxious and non-clinical controls. *Behavioural and Cognitive Psychotherapy, epub ahead of print* https://doi.org/10.1017/S135246581600031X

Salkovskis et al, in preparation. A randomised controlled trial of cognitive behaviour therapy versus ERP for OCD.

Santana, L., Fontenelle, J. M., Yucel, M., & Fontenelle, L. F. (2013). Rates and correlates of nonadherence to treatment in obsessive-compulsive disorder. *Journal of Psychiatric Practice, 19*(1), 42–53. doi: http://dx.doi.org/10.1097/01.pra.0000426326.49396.97

Savage, C. R., Keuthen, N. J., Jenike, M. A., *et al.* (1996). Recall and recognition memory in obsessive-compulsive disorder. *Journal of Neuropsychiatry and Clinical Neurosciences, 8*(1), 99–103.

Schwartz, C., Schlegl, S., Katrin Kuelz, A., & Voderholzer, U. (2013). Treatment-seeking in OCD community cases and psychological treatment actually provided to treatment-seeking patients: A systematic review. *Journal of Obsessive-Compulsive and Related Disorder, 2*, 448–56. doi: http://dx.doi.org/10.1016/j.jocrd.2013.10.006

Seaman, C., Oldfield, V. B., Gordon, O., Forrester, E., & Salkovskis, P. M. (2010). The impact of symptomatic hoarding in OCD and its treatment. *Behavioural and Cognitive Psychotherapy, 38*(2), 157–71. doi: http://dx.doi.org/10.1017/S1352465809990695

Shafran, R., Thordarson, D. S., & Rachman, S. (1996). Thought-action fusion in obsessive compulsive disorder. *Journal of Anxiety Disorders, 10*(5), 379–91. doi: http://dx.doi.org/10.1016/0887-6185%2896%2900018-7

Sher, K. J., Frost, R. O., & Otto, R. (1983). Cognitive deficits in compulsive checkers: an exploratory study. *Behaviour Research and Therapy, 21*, 357–63.

Simpson, H., Foa, E. B., Liebowitz, M. R., *et al.* (2013). Cognitive-behavioral therapy vs risperidone for augmenting serotonin reuptake inhibitors in obsessive-compulsive disorder: A randomized clinical trial. *JAMA Psychiatry, 70*(11), 1190–9. doi: 10.1001/jamapsychiatry.2013.1932

Simpson, H. B., Marcus, S. M., Zuckoff, A., Franklin, M., & Foa, E. B. (2012). Patient adherence to cognitive-behavioral therapy predicts long-term outcome in obsessive-compulsive disorder [Letter]. *Journal of Clinical Psychiatry, 73*(9), 1265–6. doi: http://dx.doi.org/10.4088/JCP.12l07879

Skapinakis, P., Caldwell, D. M., Hollingworth, W., *et al.* (2016). Pharmacological and psychotherapeutic interventions for management of obsessive-compulsive disorder in adults: A systematic review and network meta-analysis. *The Lancet Psychiatry, 3,* 730–9. doi: http://dx.doi.org/10.1016/S2215-0366%2816%2930069-4

Srivastava, S., Bhatia, M., Thawani, R., & Jhanjee, A. (2011). Quality of life in patients with obsessive compulsive disorder: A longitudinal study from India. *Asian Journal of Psychiatry, 4*(3), 178–82. doi: http://dx.doi.org/10.1016/j.ajp.2011.05.008

Steketee, G. (2005). Psychometric validation of the obsessive belief questionnaire and interpretation of intrusions inventory—part 2: Factor analyses and testing of a brief version. *Behaviour Research and Therapy, 43*(11), 1527–42. doi: http://dx.doi.org/10.1016/j.brat.2004.07.010

Steketee, G., & Foa, E. B. (1985). Obsessive-compulsive disorder. *Clinical Handbook of Psychological Disorders: A step-by-step treatment manual* (pp. 69–144). New York, NY: Guilford Press; US.

Steketee, G., Frost, R., Bhar, S., *et al.* (2003). Psychometric validation of the Obsessive Beliefs Questionnaire and the Interpretation of Intrusions Inventory: Part I. *Behaviour Research and Therapy, 41*(8), 863–78. doi: http://dx.doi.org/10.1016/S0005-7967%2802%2900099-2

Steketee, G., Frost, R. O., & Cohen, I. (1998). Beliefs in obsessive-compulsive disorder. *Journal of Anxiety Disorders, 12*(6), 525–37. doi: http://dx.doi.org/10.1016/S0887-6185%2898%2900030-9

Stengler, K., Olbrich, S., Heider, D., Dietrich, S., Riedel-Heller, S., & Jahn, I. (2013). Mental health treatment seeking among patients with OCD: Impact of age of onset. *Social Psychiatry and Psychiatric Epidemiology, 48*(5), 813–19. doi: http://dx.doi.org/10.1007/s00127-012-0544-3

Stengler-Wenzke, K., Kroll, M., Matschinger, H., & Angermeyer, M. C. (2006a). Quality of life of relatives of patients with obsessive-compulsive disorder. *Comprehensive Psychiatry, 47*(6), 523–7. doi: http://dx.doi.org/10.1016/j.comppsych.2006.02.002

Stengler-Wenzke, K., Kroll, M., Matschinger, H., & Angermeyer, M. C. (2006b). Subjective quality of life of patients with obsessive-compulsive disorder. *Social Psychiatry and Psychiatric Epidemiology, 41*(8), 662–8. doi: http://dx.doi.org/10.1007/s00127-006-0077-8

Stewart, S., Beresin, C., Haddad, S., Stack, D. E., Fama, J., & Jenike, M. (2008). Predictors of family accommodation in obsessive-compulsive disorder. *Annals of Clinical Psychiatry, 20*(2), 65–70.

Stewart, S., Yu, D., Scharf, J., *et al.* (2013). Genome-wide association study of obsessive-compulsive disorder. *Molecular Psychiatry, 18*(7), 788–98. doi: http://dx.doi.org/10.1038/mp.2012.85

Stobie, B., Taylor, T., Quigley, A., Ewing, S., & Salkovskis, P. M. (2007). 'Contents may vary': A pilot study of treatment histories of OCD patients. *Behavioural and Cognitive Psychotherapy, 35*(3), 273–82. doi: http://dx.doi.org/10.1017/S135246580700358X

Subramaniam, M., Abdin, E., Vaingankar, J. A., & Chong, S. A. (2012). Obsessive-compulsive disorder: Prevalence, correlates, help-seeking and quality of life in a multiracial Asian population. *Social Psychiatry and Psychiatric Epidemiology, 47*(12), 2035–43. doi: http://dx.doi.org/10.1007/s00127-012-0507-8

Swedo, S. E., Pietrini, P., Leonard, H. L., *et al.* (1992). Cerebral glucose metabolism in childhood-onset obsessive-compulsive disorder: Revisualization during pharmacotherapy. *Archives of General Psychiatry, 49*(9), 690–4.

Tallis, F., Pratt, P., & Jamani, N. (1999). Obsessive compulsive disorder, checking, and non-verbal memory: A neuropsychological investigation. *Behaviour Research and Therapy, 37*(2), 161–6. doi: http://dx.doi.org/10.1016/S0005-7967%2898%2900075-8

Taylor, S. (2011). Etiology of obsessions and compulsions: A meta-analysis and narrative review of twin studies. *Clinical Psychology Review, 31*(8), 1361–72. doi: http://dx.doi.org/10.1016/j.cpr.2011.09.008

Taylor, S. (2013). Molecular genetics of obsessive-compulsive disorder: A comprehensive meta-analysis of genetic association studies. *Molecular Psychiatry, 18*(7), 799–805.

Taylor, S., Abramowitz, J. S., & McKay, D. (2005). Are there interactions among dysfunctional beliefs in obsessive compulsive disorder? *Cognitive Behaviour Therapy, 34*(2), 89–98.

Taylor, S., Abramowitz, J. S., McKay, D., *et al.* (2006). Do dysfunctional beliefs play a role in all types of obsessive-compulsive disorder? *Journal of Anxiety Disorders, 20*(1), 85–97. doi: http://dx.doi.org/10.1016/j.janxdis.2004.11.005

Thompson-Hollands, J., Edson, A., Tompson, M. C., & Comer, J. S. (2014). Family involvement in the psychological treatment of obsessive-compulsive disorder: A meta-analysis. *Journal of Family Psychology, 28*(3), 287–98. doi: http://dx.doi.org/10.1037/a0036709

Timpano, K. R., Keough, M. E., Mahaffey, B., Schmidt, N. B., & Abramowitz, J. (2010). Parenting and obsessive compulsive symptoms: Implications of authoritarian parenting. *Journal of Cognitive Psychotherapy, 24*(3), 151–64. doi: http://dx.doi.org/10.1891/0889-8391.24.3.151

Toates, F. (1995). Cognition and evolution: An organization of action perspective. *Behavioural Processes, 35*(1–3), 239–50. doi: http://dx.doi.org/10.1016/0376-6357%2895%2900058-5

Tolin, D. F., Abramowitz, J. S., Brigidi, B. D., Amir, N., Street, G. P., & Foa, E. B. (2001). Memory and memory confidence in obsessive-compulsive disorder. *Behaviour Research and Therapy, 39*(8), 913–27.

Tolin, D. F., Abramowitz, J. S., Brigidi, B. D., & Foa, E. B. (2003). Intolerance of uncertainty in obsessive-compulsive disorder. *Journal of Anxiety Disorders, 17*(2), 233–42.

Tolin, D. F., Abramowitz, J. S., Hamlin, C., Foa, E. B., & Synodi, D. S. (2002). Attributions for thought suppression failure in obsessive-compulsive disorder. *Cognitive Therapy and Research, 26*(4), 505–17.

Tolin, D. F., Brady, R. E., & Hannan, S. (2008). Obsessional beliefs and symptoms of obsessive–compulsive disorder in a clinical sample. *Journal of Psychopathology and Behavioral Assessment, 30*(1), 31–42. doi: http://dx.doi.org/10.1007/s10862-007-9076-7

Tolin, D. F., Worhunsky, P., & Maltby, N. (2006). Are 'obsessive' beliefs specific to OCD?: A comparison across anxiety disorders. *Behaviour Research and Therapy, 44*(4), 469–80. doi: http://dx.doi.org/10.1016/j.brat.2005.03.007

Torres, A. R., Prince, M. J., Bebbington, P. E., *et al.* (2006). Obsessive-compulsive disorder: Prevalence, comorbidity, impact, and help-seeking in the British National Psychiatric Morbidity survey of 2000. *American Journal of Psychiatry, 163*(11), 1978–85.

Torres, A. R., Ramos-Cerqueira, A. T. A., Ferrao, Y. A., Fontenelle, L. F., do Rosario, M. C., & Miguel, E. C. (2011). Suicidality in obsessive-compulsive disorder: Prevalence and relation to symptom dimensions and comorbid conditions. *Journal of Clinical Psychiatry, 72*(1), 17–26. doi: http://dx.doi.org/10.4088/JCP.09m05651blu

Trzaskowski, M., Zavos, H. M., Haworth, C. M., Plomin, R., & Eley, T. C. (2012). Stable genetic influence on anxiety-related behaviours across middle childhood. *Journal of Abnormal Child Psychology, 40*(1), 85–94. doi: http://dx.doi.org/10.1007/s10802-011-9545-z

van Grootheest, D. S., Cath, D. C., Beekman, A. T., & Boomsma, D. I. (2007). Genetic and environmental influences on obsessive-compulsive symptoms in adults: A population-based twin-family study. *Psychological Medicine, 37*(11), 1635–44. doi: http://dx.doi.org/10.1017/S0033291707000980

Veale, D., Miles, S., Smallcombe, N., Ghezai, H., Goldacre, B., & Hodsoll, J. (2014). Atypical antipsychotic augmentation in SSRI treatment refractory obsessive-compulsive disorder: A systematic review and meta-analysis. *BMC Psychiatry, 14,* 317.

Verwoerd, J., de Jong, P. J., Wessel, I., & van Hout, W. J. (2013). 'If I feel disgusted, I must be getting ill': Emotional reasoning in the context of contamination fear. *Behaviour Research and Therapy, 51*(3), 122–7. doi: http://dx.doi.org/10.1016/j.brat.2012.11.005

Wahl, K., Kordon, A., Kuelz, K., Voderholzer, U., Hohagen, F., & Zurowski, B. (2010). Obsessive-compulsive disorder (OCD) is still an unrecognised disorder: A study on the recognition of OCD in psychiatric outpatients. *European Psychiatry, 25*(7), 374–7. doi: http://dx.doi.org/10.1016/j.eurpsy.2009.12.003

Wahl, K., Salkovskis, P. M., & Cotter, I. (2008). 'I wash until it feels right': the phenomenology of stopping criteria in obsessive-compulsive washing. *Journal of Anxiety Disorders, 22*(2), 143–61.

Warwick, H. M., & Salkovskis, P. M. (1990). Unwanted erections in obsessive-compulsive disorder. *British Journal of Psychiatry, 157,* 919–21.

Weissman, M. M., Bland, R. C., Canino, G. J., *et al.* (1994). The cross national epidemiology of obsessive compulsive disorder: The Cross National Collaborative Group. *Journal of Clinical Psychiatry, 55*(3, Suppl), 5–10.

Wheaton, M. G., Abramowitz, J. S., Berman, N. C., Riemann, B. C., & Hale, L. R. (2010). The relationship between obsessive beliefs and symptom dimensions in obsessive-compulsive disorder. *Behaviour Research and Therapy, 48*(10), 949–54. doi: 10.1016/j.brat.2010.05.027

Whittal, M. L., Robichaud, M., Thordarson, D. S., & McLean, P. D. (2008). Group and individual treatment of obsessive-compulsive disorder using cognitive therapy and exposure plus response prevention: A 2-year follow-up of two randomized trials. *Journal of Consulting and Clinical Psychology, 76*(6), 1003–14. doi: http://dx.doi.org/10.1037/a0013076

Whittal, M. L., Thordarson, D. S., & McLean, P. D. (2005). Treatment of obsessive-compulsive disorder: Cognitive behavior therapy vs. exposure and response prevention. *Behaviour Research and Therapy, 43*(12), 1559–76. doi: http://dx.doi.org/10.1016/j.brat.2004.11.012

Woods, C. M., Vevea, J. L., Chambless, D. L., & Bayen, U. J. (2002). Are compulsive checkers impaired in memory? A meta-analytic review. *Clinical Psychology: Science and Practice, 9*(4), 353–66. doi: http://dx.doi.org/10.1093/clipsy/9.4.353

Wolpe J. (1958). *Psychotherapy by Reciprocal Inhibition.* Stanford, CA: Stanford University Press, 239 pp.

World Health Organization (2014). *The ICD-10 Classification of Diseases and Related Health Problems,*(10th revision). Apps who.int/classifications/icd10/browse/2014/en#/F42

Chapter 2

When you meet: assessing obsessive-compulsive disorder

2.1 Assessment leading to understanding: the preliminaries

The key to assessment is not to engage your client or patient, but rather to engage with them. An assessment is always a two-way process; as a therapist, you are both assessing people with obsessive–compulsive disorder (OCD) and being assessed by them. The person with OCD has often made a long and difficult journey to the point of seeing you, and they often have a range of doubts and fears about both the possibilities of therapy and how things will work with you, the therapist. At an assessment, we are typically asking people to share their deepest doubts and fears to a complete stranger very quickly. The big surprise is that they will often do so even at the earliest stages, but it is up to the individual therapist to do what they can to make this as easy and unthreatening as possible. For treatment to be most effective and efficient, an atmosphere of mutual trust has to be built, and this begins with the process that therapists call assessment, which could more appropriately be referred to as the beginning of the sharing of information. Part of this process is inviting the person with OCD to share their story with you.

A good way to start the assessment is to agree on how communications will work, starting with exchanging preferred names. The therapist, when introducing him or herself, can offer (if requested) to share something about his or her training and experience, his or her supervisory arrangements, and so on. It is very helpful at this stage to ask the person attending the assessment whether he or she might have any questions to ask. If the person seems to be ill at ease (and most will be anxious about meeting you for the first time), ask whether there is anything that you can do or tell the person about that might make him or her feel more comfortable. The therapist should set the scene by indicating what is going to happen in the session.

Assessment thus begins the process of engagement and building a collaborative pattern of working, with the explicit aim of developing an understanding of the person's problems, including, but not necessarily confined to, their obsessional issues, with the aim being to underpin the cognitive-behavioural treatment of OCD. That is to say, assessment *is* the beginning of treatment. Whatever your level of experience as a therapist, it is essential to be well informed about OCD, its contexts and causes, and understand how difficult it can be to live with this problem.

In some instances, people will be telling you the detail of their difficulties for the first time. They may not conceptualize the problem as OCD, or even find it in some way risky to do so. People with OCD may have experienced negative reactions from others when disclosing problems in the past, which may have included minimization, misunderstanding, or ridicule of their difficulties, or even shock when they have described particular obsessions. As a result of their beliefs and/or such experiences, they may be particularly sensitive to your reactions. The overall aim of the initial meeting, once you have established that the problem is OCD, is therefore to convey a sense that the person's difficulties are serious but understandable and treatable. Another aim of the assessment is to gain a thorough clinical picture of the main presenting problem(s), comorbidity, and contextual factors that are relevant to the problem, and other factors that may affect the person's ability to participate in treatment. Gaining a sense of the person's resources and resilience will also aid in both of these aims. You want to get to know who they are as well as what problems they have.

In a thorough assessment it is helpful to begin by asking about the *main problem* that has brought the person to therapy—this is often, but not always, the most troubling *obsessions, doubts, images, or sensations*, and the associated compulsions, observable or covert. It is helpful to enquire about places and activities that the person avoids or has difficulty with, as well as building a picture of how the problem has an impact on the full range of the person's current functioning. This will enable you to begin to build a picture of the person's life and difficulties in context; what (s)he can and cannot do, or can only do in a limited way. Structured interviews and checklists can help with gathering this information, but it is not always helpful to use these in an obvious way early on while the relationship is forming. Opening questions can include:

'Could you tell me in your own words what has brought you here today?'

'In what ways is the problem impacting on what you can or cannot do?'

'Perhaps you could talk me through a typical day, describing how the OCD gets in the way. Which would be a good day to choose?'

Intrusive thoughts: sometimes people are very clear about the thoughts that are troubling them. If they are afraid of becoming contaminated or contracting a disease they may talk about the danger and the fears they have rather than discuss their thoughts per se. A difficulty sometimes experienced in assessment is when it is not clear what the intrusions are. In such instances, people may often refer to 'my thoughts' repeatedly in the room, but will not specify what they are. Usually, reluctance to describe intrusions results from specific beliefs about what might happen if they described their thoughts (e.g. the therapist will think they are mad or bad, will laugh, or that saying things out loud will make the thoughts worse, the feared outcome becomes more likely to happen, and so on). To identify such factors the therapist should indicate a degree of understanding:

> 'Many people with this type of problem find it difficult to mention what their thoughts are about, often because they think that it is risky to do so, or they find their thoughts uncomfortable, frightening, or embarrassing. Does that type of idea ever cross your mind? … What do you think is the worst thing that would happen if you mentioned them to me?'

It can often be helpful to normalize the type of thoughts by giving clinical examples that the therapist judges are likely to be similar to the person's experience; for example, by saying:

WALTER: 'I'm having some thoughts, thoughts that really bother me.'

THERAPIST: 'Are they about something awful happening?'

WALTER: 'Well … kind of. I can't talk about them.'

THERAPIST: 'It sounds like these thoughts are very upsetting for you, and difficult to talk about. That often happens; it can be very difficult to discuss the kind of thoughts that are especially upsetting. Often, people come to see me about thoughts which they haven't even told their own family about, because the thoughts seem so awful to them. Have you ever been able to tell anyone about these thoughts?'

WALTER: 'No. It's … very difficult. Do other people really have thoughts they can't talk about?'

THERAPIST: 'Yes. Very often people find it easiest to tell me first why the thoughts are difficult to talk about. Of course, there are lots of things which may make talking difficult. For example, sometimes people worry that I'll think they are crazy, or that I will think they are bad. Other times it's that the thoughts themselves are embarrassing, or people think I'll be shocked. What is the worst thing about these thoughts for you?'

WALTER: 'I'm very worried … that you'll think I'm bad and have me locked up. Because the thoughts are so bad; I don't think anyone else has thoughts this bad; you might think I'm dangerous.'

THERAPIST: 'Would it be helpful to you if I told you about some of the worrying kinds of thoughts that other people have?'

The therapist might give some examples of the types of thought experienced in clinical and non-clinical populations (e.g. Rachman and de Silva (1978)), stressing their alienness to the person having them and introducing the idea of the importance of meaning.

THERAPIST: 'There is a very important thing to remember about these kinds of thoughts: the people who get most upset about a particular thought are the people for whom it is most difficult; for instance, if you have strong religious beliefs you are more likely to get upset by blasphemous thoughts; if you are very gentle you will get upset about violent thoughts or impulses. Think about someone who deliberately gets into fights a lot; do you think violent thoughts upset them?'

WALTER: 'No, I see what you mean. But would you take someone's child away from them if they had thoughts about doing awful things to them?'

THERAPIST: 'One of the most important features of these kinds of thoughts is how upset they make the person having them. It might seem odd, but very often the thoughts happen because you are trying hard not to have them. Could you try right now *not* to think about a giraffe.' (Pause) 'What happened?'

WALTER: 'I had a picture of a giraffe!'

THERAPIST: 'Right, that's what happens with a thought that is not upsetting when you try not to have it. If the thought is upsetting, then it comes on even more than that. Would it be sensible to take someone's child away from them because they were trying not to think about harming them?'

WALTER: 'That's just what I do. I try really hard not to have these thoughts and they just keep on coming. Then I try to wipe them out. It's really difficult.'

THERAPIST: 'If you think about what you just did with the thought of the giraffe, what does that tell you about why they keep on coming?'

Rather than making direct guesses it is usually better to elicit and discuss worries about disclosing the obsessional thoughts, using examples that appear to have some similarity to the person's own difficulties. It will be important to get detail of the thoughts when drawing out the formulation later on in therapy.

Throughout assessment, there should be, where this is correct, a subtext (sometimes even explicitly) from the therapists which runs: 'What you are describing is familiar to me; I am not shocked or otherwise disturbed by what I am hearing, which I have heard before. It makes sense to me and I am comfortable with working with you on these issues.' To a substantial degree, this is conveyed both through the line of questioning adopted by the therapist and by the non-verbal cues they provide.

Overt rituals: in general, people's descriptions of their problems are influenced by familiarity, so that they may omit details which seem trivial or normal to them but are crucial to therapy. For example, the person with OCD might mention handwashing but not mention that they pick things up using tissues or never touch doors with their hands because of fears of contamination.

Covert/mental rituals: one of the more difficult tasks can be assessment of mental rituals. These—often more subtle—safety-seeking behaviours can be elicited through careful questions about recent occasions on which the thought occurred, focussing on thoughts or images the person tried to form in their mind, or any other mental activity that they deliberately tried to form or carry out, e.g. 'Did you try to get any other thoughts? Did you try to think things to put the thought right?' Asking the person to provoke or form their usual intrusion can also be helpful. These strategies can also elicit reports of cognitive avoidance and thought suppression.

Gaining a sense of how the problem developed and whether it has waxed and waned can be very informative, and can help both in building up your understanding and also in conveying the notion that the problem is understandable. It can also provide useful information on stressors and protective factors. However, the priority is on gaining an understanding of what is happening at present (see Section 2.9, Spotlight on supervision).

2.2 Other forms of the problem/foci of worries

OCD can present with a wide variety of symptoms, even within an individual at a single timepoint, and can often show patterns of change over time. Enquiring about all forms of the problem is helpful to gain a full clinical picture. Checklists of common obsessions and compulsions, such as the checklist that accompanies the Yale–Brown Obsessive Compulsive Scale (YBOCS; Goodman *et al.*, 1989), can be very useful in gaining a good understanding of present and historical obsessional problems.

2.3 Diagnosis in the room—determining what is OCD and what is not

It is clear that diagnosis is a mixture of blessing and curse. Psychiatric diagnosis will not tell you what the person's problem is; only careful listening to his or her story will do that. However, it will tell you where to begin to look. The fundamental phenomena of OCD have probably remained the same for centuries, but details of the diagnostic criteria for OCD have changed over time; for example, dropping the stipulation that the obsessions are not worries that are related to 'real life' problems. The two main diagnostic systems, *DSM* and *ICD* (*Diagnostic and Statistical Manual of Mental Disorders* and *International Classification of Diseases*), are not exactly the same and there is a certain degree of subjectivity in ascertaining the level of interference in the person's life. Our approach in a clinical context is therefore to take the spirit rather than the letter of diagnosis. In this context, it can also be helpful to find out how the person with OCD views the diagnostic process, and whether or not it is important to them. It would then be appropriate to communicate your own views regarding the value and problems of diagnosis, being mindful of the potential utility of diagnosis in accessing services etc., and the potential negative labelling effects that can be associated with diagnosis.

Having a common language to describe OCD is useful in the context of research. However, as a clinician, establishing the detail of the lived experience of OCD will tell you much more.

2.4 **OCD in context**

Getting a picture of the individual cultural context is essential for understanding and diagnosing OCD in every person. This provides relevant information as to the kinds of beliefs and experience that may have influenced the problem, and a sense of what is culturally normative. This does not simply refer to broadly defined culture, but includes 'microculture' such as families and peer groups. This may be particularly important in the case of OCD related to cultural factors, such as religion. Having some familiarity with the religious beliefs and practices of the person and the religion is helpful in building a *shared understanding* of what is excessive. If you are not very familiar with the religion in question, a stance of honest curiosity can help build a shared understanding of what is excessive. Helpful questions for the therapist to bear in mind include (see Abramowitz and Jacoby, 2014, for further discussion):

Does the compulsive behaviour go far beyond the requirements of religious guidance?

Does the person's spouse/sibling/parent practise the religion in the same way?

Does the compulsive behaviour have a narrow or overly trivial focus?

Are the requirements of work, prayer, and family demands ignored or not receiving enough attention because of a focus on the difficulties with religious practice?

These types of reflections about levels of interference and what is normative may also be useful where the OCD is interfering with work in a role that requires significant responsibility and accuracy, such as medicine or pharmacy. Asking if the person's colleagues would take the same precautions can yield useful information.

As well as areas that may be affected by the person's OCD, it is important to check for the presence of other stressors that may be having an impact on the problem, e.g. general levels of stress or the person's ability to come to, or engage with, therapy. These may include difficulties with finances, relationships, immigration, work, housing, or caring responsibilities for spouse, parents, or children. Past stressors can be important including post-traumatic stress disorder (PTSD); note that in mental contamination it is likely that associations based on past memories may be crucial to both understanding and treatment of the obsessional problem (see Section 4.3). Assessing levels of alcohol and drug use is also important in this regard and as part of a risk assessment.

Home visits and contact with alternative informants can provide important information as to the problem in context. Sometimes the information gleaned can seem paradoxical; for example, people with contamination obsessions who live in unclean situations because they are avoiding cleaning owing to the time and distress involved in complicated washing rituals, or who have a small designated uncontaminated area of their room because of the overwhelming demands of keeping the whole room clean. As assessment and treatment progresses, you will gain a shared understanding of the internal logic of these situations.

2.5 **Other comorbid diagnoses**

Comorbidity is high in OCD, with 62–90% of people with OCD also found to be suffering from another *DSM-IV* Axis I disorder (Crino *et al.*, 2005; Fireman *et al.*, 2001; Ruscio *et al.*, 2010; Torres *et al.*, 2006). Rates of comorbidity with depression range from 37% to 63%, and other anxiety disorders, including generalized anxiety disorder (GAD), from 20% to 76% (Abramowitz and Foa, 1998; Crino *et al.*, 2005; Ruscio *et al.*, 2010; Torres *et al.*, 2006). It will be important to establish levels of depression and anxiety in the assessment, helped by instruments such as the GAD-7 (Spitzer *et al.*, 2006) and PHQ-9 (Kroenke and Spitzer, 2002).

These problems may require treatment in their own right. It is useful to ask the person their own view of how dependent the issues are: 'if you no longer had OCD, do you think depression/GAD, etc. would still be a problem?'

In addition, mood can play an important role in maintaining aspects of the problem. In a sample of people with OCD, Ricciardi and McNally (1995) found that comorbid depression was linked to higher rates of obsessions but not compulsions. This study noted that, in 85% of their sample, OCD preceded (65%) or began at the same time (20%) as mood disorder. However, a large epidemiological study found that mood disorders were almost as likely to precede (40.2%) as to follow OCD (45.6%) (Ruscio *et al.*, 2010).

People with OCD clearly can and do experience other worries alongside their obsessions, and those with greater responsibility beliefs may be more prone to pathological worry in addition to OCD (Abramowitz and Foa, 1998). Within non-clinical individuals, obsessions have been shown to differ significantly from everyday worries in terms of being less frequent, more ego-dystonic, and more imagery based (Langlois *et al.*, 2000; Lee *et al.*, 2005).

A diagnostic screener such as the Structured Clinical Interview for DSM-5 (SCID screener; First *et al.*, 1995) or the Psychiatric Diagnostic Screening Questionnaire (PDSQ; Zimmerman and Mattia, 2001) can provide helpful information as to other difficulties that are present at a clinical or subclinical level. It is important to follow up scores above threshold on any self-report screening tool with a clinical interview. Symptoms identified as 'present' on a screener may ostensibly look like another disorder but on questioning might be directly related to the OCD. For example, 'panic attacks' are often mentioned by people with OCD, but these tend to be situationally triggered (as opposed to 'out of the blue'). Further examples of this diagnostic overlap are provided in Table 2.1.

It is very important to ascertain the phenomenology of the problem, as misdiagnosis can be damaging and prevent access to appropriate treatment (Challacombe and Wroe, 2013).

2.6 **Personality**

Sometimes it can be useful to establish whether the person meets criteria for common 'personality disorders' such as obsessive-compulsive (OCPD), avoidant, paranoid, dependent, and borderline. The criteria for some personality disorders, particularly OCPD and avoidant personality disorder, may overlap with the experience of OCD itself (see Section 4.1). Enquiring about personality, particularly in the context of gaining developmental information, can help to elucidate whether longstanding traits may play a role in maintaining the problem. Despite common clinician beliefs to the contrary, the presence of any personality issues does not in itself necessarily interfere with cognitive-behavioural therapy (CBT; Dreessen and Arntz, 1998; Dreessen *et al.*, 1997), although there is evidence that applying the label of comorbid personality disorder, even inaccurately, may adversely impact on therapist expectancies (Lam *et al.*, 2015). Moreover, in OCPD, there is now some evidence that the presence of a perfectionism-based set of reactions that may have a positive effect on

Table 2.1 Key phenomena distinguishing OCD from other disorders commonly misdiagnosed as OCD

ICD/DSM disorder	Core features	Similar features but occur in context of OCD
Panic disorder	Intense anxiety that occurs out of the blue, manifesting as a constellation of physical symptoms (e.g. shortness of breath, dissociation, racing heart, sweating, nausea), which are feared to relate to a catastrophic outcome. Reach a peak within 5–10 minutes and occur three times a week for 1-month period	Intense anxiety (which is likely to include physical symptoms), but occurring in situations where obsessions are triggered; e.g. anxiety when something becomes 'contaminated' or when an obsession of harm occurs in the presence of a child. Severe avoidance in OCD can closely resemble agoraphobia
Social phobia	Specific fear of social situations owing to fear that the person will do or say something embarrassing or humiliating such as blushing or stuttering	Concern about the social consequences of obsessional behaviour, e.g. people will think I'm mad if they saw me doing a ritual
Generalized anxiety disorder	Excessive worry about a number of topics that is experienced as uncontrollable, pervasive (over 50%) of time and of at least 6 months' duration	Worry confined to a narrow range of topics. Content of obsession rather then worrying about it is the problem
Health anxiety	Excessive worry and preoccupation about symptoms of illness and persistent belief that the person is ill	Worry focussed on the causes of illness rather than symptoms, and worry about the risks of getting ill. Realistically, OCD and health anxiety overlap at times
Depressive disorder	Repetitive negative thoughts that the person is worthless, guilty, etc., persistent and pervasive sad mood, interference in sleep, concentration, appetite. Note: subclinical intrusive thoughts can occur in the context of depression	Repetitive negative thoughts that the person interprets as meaning they may be a bad person. Note: depression is a common comorbidity with OCD
Eating disorders	Preoccupation with and high value placed on weight and shape. Avoidance or restriction of food intake. May be accompanied by a binge/purge cycle	Avoidance or restriction of food owing to obsessional rules; e.g. I will only eat food from sealed packets to avoid contamination, not able to eat when obsessions are present, not eating as a ritual

Table 2.1 Continued

ICD/DSM disorder	Core features	Similar features but occur in context of OCD
Phobia of vomiting (sometimes mistaken for OCD or an eating disorder)	Specific fear that the person will contract an illness or eat something that will cause them to vomit. Appraisal of the experience of vomiting as uncontrollable, distressing, and extremely aversive. Attention and behaviour revolves around this fear	Fears of becoming ill not limited to vomiting
Schizophrenia or psychosis (including postpartum psychosis)	Constellation of positive symptoms (e.g. delusions, hallucinations, disordered thinking) and negative symptoms (e.g. withdrawal, apathy). Can be sudden and acute onset	Intense anxiety, distress, and doubts about safety and threat. Not disordered thinking. Can be sudden and acute onset. Strongly held beliefs (especially when anxious), not delusional; examine how they are formed

treatment outcomes (Gordon *et al.*, 2015). The point of assessing personality issues is so that, when the assessment is summarized as a prelude to beginning treatment, these can be discussed as potential areas for the person to work with if they wish. For some, such issues may also indicate areas of strength and resources they can bring into treatment; for example, in 'OCPD' it seems likely that persistence (rather than perseveration) will help the person push through the difficult periods in treatment.

2.7 **Assessing risk**

Some clinicians can become overly anxious over risk issues. This is because OCD is often characterized by unwanted intrusive thoughts and doubts regarding sexual, violent, or otherwise 'unacceptable' thoughts. These thoughts are experienced as repugnant and distressing; they often lead the person to wonder what they mean and fear that they may act on them despite their sense that the thoughts do not fit with their values (are ego-dystonic). They may then take measures, including avoidance and compulsions, to ensure their thoughts do not 'come true'. However, the content of intrusive thoughts can cause alarm amongst some professionals with less understanding of OCD, who may feel it is necessary to err on the side of caution and instigate risk procedures. However, as Veale *et al.* (2009) put it: 'a person with OCD can be harmed by an incorrect or unduly lengthy risk assessment, responding with increased doubts and fears about the implications of their intrusive thoughts. At best this will lead to greater distress, avoidance and compulsive behaviours, and mistrust of health professionals; at worst, to complete decompensation of the patient or break-up of the family (Veale *et al.*, 2009). The risk of people acting directly on their intrusive thoughts has been termed '*primary risk*' by Veale *et al.* (2009), whilst indirect effects, arising from the fact of suffering from OCD, is '*secondary risk*'. Secondary risk is something also present in most untreated or undertreated psychiatric and psychological problems, and links to the degree of impairment, distress, and damage to quality of life.

The NICE (The National Institute for Health and Care Excellence) guidelines (National Collaborating Centre for Mental Health, 2005: p.15) state that:

> 'If healthcare professionals are uncertain about the risks associated with intrusive sex-ual, aggressive or death-related thoughts reported by people with OCD, they should consult mental health professionals with specific expertise in the assessment and man-agement of OCD. These themes are common in people with OCD at any age, and are often misinterpreted as indicating risk.'

Primary risk is therefore typically very low, but problems can be caused by assessing it as high. Once you have established a diagnosis of OCD, it may some-times be necessary to help other professionals understand that people with OCD do not act on obsessions, e.g. to smother a baby or push someone in front of a train. It is important to note that comorbidity does occur and someone with OCD of one subtype may have problematic thoughts that are not part of OCD at all.

Another recommendation of the NICE guidelines is:

> 'In people who have been diagnosed with OCD, healthcare professionals should assess the risk of self-harm and suicide, especially if they have also been diagnosed with depression. Part of the risk assessment should include the impact of their compulsive behaviours on themselves or others.'
>
> (NICE guideline CG31, 1.4.1.2, p.11)

As mentioned, the risks resulting from OCD-driven behaviours, or the des-peration caused by or experienced alongside the problem, have been termed secondary risk. These risks may be much less obvious as they are often unin-tended consequences of following compulsions or rules or preoccupation with obsessions. Examples of secondary risk include overuse of cleaning products to the point that the environment is toxic to the person and others who inhabit it, use of inappropriate cleaning products such as bleach directly on skin, or on the skin of children, and avoiding water and food owing to contamination fears. In the case of intrusive thoughts of harm, examples may include avoidance of time with their own children. Secondary risks include the impact on family mem-bers, who may be drawn into rituals or support avoidant behaviour. The effects of obsessional behaviour may be of increased dependence on others, conflict, or isolation from other people, which may in turn cause or exacerbate OCD and depression. Clinicians will need to recognize and understand secondary risks carefully to make a decision as to whether additional management or risk assessment is required and whether treatment should be prioritized.

Some obsessions do concern a fear of self-harm or suicide and, as with other unwanted intrusive thoughts, people take measures to avoid acting on these thoughts. However, self-harm can be used by people with OCD as a strategy to manage other intrusive thoughts or difficult feelings.

Depression and hopelessness increase risk of self-harm and suicide. OCD severity, depressive symptoms, comorbidity, and a history of suicide have been associated with increasing suicidality in OCD (Angelakis *et al.*, 2015). Of those with OCD in the British comorbidity survey, 25.7% had attempted suicide, while 63.3% had experienced suicidal thoughts (Torres *et al.*, 2006). Similarly, Torres *et al.* (2011) reported that 36% of their sample had experienced lifetime suicidal thoughts, 20% had made plans, and 10% had made attempts.

Levels of drug and alcohol use should be ascertained as part of the assessment, along with any increase in risk to self or others as a result of being in a disinhibited state. Sometimes drugs or alcohol are used to manage anxiety. Dependence on drugs or alcohol and the physiological and emotional disturbance caused will make it difficult for the person to engage in CBT.

Veale *et al.* (2009) provide an excellent discussion of identifying and managing risk issues in OCD.

2.8 **Assessing severity: clinician-rated and questionnaire measures**

Self-report questionnaires are used to supplement the basic clinical interview, and are a helpful shorthand way of obtaining a range of detail about the person's problem and screening for specific factors. It is helpful to send these ahead of the first appointment with an explanatory letter and the offer of discussion should there be concerns. When these are brought to the first session, it can save some time, particularly if the questionnaires sent include some broad screeners as well as symptom measures. As therapy progresses, they can be used to evaluate key changes in outcomes on a session-by-session basis, to identify the extent of clinical changes and any residual or unchanged problems, and to help target key maintaining factors.

Some of the most useful self-report symptom measures include the Obsessive-Compulsive Inventory (Foa *et al.*, 1998); general beliefs concerning responsibility are measured using the Responsibility Assumptions scale, whilst the Responsibility Interpretations Questionnaire is used to assess specific appraisals of intrusions (Salkovskis *et al.*, 2000) Note that these measures are included in the appendices.

The YBOCS scale (Goodman *et al.*, 1989) is the most widely used clinician-administered interview schedule, and can be readily integrated into diagnostic assessments. Although it has some problems as a broad measure, it includes both a symptom checklist and an interview to measure severity. A self-report version is also available. Note that some experience with OCD is required to make valid and reliable ratings.

2.8.1 Idiosyncratic measures

Idiosyncratic ratings, e.g. of specific beliefs about negative outcomes, of discomfort, of the urge to neutralize are always relevant. During treatment, they provide important information about how subjective responses change both within sessions and between sessions as treatment progresses. Asking at assessment provides a 'baseline' measure. For some individuals you can record *behavioural byproducts:* these are incidental correlates of the obsessional behaviour that indicate its extent and are easy to measure, especially in people with OCD who engage in excessive washing/cleaning. Examples are the amount of soap, toilet paper, or cleaning materials bought each week.

2.9 Spotlight on supervision: problems in getting a good assessment

'*My client feels that the answer lies in finding out why (s)he developed OCD and I'm finding it hard to get information about his/her current problem.*'

Sometimes the person with OCD may become increasingly preoccupied with the idea that the best way to solve their present problems is to identify the origins. After all, how is it possible to treat a problem if we do not know for sure how it started? In such cases, drawing a distinction between the origins of a problem and the factors that maintain it is often a good way of dealing with these ideas. Consider using the following metaphor:

> 'Imagine you have woken in hospital with a broken leg. You have no recollection of how you broke it. There is no need to know the cause of the fracture to mend the break. In fact, the leg usually heals itself; what the doctors do is identify and deal with anything that might slow down or prevent the normal healing process. Once you are back on your feet, however, you might want to consider how the leg got broken. It may have been a complete accident, in that you stumbled and fell for no obvious reason. However, it might be that you tripped because there is a section of loose stair carpet, so that one day soon it will happen again. If that's the case, you would want to fix the carpet.'

Using Socratic questioning when sharing this metaphor can enhance its impact. As described in Section 1.8.3, in some cases there are general and enduring belief factors that may have made the person prone to developing OCD, and which may not fully change in the course of treatment. At a later point in therapy it can be helpful to identify and deal with these.

2.10 Ending the assessment: OCD is the main problem—what happens next?

Current guidelines in the UK are based on the stepped care approach, which encompasses low intensity and high intensity intervention. Deciding if a person is suitable for low intensity intervention is based on the severity of his or her problem. NICE guidelines recommend that, if the person is suffering from moderate to severe OCD, a high intensity approach is warranted in the first instance (see the *Oxford Guide to Low Intensity CBT Interventions* for more information on other CBT-based approaches with OCD; Bennett-Levy *et al.*, 2010). We take the view that, where possible and assuming that patients have accessed at least one self-help book or package themselves, it is appropriate to offer higher intensity treatment of the type described here.

It can help to ascertain preliminary goals for treatment. This can refocus the discussion on the benefits of undertaking therapy and can help reorientate towards change after a long discussion of the problem (see Section 3.4 on Goals).

2.10.1 End of assessment checklist

Does the person have OCD?

Assessment questionnaire scores

Does the person have other comorbid conditions?

What are the main priorities and goals for treatment?

Are there any other factors that may get in the way of CBT? (e.g. Can the person attend regular sessions?)

References

Abramowitz, J. S., & Foa, E. B. (1998). Worries and obsessions in individuals with obsessive-compulsive disorder with and without comorbid generalized anxiety disorder. *Behaviour Research and Therapy, 36*(7–8), 695–700.

Abramowitz, J. S., & Jacoby, R. J. (2014). Scrupulosity: A cognitive-behavioral analysis and implications for treatment. *Journal of Obsessive-Compulsive and Related Disorders, 3*(2), 140–9. doi: http://dx.doi.org/10.1016/j.jocrd.2013.12.007

Angelakis, I., Gooding, P., Tarrier, N. & Panagioti, M. (2015). Suicidality in obsessive compulsive disorder (OCD): A systematic review and meta-analysis. *Clinical Psychology Review, 39,* 1–15. doi: http://dx.doi.org/10.1016/j.cpr.2015.03.002

Bennett-Levy, J., Richards, D., Farrand, P., Christensen, H., Griffiths, K., Kavanagh, D., *et al.* (2010). *Oxford Guide to Low Intensity Interventions.* Oxford: Oxford University Press.

Challacombe, F. L., & Wroe, A. L. (2013). A hidden problem: consequences of the misdiagnosis of perinatal obsessive-compulsive disorder. *British Journal of General Practice, 63*(610), 275–6. doi: http://dx.doi.org/10.3399/bjgp13X667376

Crino, R., Slade, T., & Andrews, G. (2005). The changing prevalence and severity of obsessive-compulsive disorder criteria from DSM-III to DSM-IV. *The American Journal of Psychiatry, 162*(5), 876–82. doi: http://dx.doi.org/10.1176/appi.ajp.162.5.876

Dreessen, L., & Arntz, A. (1998). The impact of personality disorders on treatment outcome of anxiety disorders: Best-evidence synthesis. *Behaviour Research and Therapy, 36*(5), 483–504. doi: http://dx.doi.org/10.1016/S0005-7967%2898%2900026-6

Dreessen, L., Hoekstra, R., & Arntz, A. (1997). Personality disorders do not influence the results of cognitive and behavior therapy for obsessive compulsive disorder. *Journal of Anxiety Disorders, 11*(5), 503–21. doi: http://dx.doi.org/10.1016/S0887-6185%2897%2900027-3

Fireman, B., Koran, L. M., Leventhal, J. L., & Jacobson, A. (2001). The prevalence of clinically recognized obsessive-compulsive disorder in a large health maintenance organization. *The American Journal of Psychiatry, 158*(11), 1904–10. doi: http://dx.doi.org/10.1176/appi.ajp.158.11.1904

First, M. B., Spitzer, R. L., Gibbon, M., & Williams, J. B. W. (1995). *Structured Clinical Interview for DSM-IV Axis-I disorders (SCID-IP).* Washington, DC: American Psychiatric Press.

Foa, E. B., Kozak, M. J., Salkovskis, P. M., Coles, M. E., & Amir, N. (1998). The validation of a new obsessive-compulsive disorder scale: The Obsessive-Compulsive Inventory. *Psychological Assessment, 10*(3), 206–14.

Goodman, W. K., Price, L. H., Rasmussen, S. A., Mazure, C., Fleischmann, R., Hill, C. L. *et al.* (1989). The Yale-Brown Obsessive Compulsive Scale: I. Development, use, and reliability. *Archives of General Psychiatry, 46*(11), 1006–11.

Gordon, O., Salkovskis, P.M., & Bream, V. (2015). The impact of obsessive compulsive personality disorder on cognitive behaviour therapy for obsessive compulsive disorder. *Behavioural and Cognitive Psychotherapy, 44*(4), 444–59.

Kroenke, K., & Spitzer, R. L. (2002). The PHQ-9: a new depression diagnostic and severity measure. *Psychiatric Annals. 32,* 509–15.

Lam, D. C., Poplavskaya, E. V., Salkovskis, P. M., Hogg, L. I., & Panting, H. (2015). An experimental investigation of the impact of personality disorder diagnosis on clinicians: Can we see past the borderline? *Behavioural and Cognitive Psychotherapy, 44*(3), 361–73. doi: http://dx.doi.org/10.1017/S1352465815000351

Langlois, F., Freeston, M. H., & Ladouceur, R. (2000). Differences and similarities between obsessive intrusive thoughts and worry in a non-clinical population: Study 1. *Behaviour Research and Therapy, 38*(2), 157–73. doi: http://dx.doi.org/10.1016/S0005-7967%2899%2900027-3

Lee, H.-J., Lee, S.-H., Kim, H.-S., Kwon, S.-M., & Telch, M. J. (2005). A comparison of autogenous/reactive obsessions and worry in a nonclinical population: A test of the continuum hypothesis. *Behaviour Research and Therapy, 43*(8), 999–1010. doi: http://dx.doi.org/10.1016/j.brat.2004.06.017

National Collaborating Centre for Mental Health (2005): *CG31. NICE Guidance on OCD.* London: The British Psychological Society and the Royal College of Psychiatrists.

Rachman, S., & de Silva, P. (1978). Abnormal and normal obsessions. *Behaviour Research and Therapy, 16*(4), 233–48. doi: http://dx.doi.org/10.1016/0005-7967%2878%2990022-0

Ricciardi, J. N., & McNally, R. J. (1995). Depressed mood is related to obsessions, but not to compulsions, in obsessive-compulsive disorder. *Journal of Anxiety Disorders, 9*(3), 249–56. doi: http://dx.doi.org/10.1016/0887-6185%2895%2900006-A

Ruscio, A., Stein, D., Chiu, W., & Kessler, R. (2010). The epidemiology of obsessive-compulsive disorder in the National Comorbidity Survey Replication. *Molecular Psychiatry, 15*(1), 53–63. doi: http://dx.doi.org/10.1038/mp.2008.94

Salkovskis, P. M., Wroe, A. L., Gledhill, A., Morrison, N., Forrester, E., Richards, C., *et al.* (2000). Responsibility attitudes and interpretations are characteristic of obsessive compulsive disorder. *Behaviour Research and Therapy, 38*(4), 347–72.

Spitzer, R. L. *et al.* (2006). A brief measure for assessing generalized anxiety disorder: the GAD-7. *Archives of Internal Medicine, 166*, 1092–7.

Torres, A. R., Prince, M. J., Bebbington, P. E., Bhugra, D., Brugha, T. S., Farrell, M., *et al.* (2006). Obsessive-compulsive disorder: Prevalence, comorbidity, impact, and help-seeking in the British National Psychiatric Morbidity survey of 2000. *American Journal of Psychiatry, 163*(11), 1978–85.

Torres, A. R., Ramos-Cerqueira, A. T. A., Ferrao, Y. A., Fontenelle, L. F., do Rosario, M. C., & Miguel, E. C. (2011). Suicidality in obsessive-compulsive disorder: Prevalence and relation to symptom dimensions and comorbid conditions. *Journal of Clinical Psychiatry, 72*(1), 17–26. doi: http://dx.doi.org/10.4088/JCP.09m05651blu

Veale, D., Freeston, M., Krebs, G., Heyman, I., & Salkovskis, P. (2009). Risk assessment and management in obsessive-compulsive disorder. *Advances in Psychiatric Treatment, 15*, 332–43.

Zimmerman, M., & Mattia, J. I. (2001). A self-report scale to help make psychiatric diagnoses: The Psychiatric Diagnostic Screening Questionnaire. *Archives of General Psychiatry, 58*(8), 787–94. doi: http://dx.doi.org/10.1001/archpsyc.58.8.787

Chapter 3

Cognitive-behaviour therapy for obsessive-compulsive disorder

As already described, obsessive-compulsive disorder (OCD) can affect people in a wide variety of ways and cognitive-behaviour therapy (CBT) for OCD therefore requires a personalized and flexible approach, reflecting the needs of the person and their context. Such an approach is best described as 'semi-idiographic' because, although the underpinning principles are shared, the details are specific to each individual. The aim of this section is not to provide a rigid or prescriptive session-by-session protocol but rather a guide through the stages of CBT for OCD, which need to be taken in the order given. These follow on from assessment, as previously described (see Chapter 2), and are: (i) engagement and formulation; (ii) setting up the choice to change actively; (iii) supporting and building on the person's efforts to change; and (iv) longer term maintenance and relapse prevention strategies, including helping the person to reclaim their life. In practice, engagement, normalizing, and formulating take place, beginning with the assessment, and continue to evolve throughout the entire course of therapy. The main focus of the middle phase is building on the formulation and helping the person with OCD choose to change, then working on active change strategies, using discussion and behavioural experiments. This is followed by consolidating, extending, generalizing and maintaining gains, and helping the person with OCD to 'become their own therapist'.

We will be discussing these phases and the elements of therapy using examples from Walter (rumination), Lydia (checking), Saul (not just-right experiences), Jessie (contamination), and Jane (religious).

3.1 The 'nuts and bolts' of therapy

3.1.1 How therapy works

Before going further into the 'how to' of treatment, we should consider how psychological treatment works in terms of the overarching principles (derived from Salkovskis, 1996, 1997). This is rather simple in principle, but more complex in application. It is particularly important to bear this issue in mind with the treatment of OCD, although it can also be applied to other anxiety problems.

It starts from the basic cognitive premise that people suffer from anxiety because they think situations are more dangerous than they really are, and have become 'stuck' in this perception. What any effective treatment does is to help the person to consider and apply alternative, less threatening, explanations of their problem. If such alternative explanations are to be helpful, then, on consideration and discussion, they have to fit in with the person's past experience (Salkovskis, 2010). Going further, the alternative also has to survive the person's future experience; that is, it has to be able to be tested. This conceptualization helps us make sense of CBT as the integration of cognitive and behavioural therapy; the cognitive component relates to the generation of the alternative explanation (the formulation followed by theory A/B), drawing on the person's experience of his or her problem. In discussion, it will become clear that aspects of the formulation/alternative explanation are neither confirmed nor disconfirmed by the person's experience, which is where behavioural experiments come in; these are ways of structuring and gathering *new* information which informs the validity of the formulation. As we will see in Section 3.7, such behavioural experiments can involve exposure, but can also involve gathering information about other types of psychological effects involved in the maintenance of the person's OCD, such as selective attention, thought suppression, and so on.

This means that good therapy is fundamentally about two (or sometimes more than two) people working together to *find out how the world really works*. As will be discussed in Section 3.2, the atmosphere sought is that of two experts working on the problem in close collaboration; the therapist as the expert in OCD, the person with OCD as the expert in his or her own experience. Putting these two types of expertise together will allow treatment to progress, and, most importantly, be owned by the individual with OCD, rather in the way that the athlete rather than the coach deserves credit for their sporting performance. This means, in a way, that the therapist does not do the treatment, but rather seeks to arrange things so that the person with OCD can make changes to overcome their anxiety and reclaim their life.

3.1.2 **How therapy is performed**

The technical principles of CBT include a collaborative and active style, use of an idiosyncratic formulation, being goal-orientated and problem-focussed, working in a structured and time-limited fashion to identify, evaluate, and respond to cognitions, and use of a variety of techniques to elicit cognitive and behavioural change (Beck, 2011). It is useful to be aware of Roth and Pilling's (2007) competence framework, which includes generic competences relevant to all psychological therapies, basic CBT competences, specific core CBT techniques employed in most forms of CBT, problem-specific competences, and metacompetences. See Section 4.7 for further discussion of OCD-specific competences.

CBT for OCD has some distinctive features, although many of these can also be applied to other problems. These include the use of metaphor (Box 3.1), analogy, imagery, and, at times, humour. A truly collaborative, exploratory, and experiential style in therapy underpins the specific strategies described in this chapter. Use of homework is critical—everything that occurs within and outside the session is an opportunity to stand up to OCD and break free of the problem. Homework should be agreed at every session and *always* discussed in the following session, focussing on what has been learned and what that means. This explicitly includes identification of the fact that at times the homework set may be difficult or even not possible, in which case discussion of what happened will be particularly helpful. See Kazantzis and L'Abate (2006) for further discussion.

3.1.3 Recording sessions

Therapists often record sessions as part of their own supervision and self-reflection. Encouraging the individual with OCD to audio record sessions from the start will facilitate an active engagement in tackling problems outside of the therapy sessions—listening to the session for homework is set as a regular task. Most people can now make audio recordings on their phones, overcoming many governance issues. As well as the recording it is useful to encourage taking notes of key points during a session. It is important to explain clearly the rationale for recording sessions: a recording aids recall (without recording only about 10% of an hour's discussion will be remembered), allows further reflection on the content, and summarizing in terms of note-taking and 'what I have learned', 'what I disagreed with', and 'what I was unclear about'. Recording also allows for processing of the content of the session in a less anxious state; if therapy is done well, the individual with OCD will experience high levels of emotion, which can make it difficult to make sense of what is being discussed. Listening to the recording after the session will generate questions, ideas, and promote further advances in understanding. In a survey of therapists and their clients with OCD who recorded sessions in this way, Shepherd *et al.* (2009) found that

Box 3.1 Using metaphors—the OCD bully

'Cognitive therapy has, as a central task, the aim of transforming meaning to further the client's goals and help journey towards a more helpful, realistic and adaptive view of the self and the world. Metaphor should therefore be a powerful companion.'

Stott *et al.* (2010). *Oxford Guide to Metaphors in CBT*, p.14.

Stott *et al.* (2010) describe how metaphors are invaluable communication tools in the face of the 'inexpressibility' of a concept. Furthermore, metaphors provide 'compactness' of expression (where a complex and detailed idea can be represented in the metaphor). Metaphors also provide 'vividness', using rich and distinctive imagery that facilitates recall at other times. Metaphors also provide an ideal base for guided discovery.

The OCD bully metaphor is a striking example of these three features—a vivid and memorable image that provides a succinct summary of the insidious and frightening way that OCD takes over. The numerous other metaphors described here and in the *Oxford Guide to Metaphors* provide lively and engaging moments in therapy, and then can become part of a shared understanding and language between you and the person with OCD.

The bully metaphor

Think of a school-age child that you know—imagine him or her going to school and being accosted by a bully who demands his or her lunch money. Frightened, (s)he gives it to the bully and runs away. The next day the bully asks for the money again, and continues to do so all week. The following week, the bully asks for an extra pound each day. The child has to steal the money from his or her mother's purse for fear of the bully hurting him or her. What would you advise the child to do? Get some help, tell the teacher— ultimately stand up to the bully and stop giving him or her the money. This is a frightening prospect, but bullies are 'all mouth and no trousers'—once you stand up to them, they go away. The alternative is to give in to the bully every day, with greater and greater demands.

This is a relatively transparent metaphor; the bully is the OCD, and the increasing amounts of money demanded represent the increasing time and effort OCD takes over time with accompanying distress. Standing up to the bully involved engaging in behavioural experiments and proving that the threats OCD makes are empty and untrue. The metaphor can be adapted to involve an extortionist, a dictator, an abusive partner, or other character that is meaningful to the person with OCD. It is worth spending time getting this metaphor across as it is then shorthand throughout treatment for having the bravery to stand up to a frightening foe.

90% of clients reported listening to recordings between therapy sessions to some extent. The majority reported discussing the recordings with their therapist. Clients typically planned to keep the recordings after therapy ended. Most clients and therapists endorsed positive attitudes towards the use of recordings. Both clients and therapists regarded the use of recordings for therapist peer supervision purposes favourably. Similar advantages (e.g. improving memory for sessions) and disadvantages (e.g. practical issues and feeling self-conscious) of recordings were generated by clients and therapists. Interestingly, therapists were more likely than clients to express concern about patients being distressed by listening to recordings.

The therapist can suggest that the person with OCD keep a notebook; at the front (s)he can record, for each session 'What I learned from today's session'; we find it helpful to do this in the form of between six and ten bullet points. (S)he can also record any homework and its outcome in terms of what was learned. At the back of the notebook, (s)he notes anything that (s)he was unclear about or, on listening to the recording, disagreed with. The person can also transfer their formulation and other important pieces of information into the notebook, which then can be used as a 'personal therapy manual', useful for consolidation and relapse prevention. Often it is useful to begin sessions by reviewing the most recent entries in the notebook; this can also be helpful to orientate the therapist.

3.1.4 Setting parameters

It is important to establish how many sessions you have available, the time-frame in which you expect these to be completed, and how frequently and for how long you will meet. Typically a course of CBT for OCD will be around 12 sessions plus follow-ups, although, for more severe OCD, or when it focusses mostly on home, some longer 'outreach' sessions may need to be added. This helps manage expectations and maintain the momentum of the sessions.

3.2 Developing a shared understanding: formulation

One of the first elements of CBT for OCD is developing a formulation, which should happen in the initial sessions. In Section 1.1 we saw examples of the cognitive-behavioural model of OCD for people with a variety of OCD problems: Walter (rumination), Lydia (checking), Saul (not just-right experiences), Jessie (contamination), and Jane (religious). We will be building on these cases in this section, starting with how to derive the formulation.

Your formulation will be your roadmap, guiding you through the process of working with the person to overcome the difficulties. Formulation is essentially finding a way to make sense of what is keeping the problem going in the here-and-now (and, usually later in therapy, possibly also what contributed to its development). It is the person's guide to what is unhelpful about what (s)he currently does and therefore what needs to change. It is essential not to rush through this process, which you may feel pressurized to do, particularly if the person with OCD is keen to go home with some advice on 'what to do'. Understanding the problem is the bedrock of change; get it wrong and therapy will be suboptimal.

The process of developing a good formulation is a collaborative one, which continues throughout the course of therapy. It is sometimes helpful to introduce it as the joining of two areas of expertise. The person with OCD is the 'expert' on their own experience, while the therapist will have knowledge of a psychological model for understanding what maintains the person's difficulties and is instrumental in linking the person's experiences to the theoretical model. You will need to work in partnership to develop an idiosyncratic formulation, based on such a model. Empathy and curiosity are key to this process—a genuine desire to understand how it feels to be this person and why they have got to this point is required.

As you conducted the assessment, you will already have gathered lots of important data from your first meeting which relates to key aspects of the cognitive-behavioural model. Keep this information in mind as it will be helpful in refining your emerging formulation.

The process of developing an idiosyncratic formulation explicitly and collaboratively with your client begins with reviewing a *recent, specific, typical* example of his or her OCD; if the person indicates that there is a range of 'types' of OCD, consider going through the process with further examples. If you do this, help the person to identify the similarities and differences between examples and what these might mean. Note that one of the main problems new therapists have when trying to develop a shared understanding is that they drift off the specific example, getting information about the person's ideas about what generally happens rather than a specific memory of what did happen on that particular occasion. The frequent use of summaries, reminding both the individual with OCD and the therapist of the specific incident, prevents this from happening.

> *Recent*—it will be easier to recall details of how the person felt, the thoughts that went through his or her mind and how (s)he responded—the 'devil is in the detail', so the easier it is to recollect, the more likely you and the person are to identify important details. Explain that you want an account of his or her recollection as it happened rather than their guesses about what might have been going on.

Specific—clients will often describe a range of examples to give a picture of their obsessional difficulties, sometimes flitting between examples. Remaining focussed on one specific example at a time is important to ensure the inclusion of important details. The use of summaries and orientating to the present is particularly important here; for example, 'So yesterday, when you had the thought "that looks like blood" at 3 o'clock, what did that mean to you right then?'

Typical—to develop a formulation that will be helpful in guiding treatment, it is crucial that it is based on an example that reflects how the person's OCD is experienced most of the time.

It is also important to draw this out together rather than drawing out the model independently in your notes or providing a pre-prepared model (Figure 3.1). Perhaps get a sheet of paper out on the table between you, or better still use a whiteboard if you have one available. This can be photographed using the person's mobile phone and re-drawn by them later, as a separate sheet or in their notebook. Key CBT skills are crucial here—remember to be collaborative, use guided discovery, be curious, don't assume anything, and continue to check

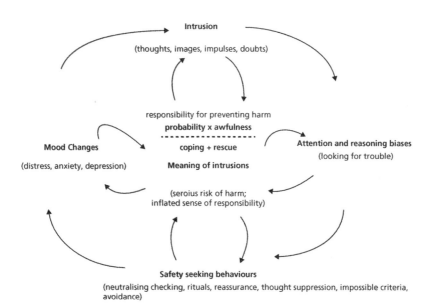

Figure 3.1 Cognitive-behavioural model of the maintenance of OCD.
Data from Paul M. Salkovskis, Obsessional-compulsive problems: A cognitive-behavioural analysis, *Behaviour Research and Therapy, 23*(5), 571–83, doi:10.1016/0005-7967(85)90105-6, 1985, Elsevier Ltd.

out your understanding as you progress. Throughout reflect empathically on how the person might be reacting emotionally.

THERAPIST: So, Walter, can you think of when the problem has really bothered you, perhaps from the last few days? Try and pick an example that gives a good idea of how this typically works, in terms of the effect it has on you and what it gets you to do.

WALTER: Yes, there was yesterday watching the news and this morning travelling here and in the waiting room. It always goes the same way though.

THERAPIST: What I'm going to ask you to do is to just focus on one particular incident at a time. We'll probably look at two or three different examples, but I'm going to ask you to talk me through each example, one at a time. So, which of those do you think we could start with? Maybe think about which one made you feel most distressed or got you doing lots of things to try and make yourself feel okay.

WALTER: Well, on the way here today, there was a copy of a newspaper on the bus and there was a big headline about another scandal. And then it all started again. I turned the newspaper over and tried to read my book, but it was no use, and before I knew it I was going through lots of other things in my head from ages ago trying to work out whether I'd done something wrong. Then this woman came and sat next to me with her child and I had to get up straight away and got off at the next stop. I felt sick.

THERAPIST: So, I'm just going to get you to slow down and we're going to go through it really slowly, a bit like playing it back in slow motion, and I'll hit the pause button every now and then to ask you more questions. So, let's start at the point just before you started to feel anxious on the bus. Was that before you got on the bus or once you were on the bus?

WALTER: While I was waiting for the bus a load of school kids arrived. And I thought 'oh no—this is all I need!'

THERAPIST: So, the trigger was the school kids arriving at the bus stop. Let's note that down.

> **Trigger**
> School kids at bus stop

THERAPIST: So, you thought 'oh no—that's all I need!'—why was that? Why did it upset you?

WALTER: Well, because I knew what was coming next—the usual torment.

THERAPIST: So, when the school kids arrived at the bus stop, what did you think?

WALTER: Keep your distance, Walter—don't look at them.

THERAPIST: Why was it important for you to keep your distance?

WALTER: It's the usual thing—thinking that maybe I fancy them.

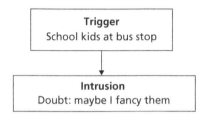

THERAPIST: Okay—so that was the thought that popped into your head when you saw the schoolkids?

WALTER: Yes.

THERAPIST: Okay—let's note that down.

THERAPIST: At that time, how much did you believe, out of 100, that you might fancy them?

WALTER: Eighty per cent.

THERAPIST: And when you thought at that time that there was an 80% chance that you might fancy them, how did that make you feel right then?

WALTER: Awful, guilty, and frightened.

THERAPIST: Okay, so there on the bus you believed 80% that you might fancy those kids, so not surprisingly you felt awful about that. What happened next?

WALTER: I turned my back to them so I wouldn't be able to see them.

THERAPIST: Why was it important for you to do that right then?

WALTER: In case I'm a paedophile. Maybe I'm a paedophile and don't realize— this will torment me everyday until I die.

THERAPIST: Okay—so that's what you concluded once you'd had the intrusive thought? What an upsetting thing to think; this is so difficult for you. Let's note that down too.

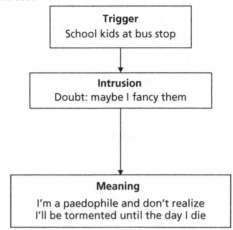

THERAPIST: So, not surprisingly, the idea that you could be a paedophile without realizing is what made you turn your back to them—that's what it meant to you at the time. Let's add that here.

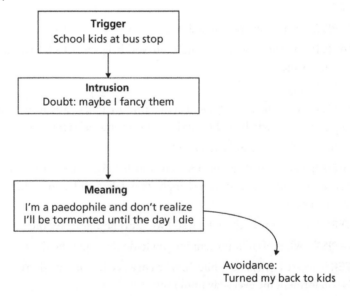

THERAPIST: Did you do anything else?

WALTER: Luckily the bus came. So, I waited to see if they got on the bus before getting on. I always wait for the next bus if there's loads of kids getting on.

THERAPIST: So let's note that too. Was there anything you tried *not* to do at that time?

WALTER: Yes, I did my best to keep my eyes outside the bus.

THERAPIST: How were you feeling at this point?

WALTER: Awful!

THERAPIST: That must have felt terrible. What kind of awful was that? Were you feeling anxious?

WALTER: Yes—and disgusted with myself too.

THERAPIST: Okay, so let's add how this affected the way you were feeling.

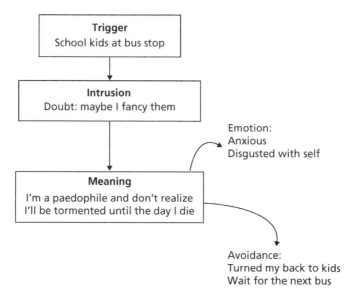

THERAPIST: What happened next?

WALTER: I sat down at the back where it was quiet and there was a newspaper lying there with a headline about a new investigation into historical abuse.

THERAPIST: What effect did that have?

WALTER: I got the usual images of being carted off by the police for questioning.

THERAPIST: Okay, so it sounds like there's another trigger, followed by another intrusion—let's add these.

THERAPIST: So when you had that image, what did you make of it?

WALTER: Well, I couldn't bear thinking that could happen to me too. So I started going through those events from the past, trying to work out whether I'd done anything wrong.

THERAPIST: What made it so important for you to do that at that time?

WALTER: I needed to be sure I hadn't done anything wrong.

THERAPIST: What would it be like if you didn't trawl through your memory?

WALTER: I'd be in torment with the not knowing. I wouldn't be able to rest easy—always waiting for that knock on the door.

THERAPIST: Okay, so that's important—let's add this too. The idea that you'll be living in torment until you can be sure.

THERAPIST: … and this is what gets you trawling through your memory. Let's add that too.

THERAPIST: Did you pay more attention to particular parts of your body there and then? Were you checking for any signs of arousal?

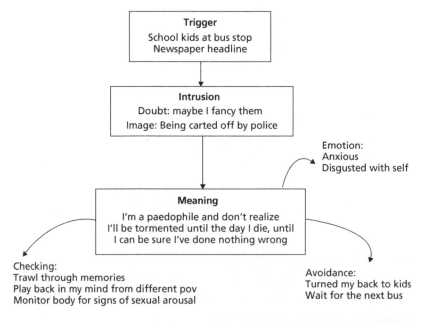

The therapist continues to carefully elicit all the different aspects of the model relevant to the person. Note that, from time to time, normalizing elements are introduced; for example, 'so its not surprising that …'

Remember to ask for a belief rating of the meaning: 'how convincing did that [meaning] seem to you at the time?' (Figure 3.2a; Table 3.1).

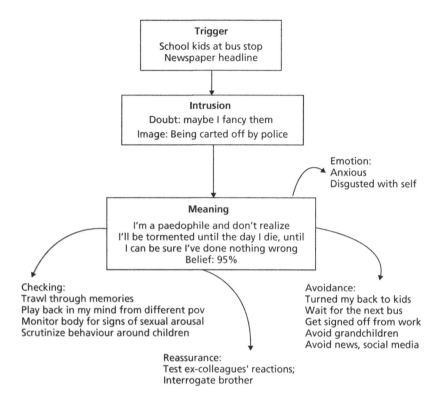

Figure 3.2a Walter's formulation without loops closed.

Table 3.1 Useful questions to elicit details of the formulation

Situation	When was the last time you were troubled by the problem? Where were you, what were you doing at the time? What kind of mood were you in that day?
Intrusion	What was the first thing you noticed? What was the first sign of trouble? (i.e. an intrusive thought, image or doubt, often triggered by something going on around the person)
Appraisal/ meaning/belief	When you thought this, what did that mean to you at that moment? Is that the worst thing that could have happened? What is the worst thing about that? (Appraisal is particularly important, and it can be helpful to 'downward arrow' the meanings identified)
Reactions/ safety-seeking behaviours/ compulsions/ rituals	When you thought (appraisal), how did you react to that? What did that make you want to do? How did it make you feel? What did you pay attention to? What did you want to achieve? Did you try and avoid doing anything?

A key aim here is to convey that these reactions are an understandable and indeed proportionate response to the belief in the centre of the formulation. This can be done as part of summarizing.

3.2.1 The solution has become the problem

Having identified the key threat appraisals and safety-seeking strategies, it is important to help the person with OCD understand what is maintaining the problem—what (s)he started doing to try to feel safe and reduce threat is actually having the *opposite effect*. For this reason it is crucial to have the central threat appraisal at the heart of the diagram as it is this *belief* which both drives and is in turn reinforced by the responses. Identifying the vicious circles caused by the emotional and behavioural reactions is key to forming the petals of the distinctive 'vicious flower' formulation for OCD—getting arrows back into the belief. If there are multiple examples of each element, then use multiple 'petals'; e.g. for emotional responses, behaviours, and so on.

People are often surprised as to the number, variety, and extent of the processes that are reinforcing their sense of threat, responsibility, and danger. It can be useful to emphasize that, although some processes are deliberate and a choice (such as compulsions and avoidance), some are simply reactive and automatic (such as anxiety). Furthermore, some start as automatic; for example, attentional focus on 'threat', and become controlled—deliberately paying attention to certain aspects of their own behaviour or to the surrounding environment. The point here is that each and every one of the processes involved serves to maintain and reinforce belief in threat.

There is a general 'formula' for helping the person identify the 'loop back' for each response (Figure 3.2b); at its simplest, it is asking 'so, when you thought that this is what the intrusion meant you responded in this way *(specify)*; at that time, what was the effect of that on the meaning? Did it make it weaker or stronger? Can you tell me more about how that might work?' and so on (Table 3.2). It continues to be helpful to include in summaries empathic and normalizing responses, along the lines of 'so its not surprising that …' or 'that makes sense because …'.

The 'who wants to be a millionaire' metaphor is an accessible way to explain the research findings described in Box 3.2. On the TV show, the contestant is asked to pick one of four answers to win a large sum of money; the show host says 'are you sure?' The contestant usually looks visibly nervous at this point, and wavers. The host says 'is that your final answer?' and the tension builds. This is a real world illustration of mental checking and self-reassurance actually decreasing confidence and increasing anxiety. Sometimes the contestant will choose an option to 'phone a friend'—an approximate equivalent of reassurance.

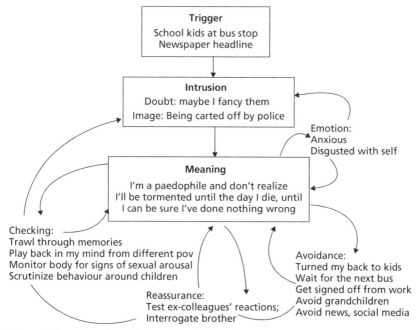

Figure 3.2b Walter's formulation with the loops ('petals') closed.

It can be useful to ask what effect the processes have on the frequency of the triggering thoughts, your starting point for the formulation. They are all likely to increase it; adding this final circle around the whole diagram can help to re-emphasize the OCD trap that the person is in. Your client may notice that some of the maintaining processes you have identified together also influence each other, in which case you could continue to draw even more lines on the figures.

3.2.2 Spotlight on supervision: formulation

3.2.2.1 Supervision issue: I can't understand the model, there are too many arrows

It is easy to be daunted by formulation when you are new to treating OCD. The cognitive model of OCD is the same as any other cognitive model of mood or anxiety:

Event → appraisal of event → response (automatic and controlled) → consequences of the response

For example, for depression:

Event: getting a job rejection → appraisal of event: thinking 'I'm a total failure' → response: automatic: feeling heavy and low; controlled: going to bed for the day → consequences of the response: feeling more like a failure for being in bed all day

Table 3.2 Useful questions to get the arrows back in to the belief

Anxiety	When you felt anxious, what did the anxiety do to the idea that [you were responsible for preventing something bad happening]? When you feel anxious about an exam, do you feel it's something important that could affect your life? Do you feel more or less sure that you are going to pass?
Rituals	What impact does doing [ritual] have in your belief that it is necessary to do it to be safe? (Remember to distinguish from the impact on anxiety.)
Impossible criteria/stopping criteria	So you do [ritual] until it feels right? What impact has that had on your belief in the long term?
Distraction	When you tried not to think about it or distract yourself, what actually happened?
Reassurance	Did seeking reassurance make you feel more or less sure [in the longer term]?
Salience/selective attention	Have you ever had a new car/been pregnant? What did you notice? If you saw more, is that because there were actually more pregnant women/Vauxhalls or was it that you paid more attention?
Avoidance	If you feel that you are not very good at parallel parking a car, what effect does avoidance have on that belief? What effect has avoidance had on what you believe about something bad happening?
Trying to be certain	Have you ever watched 'Who wants to be a millionaire? What effect does it have on the contestant's confidence when Chris Tarrant asks 'are you sure? Is that your final answer?' What do you notice the contestant tends to do? (see Box 3.2)
Reviewing actions in memory (mental checking)	Have you ever tried to remember whether or not you did something? What happens if you interrogate your memory to try to find something that didn't happen? What happens when you set yourself such an impossible task?
Reassurance	What does RE-assurance mean? I wonder if you have ever found yourself asking the same question twice? More? What do you make of that? What effect does that have on your belief?
General	When you started tuning into the idea that [you are responsible for preventing something bad happening], what effect did that have on that belief?
	Did you ever think that all these things might be making the problem worse?

Box 3.2 Research box: checking increases memory distrust

Van den Hout and Kindt (2003) used an experimental design with research participants who did not have a diagnosis of OCD. The experiment involved checking an animated virtual stove; one group was asked to do 'relevant checking' (checking the stove) and the other was asked to engage in 'irrelevant checking' (checking virtual light bulbs). 'Relevant checking' reduced the vividness and details of recollections and undermined confidence in memory. The researchers concluded that memory distrust persists as a result of checking; in OCD checking is designed to reduce uncertainty, but is a counterproductive strategy.

Radomsky and colleagues have designed many elegant studies to investigate the function of checking in OCD further. Radomsky *et al.* (2014) repeated the checking experiment with a real stove with the same findings; Radomsky and Alcolado (2010) found a similar effect for mental checking.

For example, for panic:

Event: palpitation → appraisal of event: thinking 'this means I'm having a heart attack' → response: automatic: panic; controlled: going to A&E → consequences of the response: feeling more tuned into heart sensations

For OCD:

Mental event: intrusive thought → appraisal of thought: this means something bad and I need to do something about it → response: automatic: anxiety; controlled: safety-seeking behaviours, avoidance → consequences of the response: being more tuned into the intrusive thoughts and a stronger belief that you need to do something about the thoughts.

3.3 **Normalizing**

CBT for OCD aims to help the person with OCD conclude that their intrusive thoughts, however distressing, are irrelevant to further action. Anything the person is doing to try to control, neutralize, suppress, or react to the thoughts is counterproductive, having the effect of increasing the frequency and salience of thoughts, preoccupation, and the urge to continue to use safety-seeking behaviours (SSBs). A fundamental part of therapy is modification of the way the person interprets the occurrence and/or content of their intrusions, as part of a general process of reaching an alternative, less threatening view of their intrusive thoughts and what these might mean.

Normalizing is an ongoing process that helps the person understand that it is not the thoughts themselves that are the problem, it is the meaning attached to the thoughts/the person's appraisal of the thoughts/what (s) he believes about the thoughts. Normalizing takes place from assessment onwards with empathic statements such as: 'so it's *not surprising* that you felt uncomfortable in that situation, because the thought "I'll kill my baby" came to your mind just as you were cuddling him, and you couldn't dismiss or ignore this thought as you had the horrible idea that this thought meant you were a bad person'.

Specific presentations of OCD can require specific normalizing techniques. Thinking of Saul and his 'not just-right' experiences, normalizing includes thinking about people known personally or otherwise who might have a version of these experiences. Often sports players can be spotted getting ready for a game in a particular way, i.e. putting their right shoe on first for every match. If they don't, they feel 'unlucky' or not right and would attribute losing the match to not following their ritual.

THERAPIST: Do you think other people get urges like this?

SAUL: I don't think so; I'm not sure?

THERAPIST: It's really common to have sensations like this. For example, if that picture on the wall was hung askew, some people wouldn't even notice. Some people would notice and not be bothered. Some people would notice, and would really want to straighten it, and it would keep catching their eye when we were talking. Some of those people would want to straighten it so much that they would do it—even though it is not their office, not their picture. Probably most people have an awareness of a 'not just-right' feeling and want to get things 'just-right'. For some people it is lining things up and having things 'just-so' and for other people it is doing things in a particular order or routine, or they feel that it is 'wrong'—in the absence of anything bad actually happening if they don't follow that routine.

There are many ways that normalizing is useful—the categories of normalizing discussed in Section 2.1 will be helpful with different people at different stages depending on their existing understanding of the nature of thoughts, and on how your collaborative understanding evolves.

3.3.1 People are upset by thoughts that they don't like and that don't fit with their actual values and beliefs

Who would be bothered by blasphemous thoughts? Is it possible that some people wouldn't be bothered or might even find such a thought amusing?

Given the same thought or image, different people would make a different appraisal of the thought, accompanied by a different emotional and behavioural response—a religious person might be upset and pray for forgiveness, a non-religious person would dismiss or ignore the thought and do nothing, an atheist stand-up comedian might find the thought amusing and write it into their next act. This discussion concludes that people with OCD are upset and frightened by their intrusive thoughts precisely because these represent their worst fears rather than being some reflection of actual desires or values.

3.3.2 The appraisal of a thought is dependent on context: when might a 'positive' thought be upsetting?

Imagine recalling a nice holiday or a particularly romantic evening—what are the circumstances in which these recollections are not experienced as pleasant? Imagine listening to the eulogy at a funeral service for a dear friend and having these thoughts intruding—how do you think you would react? Is it possible that the thoughts would be experienced as unwanted, unacceptable, and upsetting?

3.3.3 Intrusive thoughts are common

Research indicates that almost everyone experiences occasional unwanted and unacceptable intrusions, and that the content of these thoughts is indistinguishable between people with and without OCD (Rachman and de Silva, 1978; Salkovskis and Harrison, 1984; see Section 1.2 for more information).

3.3.4 Intrusive thoughts are useful

Intrusive unexpected thoughts play an important role in problem-solving, brainstorming, and in creative processes. Most people can think of a time when something has popped into their heads that has been helpful—remembering it is a friend's birthday or remembering to buy toilet paper on the way home. Everyday intrusive thoughts are not linear, ordered, or controlled, and that is because this kind of thinking is useful. Asking someone with OCD to imagine a world with no unexpected thoughts reveals a strange, dull, and inhuman world—no creativity, no inspiration, no spontaneity.

3.4 Developing a direction of travel: goals

Working towards defined goals is an essential element of CBT. It is useful to divide goals into short-term goals that can reasonably be achieved in two to four sessions, medium-term goals that can reasonably be achieved by the end of therapy, and long-term goals that the person would like to achieve over the next few years. Understandably, some people with OCD have a pessimistic view of the likely course of their problem, and believe that the best they can hope for is to live with a very restricted lifestyle; the goals they set will be unduly limited. For people who have suffered with OCD for a long time, being free of their obsessional problems is desired, but it might be difficult to think what life would look like. Considering the costs of OCD can help to target goals— for example, thinking about the costs of OCD in different domains, such as time, money, relationships with family and friends, ability to have emotional and physical intimacy, working/studying. Goals are constantly updated and reviewed as therapy progresses. Establishing or revisiting the goals after theory A/B helps to avoid or flush out any unachievable goals (e.g. to have no intrusive thoughts) or goals that are other 'more manageable' versions of OCD (e.g. to wash hands for 2 hours per day but not use alcogel). Long-term goals are an important focus towards the end of therapy and in the relapse prevention plan (see Section 3.9.3). Long-term goals are particularly important as they help the person to re-focus on the reason why (s)he might endure the discomfort and hard work of therapy. It is to reclaim the person's life and to re-establish his or her dreams, which typically have been given up as a result of the OCD. Engaging in treatment is a means of helping him or her to restore meaning to life when it has been eroded. Striving for these goals in many instances informs the tasks undertaken in therapy, which can be seen as steps towards reclaiming their life and all that that implies. Note that as therapy progresses the long-term goals can and should shape the shorter term goals and tasks undertaken.

3.4.1 Spotlight on supervision: goals

3.4.1.1 What do I do about a goal not to have intrusive thoughts?

Have you discussed the research papers on intrusive thoughts/had a discussion about the ubiquity and usefulness of intrusive thoughts? Is it ever possible not to have any thoughts at all? (See Sections 1.2 and 3.3.) What is getting in the way of your clients getting on board with this information? Do they not believe the research findings? Would doing their own survey help? Do they think that their thoughts are in some way worse? What kind of thoughts would a writer of horror stories have? Do their intrusive thoughts of violent or macabre acts mean that they are bad? What kind of thoughts do social workers or police officers who work in child protection have? Do their thoughts of children being abused mean that they are bad people? Once the person with OCD can change the meaning of the occurrence of thoughts then it is no longer as important not to have them.

An alternative, more helpful, goal is to have a different relationship with the thoughts—let thoughts be thoughts. The metaphor of watching waves on a beach or clouds pass overhead can be useful to illustrate this goal.

3.5 Developing an alternative understanding: theory A/theory B

Once you have worked on your roadmap, generating a shared understanding with your formulation, the next stage is identifying this as a less threatening, credible alternative understanding. At the centre of the vicious flower is the key meaning that drives the problem—the meaning has been (often) accepted as fact, and life has adapted around this meaning. The person with OCD has become convinced that something bad will happen and it is his or her responsibility to do something about it, fuelling SSBs and anxiety.

3.5.1 Developing an alternative explanation

Up until now, the person will have been generally only thinking about the problem as one of danger (we refer to their existing perspective as 'theory A'). If (s) he is thinking of the problem as danger, with a responsibility to prevent it, then it is important to remember that the person's responses to that problem are not illogical or excessive. The exercise of drawing out the formulation will have helped demonstrate the notion that the person's responses, while in keeping with the initial interpretation, actually serve to keep his or her belief in danger going. However, without any alternative to this central idea, it will be almost impossible for the person to change their behaviour, and in fact to do so is counterintuitive as the end result can only logically be to feel less safe/more irresponsible. Prior to having an alternative explanation (which we refer to as 'theory B'), the person does not have any meaningful choice in going against their OCD. Hence the limited utility of being told to just stop rituals, or of trying to 'pull yourself together'. Our experience is that people suffering from OCD are very keen indeed to 'pull themselves together'; but first they need knowledge, understanding, and support to do so.

Theory A/B works well following a particular format (Table 3.3).

Note that this is *not* presented as 'theory A is wrong, theory B is right', but rather that these are simply different ways of looking at what is happening to the person, and what needs to happen in therapy is to work out how much each one makes sense and fits with the person's understanding of his or her past experiences. Thus it is approached with curiosity rather than dogmatism. The task in therapy at this stage is to consider that maybe this responsibility/

Table 3.3 Theory A/B outline

Which is the best description of the problem I have? Which problem do I need to solve?	
Theory A **Belief rating:**	**Theory B** **Belief rating:**
What is the evidence? Why do I believe this?	
What are the implications? What do I need to do if this is true?	
What does this say about me as a person?	
What will my life be like if I carry on acting this way?	

harm interpretation (theory A) is not a fact, but an idea that can be examined, and that there may be an altogether different way of thinking about the problem. Presenting and building up an alternative 'theory B' is therefore the fulcrum of therapy, as this provides the idea that, whilst understandable given their history and responses identified in the formulation, the person's problem may be better defined as one of *oversensitivity to danger rather than one of danger itself.* Where possible, it is helpful to incorporate into theory B an attribution that counteracts the negative self-referent attributions characteristic of OCD. For example, theory B would include that she is a loving mother who understandably fears harming her child, so is oversensitive to such thoughts; in other examples that (s)he is a person who values cleanliness, is God-fearing, and so on. The alternative (theory B) also needs to be a testable idea that can then provide the scaffolding for exploring all the available evidence, including the wider context of what might be gained as well as lost from changing behaviour. This is then formulated into behavioural experiments to find out what really happens if the person does things differently and which theory may be the better fit. Finally, it provides the basis of lasting change and progress towards goals.

A key idea at this stage is that OCD has felt like a problem of genuine *danger*; the alternative is that it is better defined as a problem of *worry about danger*. It can help if theory B encompasses the counterproductive effects on anxiety and worry of treating the problem as danger (theory A). That is to say, that all the person's efforts to solve the problem of danger are making the worry problem worse.

For Saul, the barista who experiences urges to get things 'just-right', Table 3.4 shows two ways of thinking about the problem.

For the person who has bought into the idea of danger for a long time, the idea that the problem might be anything other than this may be initially

Table 3.4 Delineation of theory A and the less-threatening alternative theory B

Which is the best description of the problem I have? Which problem do I need to solve?	
Theory A	Theory B
OCD says the problem is that I must get rid of these urges and get the 'just-right' feeling or I will not be able to cope and people will think I am weird	OCD is a problem of being tuned into urges and getting the 'just-right' feeling and this causes me anxiety and makes me worry about being weird
Belief rating at the start of treatment: 50%	Belief rating at the start of treatment: 50%

dismissed as a platitude. For example, thoughts may emerge that you are fobbing the person off or just trying to reassure them. It is, of course, fine (and understandable) to be sceptical about theory B and it is often useful for the therapist to express this.

It can be helpful to frame the discussion of theory A/B in terms of the best description of the problem that the person needs to solve. This can help avoid attempts to 'prove' that one or the other is true and helps emphasize the idea that they cannot both be the answer to the question. This point becomes even clearer as the implications of each theory are drawn out ('what do I do if this is true?').

3.5.2 Building up the case: eliciting evidence for theory A and B

The first stage in examining theory A/B is collecting evidence for each. These two theories are competing (but possibly not diametrically opposite) ideas—looking for evidence to support each one often highlights that there is no real evidence for theory A. When looking for evidence it is important to encourage the person with OCD to be as unbiased as possible. Look out for double standards or acceptance of ambiguous evidence. Sources of evidence include things that have happened to the individual and others, the opinions of people who know the person, the behaviour of others in general, and information from the past, including what life was like before OCD was a problem. Other examples of spurious evidence include ambiguous and circumstantial 'evidence'—just because two things happened at the same time, it does not mean that one caused the other. Are there other occasions when the person thought about accidents and they didn't happen? Did they ever think of their brother winning the lottery? Did that happen? Why not? (See 'magical thinking' and thought–action fusion in Sections 1.4.4 and 1.8.1.7, respectively.) When considering the evidence together, encourage the person to imagine a courtroom situation, with the same high standards applied to permissible evidence. Saul was not able to generate real evidence for his theory A (Table 3.5).

As theory A has been convincing for a long time for many people with OCD, often it can feel that there is actual evidence and the challenge for the therapist is to examine this evidence and work out whether it really does support the theory.

It is important to take belief ratings at an early point in the session prior to detailed discussion. It may be that initial belief in theory B is very low—0%, often contrasting with high belief ratings in theory A. This can be useful in itself later on, for example when exploring evidence, which is typically non-existent or ambiguous for theory A and plentiful for theory B. The therapist might query this in the following way:

THERAPIST: How interesting that your belief in theory A is so high, despite any 'hard' evidence. What else do you think might explain that?

This will lead to the person seeing again that anxiety is a key maintaining factor that makes worries feel more true (see Section 1.8.1.2).

Lydia, who checks taps, locks, and emails, felt that she had quite 'good' evidence for theory A being true:

The therapist then discussed the evidence that Lydia had brought up for her theory A (Table 3.6).

Table 3.5 Building up the case: eliciting evidence for theory A and B

Which is the best description of the problem I have? Which problem do I need to solve?	
Theory A	Theory B
OCD says the problem is that I must get rid of these urges and get the 'just-right' feeling or I will not be able to cope and people will think I am weird	OCD is a problem of being tuned into urges and getting the 'just-right' feeling and this causes me anxiety and makes me worry about being weird
Belief rating at the start of treatment: 50%	Belief rating at the start of treatment: 50%
What is the evidence? ..... Why do I believe this?	
None	Once I started responding to these urges I noticed them more and I have felt more anxious and the whole problem has got worse
	I have always had a tendency to have things 'just-so'

Table 3.6 Challenging evidence for theory A

Which is the best description of the problem I have? Which problem do I need to solve?	
Theory A	Theory B
A disaster will happen if I am not careful enough Start of session: 100%	For understandable reasons I have become very sensitive to the idea of disaster and spend too much time trying to prevent it Start of session: 0%
What is the evidence? ..... Why do I believe this?	
I do feel very responsible for things (I had to look after my grandmother when my mum went to work) I once flooded a bathroom by leaving a tap dripping	

THERAPIST: I understand that you had a lot of responsibility when you were a child, which you still feel is a strong part of who you are. However, do you think this is evidence that you are more prone to disasters or that you are more sensitive to worrying about bad things happening?

LYDIA: Well, I suppose it could fit with being more sensitive. I mean, most kids don't have such a heavy weight on their shoulders and it's not a big deal if they make mistakes.

Lydia and her therapist were able to amend the evidence at this stage (Table 3.7).

It is often helpful to consider developmental and historical information here, and how that has led to the development of particular beliefs and vulnerabilities. It is helpful to be alert to contributing factors, such as stress and increases in responsibility and messages about threat, responsibility, and competence that may have been gleaned from early and subsequent experience. This may include thinking about the significance of ostensibly positive events, such as having a baby or getting a promotion, or negative events, such as losses. Further and more detailed consideration of these issues can be agreed for homework and should be part of a therapy summary towards the end (see Section 3.9.3).

3.5.2.1 Thinking it through: what are the implications for each theory?

Once you have discussed evidence for each theory and checked that the two theories are distinct and it is understood that they are competing theories (only one can be true), the next step is to consider the implications of each theory for

Table 3.7 Reviewing evidence for both theories

Which is the best description of the problem I have? Which problem do I need to solve?	
Theory A	Theory B
A disaster will happen if I am not careful enough	For understandable reasons I have become very sensitive to the idea of disaster and spend too much time trying to prevent it
Start of session: 100%	Start of session: 0%
What is the evidence? ..... Why do I believe this?	
I do feel very responsible for things (I had to look after my grandmother when my mum went to work)	Having more responsibility as a child put me on the lookout for danger and made me feel that it was my job to prevent it
I once flooded a bathroom by leaving a tap dripping	Just because this happened and a big deal was made of it, it does not mean that I am careless in general
Anxiety makes it feel very real at the time!	

what the person needs to do day to day, what it says about them as a person, and what it says for their future. Tables 3.8 and 3.9 give the implications of each theory for Saul and Lydia, respectively.

This point is an opportunity in therapy to highlight the way that SSBs have evolved to become increasingly arbitrary and at times outrageous. It is important for the person to reflect that OCD/theory A has no limits in what it demands owing to the open-ended way in which the problem is defined (e.g. a disaster

Table 3.8 The implications of each theory for Saul

What do I need to do if this is true?	
Count, order, repeat	Ignore the urges
Avoid triggering the urges—avoid tasks at work, avoid going out if possible	Tolerate the uncomfortable feeling
	Not count, order, etc.
	Carry on with my life and not avoid people or tasks
	Find out what happens when I do not get the 'just-right' feeling
What does this say about me as a person?	
I'm different, odd, weird	I'm okay
What does this say about the future?	
I'm going to have a restricted, stressful life	I'm free, relaxed

Table 3.9 The implications of each theory for Lydia

What do I need to do if this is true (implications of buying into this idea)?	
Check more and better	Do not check
Get Mike to check more	Do not involve anyone else in checking
Do more internet research about the things that can go wrong	Do not keep looking for danger
	Trust myself!!
Do fewer 'responsible' things—e.g. give up my job just in case I make a mistake	
Stay at home all the time	
Do not contact anyone	
What will my life be like if I carry on acting this way (longer term implications of buying into this)?	
Miserable!	Better! And for Mike too!

will happen if I'm not careful enough). Ask questions such as: 'How come these particular checks are adequate?' 'Why is this enough handwashing?' 'If theory A really is true, why stop there?' 'Why not tell other people to do the same?' Taken to its logical conclusion, total faith in theory A leads to an exceedingly restrictive life for the person and everyone around him or her. This can be quite an entertaining part of the session as ever more outlandish scenarios can be imagined (going to work in a decontamination suit); on other occasions it can elicit sadness and regret as the person with OCD sees how extreme and restrictive his or her behaviour already is and how the problem has increased in severity over time.

When considering the implications of theory B, it can seem simplistic to say 'ignore the worries'/'treat worries as worries'/'treat thoughts as thoughts'. You will find it helpful to recap on the nature of intrusive thoughts—that the thoughts themselves are just thoughts, not facts or premonitions, merely mental events. Having the vicious flower formulation visible serves as a reminder that it is the meaning attached to the thought that is the target.

3.5.3 Belief ratings in theory A/B

When you have completed all of theory A/B, ask for a belief rating in each theory. The theories are mutually exclusive, but at the start it is likely that there is some belief in both. Re-rate the theories in later sessions. Where changes occur (or do not) discuss what is happening.

3.5.4 Goals

If goals have already been agreed, revisit them at this stage to check for any 'theory A' ideas (i.e. getting rid of intrusive thoughts) and to flesh out other ideas now that there is a better idea of what life will look like without OCD. As treatment progresses, short-term goals are increasingly informed by medium and longer term ones as the person reclaims normal activities, helping to make behavioural experiments more meaningful.

3.5.5 Spotlight on supervision: theory A/B

'My client says both theories are worrying—if the house is going to burn down then it makes sense to worry.'

Theory B is the idea that the problem itself is one of excessive worry. Worry problems are serious and significant but are not the same as actual danger. Moreover, these explanations cannot both be true—which one is more likely to be true? It can help to strip the theory A/B right down: theory A = danger; theory B = anxiety/worry. Is this really a danger problem? Or is it a worry about a danger problem? These theories are mutually exclusive and you use opposite methods to tackle them so it is important to get this right.

3.6 Approaching active change

The fact that the person with OCD is seeking help from a therapist indicates that (s)he recognizes (s)he needs help in tackling his or her obsessional problem. As therapists, we have an important role in creating an environment in which the person feels understood. If we have succeeded in being curious and collaborative, we will have developed our idiosyncratic formulation. Having summarized the person's existing perspective on their obsessional problem (theory A) and developed an alternative perspective that reframes their obsessional problem as a 'worry problem' (theory B), we are faced with helping the person to approach and *choose* to change. Theory A/B provides common ground for a new way of thinking about (and therefore reacting to) their particular unique pattern of OCD thinking and behaving. This process is based on the principle that people experiencing OCD understandably believe that they are justified in both their fears and the actions they take to deal with them.

What follows from this process is that the person with OCD needs to take the next step, which is to choose to confront their fears—not be backed into a corner, not to be forced or cajoled, coerced, made to feel guilty, but to choose to leave OCD behind.

Choosing to confront your fears, with the intention of not reversing it, has a quite different and wonderful effect. It refocusses the person on theory B ... 'my problem is being worried about this'. Once the decision to do this is made, it never turns out to be as bad as expected in terms of anxiety/discomfort, and it quite simply works, and works wonderfully ... unless the person keeps in his or her mind that (s)he could reverse it later—to wash, check, neutralize, say a prayer.

A metaphor to describe starting active OCD treatment is to imagine being in a boat.

'If you try to incorporate a safety hatch ("I can wash later"; "I can beg God for forgiveness later"), what you are doing is opening up a safety hatch below the waterline! The water (the OCD fears) will rush in if you set sail (confronting your OCD fears) with a safety hatch open. You will sink in your OCD fears.'

If the individual with OCD builds in a return to an obsessional way of dealing with things, they will continue to suffer the anxiety, discomfort, and distress of confrontation without benefit in terms of breaking free from OCD.

In your role as a therapist, occasionally you will need to say it is okay to resist compulsions as much as possible, as this is better than giving up from the start—but that will only bring moderate, temporary gains. The 'pact with the devil' is still in place, meaning that the compulsive behaviours are still based on the assumption that they are genuinely necessary to prevent harm and responsibility. A key message is that, when you can do it, it really works, and is less difficult when you get going than you anticipate.

In the words of one person with OCD:

'I have worked out that it is so much better to feel exhausted because I have been confronting my OCD all day than because I have been giving in to my OCD all day. And I have discovered that I end up less exhausted confronting it, and can see that I might get my life back that way, rather than being a continual slave to it without hope of ever regaining control of my life.'

3.6.1 **Empathize with the person**

To truly understand OCD, feel and show genuine empathy, you may need to take some time to imagine being in the person's shoes. How would it *feel* to be faced with an alternative perspective? While logically it may make sense to experiment with living according to theory B, in reality this will *feel* risky if not downright terrifying at times. It is important to acknowledge this with the person—in his or her shoes, you would also feel scared. Psychoeducation about anxiety can support this process, although it is important to cite this in a normalizing context; there is nothing wrong with your brain, it is doing what it is supposed to do (see Box 3.3).

In the active change stage, we can return to these ideas. The way we misinterpret what is happening results in 'false alarms', which can have the effect of reinforcing a theory A response; the challenge when following theory B is to treat intrusions as having a different meaning so that they do not provoke 'false alarms'.

We can extend further, using mountain paths as a metaphor. The theory A response was developed under conditions of an anxious mindset. In

Box 3.3 Psychoeduation about the brain's 'threat alarm'

The human brain is the result of millions of years of evolution. We have many highly developed capacities that enable us to have the sophisticated lives we lead today. Consider that the human brain is responsible for the architecture around us, creation of the internet, and many wonderful works (art, music, literature). We can roughly think of our brain in terms of our 'old brain' (the more primitive part of our brain that has existed from the earliest times) and our 'new brain' (the more recently evolved capacities; for example, our ability to imagine and to reason).

Our brain has a threat-detection system called the amygdala, which is part of our 'old brain'. This 'threat alarm' is constantly on the lookout for potential threats and, if it detects anything that could be dangerous, it triggers our 'fight or flight' response, often before we are even aware of any danger. This makes sense, as the human brain's priority is to promote our survival. This threat alarm keeps us safe by making us act quickly, often before the thinking part of the brain (new brain) has noticed the danger.

When our brain's threat alarm detects any kind of danger, we find ourselves acting very quickly without thinking. This makes sense. For example, if we are about to cross a busy road that looks clear both ways, but then we hear the sound of a siren, we tend automatically to step back onto the pavement. It may be that we would have had enough time to cross the road and we may have looked both ways and worked out if it was safe to do so. However, before this 'thinking' part of our brain kicks in, our automatic response is to step back from the pavement. Our brain's threat alarm is programmed to lead us to act in a 'better safe than sorry' way. This makes sense from an evolutionary perspective. If a primitive human heard a rustle in the bushes, it made more sense always to treat this as a threat (for example, always reacting as if it was a predator, even though it may just be the sound of a bird or the breeze), as it makes sense to flee just in case it was a predator; in survival terms, nothing much is lost by running off for no reason other than wasted energy; however, the consequences are much more serious if we assume we are safe when we are not. So, as a species, we have evolved with a threat alarm that is wired to go off in response to any potentially threatening stimuli and that leads us to act in 'better safe than sorry' ways.

Sometimes our threat alarm may become oversensitive, so that it is not working effectively for us, a bit like a smoke alarm that goes off whenever the toast burns or a car alarm that goes off whenever someone walks past. So, we may need to retune our threat alarm so that it stops giving us 'false alarms'. OCD can lead us to become oversensitized to particular kinds of threats—whatever it is that is the focus of our intrusions (e.g. paedophilia, contamination). So, it may be that it takes very little to set off our threat alarm; for example, merely being around children can feel dangerous for the person with intrusions about being a paedophile. This can cause our threat alarm to trigger a 'fight or flight' response, so that we *feel* that we need to act to avoid danger and act accordingly. Over time, we may develop well rehearsed responses to these 'false alarms', which reinforces a sense of having saved ourselves in some way and makes it difficult to take the risk. The aversive experience of anxiety itself becomes a powerful reinforcer.

The power of imagination

Our new brain capacities for imagination give us wonderful scope for creativity and enjoyment in life. However, our new brain capacity for imagination and thinking can sometimes get hijacked by our old brain's threat alarm.

To illustrate the power of imagination, just consider what happens in our bodies when we watch Masterchef or other food programmes. Seeing the food on the television screen can stimulate our salivary glands and digestive system so that our body responds *as if* we are about to receive food, despite knowing that we are watching television and we may have nothing particularly appetizing to which to look forward. Similarly, if we watch a horror film, we might find ourselves feeling jumpy and maybe even checking behind doors or shower curtains! Although we know we are just watching a film and we are safe in our home, we cannot help but feel as if there is danger lurking around the corner. In a similar way, if we read erotic literature, look at erotic photos, or watch sexual scenes on television, we can feel our bodies become sexually aroused. Again, we know that we are not about to engage in sex, but our body is preparing us for this nonetheless.

These examples illustrate the powerful impact of the brain's capacity for imagination on our body's responses. Just as merely thinking about food, danger, or sex can activate the appropriate response in our body, imagining anything threatening will activate a threat response. This is very important in OCD as it can help us to understand that merely having an intrusion (e.g. doubts about locking the door, images of germs, or intrusive thoughts of sexual contact with a child) activates our threat alarm and emotional responses. Once activated, we are primed to respond in a 'better safe than sorry' way (e.g. go back to check the door is locked, continue to wash our hands until they feel clean, avoid any contact with children).

It is important to keep this in mind when tackling OCD. Treating intrusions as 'false alarms' will help the person to disengage from unhelpful responses and also to tone down the sense of threat associated with the intrusions. Essentially, treating intrusions as 'just a thought and nothing more' is key to this process. Understandably, this can prove difficult when the body's threat response is activated—a bit like staying in the building when the fire alarm is going off—this is easer to do if we know it is a false alarm. So, the way to respond to intrusions is to treat them all as false alarms.

These ideas are derived from the work of Paul Gilbert and colleagues and compassion-focussed therapy (Gilbert, 2010).

therapy, we develop an alternative perspective (theory B) under non-anxious conditions.

This can help us to make sense of why theory A seems the relevant response when we are anxious and why theory B makes sense in the therapy room when talking with the therapist (also when theory A has much less credibility), but may be difficult to apply under conditions of anxiety.

So, in therapy, the challenge is to act according to theory B under conditions of anxiety—i.e. to start treading out a 'new path'.

In-session behavioural experiments may be key to help start the person on this new and unfamiliar path—easier to do together than expecting the person to do independently for the first time.

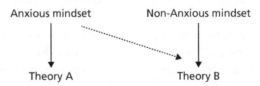

As we tread this new path, the old theory A path becomes disused and eroded so that over time the new path becomes the dominant one and becomes an easier road to take.

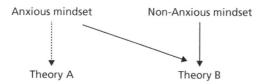

Anxious mindset   Non-Anxious mindset

Theory A   Theory B

This is also useful in illustrating the problem of 'keeping a foot in both camps'—when the individual wants to try out theory B, but is still holding on to the idea and in some way behaving as if theory A is true, meaning that in behavioural experiments, anxiety stays high.

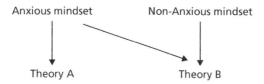

Anxious mindset   Non-Anxious mindset

Theory A   Theory B

If this happens, the theory A path continues to be used and does not erode—resulting in the person not fully finding out what happens if they stick with theory B—their OCD continues to be as anxiety-provoking as ever.

If the problem has been around for a long time (years, maybe decades), it can feel even more difficult for the person to contemplate dropping his or her theory A perspective. Take some time to imagine how it would feel to have your own reality undermined in some way. While a theory B perspective can bring a sense of liberation and relief, it can also bring a sense of bewilderment ('if only I had discovered this sooner'), loss ('I've missed out on so much') and self-criticism ('it's my own fault I've ended up in this mess'). It is important to acknowledge these feelings if they are there, and reiterate that the person was doing the best (s)he could based on his or her understanding at the time. Encourage the person to consider what (s)he would like to do, given this new understanding of the problem.

3.6.1.1 Increasing motivation for change

The fact that the person with OCD is seeking therapy indicates a desire for some change. Stages of change models (e.g. Prochaska and DiClemente, 1982) can help us understand the challenges faced at different stages of change. At precontemplation, the person with OCD may not recognize that the OCD is problematic and may indeed view his or her compulsions as essential (or at least 'helpful'). At this stage (s)he is unlikely to have sought therapy, unless of course this has been motivated by the concerns of loved ones. If so, they may have been assessed as having 'low or absent insight' in *DSM-5* terms.

The process of developing a shared understanding of the problem in the formulation that captures the person's experience and illustrates that 'the solution is the problem' is an intervention in itself. It can help the person to enter a stage of 'contemplation', where (s)he recognizes a need for change but may be unsure about whether (s)he is ready to take this step. An important role of the therapist is to help the person enter a stage of 'preparation for change', where (s)he has decided (s)he wishes to make a change and is ready to enter the 'action' phase in which (s)he is actively experimenting with living according to theory B. Here are some strategies that may help the person who continues to be doubtful to 'choose to change'.

3.6.2 **No guarantees**

Having developed an alternative explanation (theory B) of what is keeping the person's OCD going, we can frame the remainder of therapy as a period of working together to test out whether theory B offers a credible explanation for his or her experiences, including weighing up the pros and cons of each theory, including using the insurance metaphor.

THERAPIST: You've been living according to theory A for how long?

SAUL: Nearly 7 years.

THERAPIST: In that time, how well has this been working for you? What have you noticed has happened over time?

SAUL: Well, it was okay to start with, but it got worse. I ended up doing a job I don't really like just because it meant I could manage the OCD a bit more easily. I'm even struggling to hold on to that job now.

THERAPIST: That's right. The little ways of getting by have got bigger—more demanding and more time-consuming over the years, haven't they?

SAUL: I suppose.

THERAPIST: So, over the past 7 years, has living according to theory A led to any improvement in your OCD?

SAUL: No—but nothing disastrous has happened either. It feels that I've had to do more and more to make sure nothing goes wrong.

THERAPIST: What I'd like us to do together is to engage in an experiment to really test out theory B. You've been living according to theory A all this time as it seemed like the only reasonable thing to do to protect yourself. However, theory B also offers an explanation for all the things that you've been doing. You've been living according to theory A for 7 years; what do you think about testing out theory B over the next few weeks?

SAUL: I'm not sure. It feels risky. What would it involve?

THERAPIST: Well, if we look at our theory A/theory B sheet, it would essentially involve living according to theory B over the next few weeks [refer person to the section on their theory A/theory B sheet: 'what I need to do according to theory B'].

SAUL: I get what you're saying, but it feels like I'd be tempting fate. Maybe I'd be willing if you could guarantee that nothing would go wrong but you can't give me that guarantee.

THERAPIST: You're right. I can't guarantee that nothing will go wrong. But if you carry on living according to theory A, I can guarantee that your life will become more and more restricted and the OCD will get a firmer grip on your life. [Note: express concern rather than lecturing.]

SAUL: I don't think I could bear that.

THERAPIST: I don't want that for you either. This is why you've come for help. If you're willing to experiment with living according to theory B, what could the potential benefit be for you?

SAUL: Well—I could just get on with things a lot more easily.

THERAPIST: Absolutely, and what would it mean for your future? [Refer person to the section on their theory A/theory B sheet: 'what theory B predicts for my future'.]

SAUL: Yes—that paints a better future than theory A. But I couldn't bear it if everything went wrong—it would be my fault.

THERAPIST: It will feel risky and I can't offer you any guarantees. What would you say if I offered you an insurance policy that guaranteed that your house would never be burgled or damaged in any way and that nothing could ever happen to your loved ones?

SAUL: I'd take it! What's the catch?

THERAPIST: The premiums are £10,000/month.

SAUL: Well—that's ridiculous!

THERAPIST: Maybe—but it's offering an extremely high level of cover so the costs are bound to be high.

SAUL: But no one could afford that.

THERAPIST: Of course, I can't offer you any such policy. Nobody can. Nobody can guarantee you that. Insurance policies offer some compensation to help cope with the consequences when things go wrong rather than guaranteeing against things going wrong.

SAUL: I suppose so—yes.

THERAPIST: In the same way, no one can guarantee that nothing will go wrong if you give theory B a try. Living according to theory A doesn't guarantee this either really.

SAUL: But it's less likely to happen.

THERAPIST: Maybe it feels that way. But it's coming at such a great cost to you—a bit like the excessive insurance policy. You're right—things can go wrong in life—none of us has a guarantee. But what's happened is that in trying to get the nearest thing possible to a guarantee, you are constantly trying to keep things safe to the point that life has become really miserable for you. You've been trying to deal with the problem your way for the last 7 years and things seem to have got worse. How about experimenting with this for the next few weeks? At the end of the few weeks you can decide whether you wish to go back to doing things your way, according to theory A. What do you say?

3.6.3 **Pros and cons of change**

Encourage the person to engage in a process of explicitly considering the costs and benefits of changing versus not changing. For example, for Saul, the barista who had to get things 'just-so', the pros and cons of change are shown in Table 3.10.

Table 3.10 Four-way cost–benefit analysis: advantages and disadvantages of staying the same and changing

Advantages of staying the same	Disadvantages of staying the same
It feels familiar and 'safe'	Continued anxiety and stress
	Annoys my friends
	Worries my family
	Time spent repeating things
	Being late
Advantages of changing	**Disadvantages of changing**
I could start living a more normal life—free of the OCD	Anxiety
The anxiety should go	Do not know what it will be like—unknown
I will be able to perform better at work	
I could apply for a different job/start applying for training courses	
I'll be able to see my friends more	

Start this exercise together in a therapy session and ask the person to continue with it as homework. When reviewing the homework at the following session, it can be helpful to make reference to the person's therapy goals to help him or her consider any further costs of staying the same or benefits of changing that (s)he has not yet identified. Also, pay particular attention to 'advantages of staying the same' and 'disadvantages of changing', as there may be opportunities to challenge some of these ideas. Here, for example, you may be quizzical about the idea that the person feels safe due to the compulsions— this is seldom the case. It is more likely that (s)he constantly feels that the wolves are at the door.

The idea of 'digging to get out of a hole' can be useful; i.e. if you are stuck in a hole, don't keep digging (doing more SSBs), don't try a different spade (different SSBs), and don't get a friend to dig with you (reassurance/accommodation by others). Instead, get out of there.

3.6.4 **Starting behavioural experiments involving exposure and confrontation**

Although a relatively small section of this book, it is essential in all instances to include active behavioural experiments both as a way of affirming 'theory B' and helping the person to reclaim areas of life which have been blighted by OCD.

The ideal way to move to this crucial stage of confronting fears whilst refraining from compulsive behaviour (i.e. behavioural experiments involving exposure and response prevention [ERP]) is to review the theory B formulation (vicious flower) and engage the person in discussion about what the implications of it are for how (s)he should overcome OCD. Arising from this discussion the most likely conclusion is that they should 'fight the bully', 'find out what really happens', and so on. The therapist reinforces this, pointing out that if (s)he is going to do that, it has to be done in a particular way to support him or her and maximize what (s)he learns, seeking to agree the 'rules of engagement'. These vary, but usually include the following ideas:

- Anything that we do will involve teamwork
- You (the individual with OCD) will always be in control of what happens
- 'No' is always an acceptable answer; but I want permission to try to persuade when I think it is likely to be helpful
- I will never ask you to do anything with a high risk; you will, however, often feel that I am, at which point you need to remind yourself of 'theory B'
- I will never ask you to do anything I would not do myself
- In the early stages of therapy I will be with you and do things with you where possible; later this will decrease so that you are responsible for things

- I will support you with discomfort, but not reassure you about harm
- Where we are doing things together, I will keep going with you until any distress, discomfort, or anxiety has started to decrease significantly.

The choice of early tasks and the order in which problems are dealt with depends considerably on the person's confidence, the degree to which each aspect of the problem is handicapping, the extent to which a given aspect occurs in the person's normal environment and, of course, the person's readiness to carry out the task. In short, the choice should be negotiated, but with the person with OCD being asked to 'take the lead'. As a general principle, behavioural experiments should begin with a task that will provoke moderate discomfort. The target chosen should be relevant to the person's lifestyle and goals, so that success will be self-reinforcing.

Behavioural experiments are the main homework task. Given the severely distressing nature of OCD, it is important to monitor compliance with homework. Watch out for avoidance, or not being fully truthful about homework, or stopping treatment altogether. This can be avoided by 'agreeing' rather than 'setting' homework, and by the therapist explaining: 'Every time you find homework difficult we can learn more about the problem and the way it affects you. It's important that you try your hardest with all the homework we agree but, if you are not able to manage it, then it is helpful if you write detailed notes about what happened so that we can deal better with similar problems when they arise in future. Often the problems that come up are just different aspects of the obsession that we have not yet worked out.'

The individual with OCD should be in control of how these challenges will take place according to important principles that will ensure the best outcomes for them. The principles are:

1. Always look for opportunities to do the opposite of what OCD wants you to; try to do this pretty much all the time if you can.

2. Never do anything you are intending to undo. It simply means you are waiting for that moment and OCD remains in charge.

3. If, after you have done something and you find you are beginning to get overwhelmed and feel you have no choice but to undo it, seek support in holding the line from your therapist or loved ones, asking them to help and comfort you, acknowledging and focussing on your feelings of anxiety/discomfort (rather than reassuring you).

4. If you find that you are overwhelmed and undo things (i.e. engage in SSBs), wait a while then redo it (i.e. do another behavioural experiment that stands up to the problem). Best of all, redo it but even more (i.e. an anti-OCD behavioural experiment).

5. Remember what the point of doing these things is: to reclaim your life.

3.7 Change: The process of evidence gathering and discovery or, 'finding out how the world really works'

Whilst the process of gaining a shared understanding and developing an alternative, less threatening, theory (theory A/B) is a powerful therapeutic process in itself, treatment is unlikely to progress or succeed without very direct action on the part of the individual with OCD. This can be an intimidating prospect; this chapter will illustrate how to engage the individual further in this process and gain willingness to put 'theory B' to the test. What we are describing is a process of belief change that brings about a change in anxiety. This change takes place through discussion, use of metaphor, and, commonly, through behavioural experiments.

A well constructed behavioural experiment is an immensely powerful method of changing beliefs, and can range from within-session demonstrations of attention, thought suppression, impact of checking, and so on, through to intense and intensive exposure, such as dramatic behavioural experiments involving lavatories followed by sandwiches, throwing duplicate keys into bushes, and so on. *The key thing is that behavioural experiments are intended to help the person learn about how their OCD really works.* Equally, discussion in the form of guided discovery and use of metaphor through all phases of treatment provides continual opportunities for challenging the threat appraisal and building up the less-threatening alternative belief. Assessment and formulation initiate this process as the person begins to contemplate the idea that there is another way of looking at the problem; formulation and theory A/B consolidate this and working together on choosing to change sets the scene for active change. Normalizing and psychoeducation is a continuous process during the active change phase of treatment. Once you have established the idea that intrusive thoughts are normal, the next step is to let them go. When challenging OCD, anxiety is likely but will pass. Change may feel risky and outcomes may be uncertain, but to overcome the problem, uncertainty needs to be tolerated.

Many therapists find this stage difficult because the client may experience considerable distress as a result of exposure to their worst fears. However, people with OCD are usually willing to tolerate high levels of distress if they believe that treatment will be effective. Resolve tempered with understanding of the person's distress helps set the precedent for a trusting and task-orientated relationship. Failure to establish a confident and structured approach at this stage can be very difficult to correct later.

3.7.1 Which problem do I need to solve? How to find out which theory is the best fit

3.7.1.1 Behavioural experiments

A fundamental part of the process of 'finding out how the world really works' is building on the theory and actually doing things differently from the way OCD has dictated (Box 3.4).

Key points when planning behavioural experiments (BE):

- Ensure that there is a clear rationale, linked to the formulation and theory A/B
- Devise a BE that is meaningful and relevant to the person
- Don't ask the impossible; doing so undermines the sense of feeling understood and of trust
- There is no need for a hierarchy, which is both time-consuming and limiting
- Watch out for OCD behaviour undermining the impact of the BE; e.g. only touching 'contaminated' items with one hand, 'keeping track' of contamination, subtle reassurance-seeking, shifting responsibility to the therapist
- Move to planning and execution of BEs entirely by the person with OCD
- BEs are interwoven with other methods of change such as challenging of beliefs through guided discovery, use of surveys, continua, and pie charts
- Each BE can lead to another—what else do you need to find out?

3.7.2 Introducing behavioural experiments

It can be helpful to initiate this discussion in the context of theory A/B, particularly the implications. The following metaphor about faulty logic is a useful start to a discussion about how to find out 'how the world really works' when the person is not following the OCD rules.

LYDIA: But it's sensible to check and nothing bad has happened since I started it.

THERAPIST: Imagine that you are on the train between London and Edinburgh. In the corridor you see a man ripping up pieces of paper and throwing them onto the track. You ask him what he is doing:

'I'm doing it to keep the elephants off the track'

You reply that there are no elephants on the track. He replies:

'Exactly'.

LYDIA: [Laughs.]

Box 3.4 What is the difference between exposure and response prevention and behavioural experiments?

ERP is used in behaviour therapy. The individual with OCD engages in systematic, repeated, and prolonged exposure to feared situations to provoke the obsessional fear. Exposure can be in vivo or imaginal and can include exposure to the intrusive thoughts and the thoughts of subsequent catastrophic consequences. The individual does not engage in any compulsions and learns that the situation is not dangerous and that anxiety spontaneously subsides. The delivery of sessions may vary; for example, twice-weekly sessions of 90–120 minutes (Abramowitz *et al.*, 2003) to allow for prolonged exposure and extinction of anxiety. If the individual with OCD does engage in compulsions, then habituation to anxiety does not occur. Contemporary ERP also involves discussion of tolerating risk and uncertainty (Abramowitz *et al.*, 2005). Whilst individuals are introduced to their fears in a graded fashion, it is unsurprising that people decline treatment or drop out owing to the aversive nature of this experience and difficulties implementing this protocol for those with predominately mental rituals (Whittal *et al.*, 2008). The rationale for exposure can be explained as follows:

> 'Usually some anxiety occurs when you start this type of work. This is actually an important part of treatment, because often people think that the anxiety will continue and become intolerable. One of the valuable things you learn through treatment is that the anxiety does not increase to intolerable levels and it often subsides more rapidly than you might expect. Sometimes, anxiety starts to reduce within 20 minutes; more usually, half an hour to an hour. Another important thing which you will notice is that after you have done exposure two or three times, the amount of discomfort you get at first becomes less and less. This is the best indication of how the treatment is working; as time goes on, you will find you will be able to do the exposure in this way and get no discomfort at all.'
>
> See Figures 3.3, 3.4 and 3.5 (pages 123 and 124).

Behavioural experiments are defined as:

> '... planned experiential activities, based on experimentation or observation, which are undertaken by patients in or between cognitive therapy sessions. Their design is derived directly from a cognitive formulation of the problem, and their primary purpose is to obtain new information which may help to:
>
> test the validity of the patient's existing beliefs about themselves, others and the world
>
> construct and/or test new, more adaptive beliefs
>
> contribute to the development and verification of the cognitive formulation.'
>
> p.8, *Oxford Guide to Behavioural Experiments in Cognitive Therapy*, Bennett-Levy *et al.* (2004).

The main distinction is that ERP involves prolonged, systematic exposure resulting in habituation to and extinction of anxiety; behavioural experiments are designed to test and change beliefs, involving the provocation and tolerance of anxiety.

Recommended reading: Exposure-based treatment for OCD, in the *Oxford Handbook of Obsessive-Spectrum Disorders,* edited by Gail Steketee.

Of course the man believes that, because he is doing something and nothing bad has happened, this is because of his paper throwing. This fact has reinforced his belief that this behaviour was necessary. However, therapist and client usually agree that the absence of paper on the track will not lead to the presence of elephants. The man throwing the paper is engaged in some faulty reasoning, but his actions appear necessary to him to stop something bad happening.

THERAPIST: So, Lydia, what does he need to do to get out of this problem?

LYDIA: Well, I suppose he should stop throwing the paper.

THERAPIST: And what would he find out?

LYDIA: That he didn't need to do it and that he could go and do something else.

THERAPIST: And how might he feel at first?

LYDIA: Very anxious, I'm sure. But it shouldn't last forever.

THERAPIST: So why am I telling you this story?

This is a brief version of the 'builder's apprentice' described in Box 3.5. For many, the builder's apprentice may be preferred, as it is less 'jokey' and allows greater depth of exploration and guided discovery.

3.7.3 Building up theory B; disproving theory A

Some threat appraisals can be directly challenged. For example, for someone who believes that, if they look at an aeroplane in the sky and think of it falling and crashing, this will happen (an example of magical thinking/thought–action fusion), a BE to disprove theory A would be very effective. Contamination concerns can be challenged through direct contact with the sources of contamination, with specific predictions about the onset and course of the illness, i.e. if you shake hands, you will develop 'flu within 24 hours, be bedridden for 5 days, and will pass the illness to all members of your family. If this does not happen, then it provides good evidence against theory A.

Box 3.5 The builder's apprentice

On his first day at a building site, the builders played a trick on a young apprentice. They told him to hold up a wall that they had just built, telling him it would easily fall down unless he supported it, and that he had better make sure he did a good job otherwise they would have to rebuild it, or worse still, someone could get hurt. This was such a terrible idea to imagine that the apprentice 'held up' the wall for hours. After a while he began to wonder why he had never seen anyone else holding up a wall, and began to suspect that this was a joke. He very cautiously removed his hands, and found that the wall stayed up. But he kept looking over his shoulder and doubting whether it would still stand. How could he find out that the wall was solid and was not going to fall down? Perhaps give it a good push or a kick?

Going through this metaphor together with the person with OCD to identify what the person does to hold up the wall (his or her SSBs) and what (s)he needs to do to push the wall provides a way of understanding why it would be a good idea to do BEs that give really clear information as to what is happening.

Some contamination concerns are not refutable—if sitting in a building with lead windows means that at some point in the future the person will suffer the brain problems associated with lead poisoning, there is no prediction to be made that can be tested (see Section 3.7.15 on Tolerating (some) uncertainty). You can in this case generate predictions on how long the anxiety will last.

Many people will be reluctant to change the way in which they react to obsessional fears unless they can gain some convincing guarantee from the therapist that the catastrophes they fear being responsible for will not happen. Early in therapy, the focus is not on the probabilities of disaster (which in any case often tend to seem very low but very awful), but rather to have them refocus on the catastrophic impact of OCD. If we consider Lydia, who checked to prevent something bad happening.

LYDIA: I can see that the explanation we worked out could be correct. However, if I reduce or even give up checking the door, can you guarantee that my house will not be burgled?

THERAPIST: No, certainly not. However, I can offer you a different, 100% guarantee. I guarantee that, if you continue to check your door in the way you do now, you will continue to suffer from OCD for a very long time, maybe even the rest of your life.

On a similar theme:

THERAPIST: If you could be convinced that you would be cured of your obsessional problem by giving everything in your house away, would you do it?

LYDIA: (hesitating) …well, I suppose actually I can buy those things again, and I have already spent so much money in all sorts of ways on the problem.

THERAPIST: Well, the really good thing is that you don't have to give things away to achieve this; you just have to be prepared to run the same risk as everyone else.

A similar approach to this motivational issue is 'How much would you pay to get rid of your obsessional problem?' 'How much *are* you paying to make sure that you are clean/sure/etc.?' (see Section 3.6 on Presenting change as a choice).

3.7.4 **Setting up a behavioural experiment**

After discussion and thinking together, hopefully the person with OCD will be prepared to identify a particular challenge. Once you have agreed what to do, make very specific predictions of what will happen in the BE, and after the experiment, record what actually happened and what it shows (Table 3.11).

In cases of checking, such as Lydia, who feared that the house will be burgled or set on fire, BEs to test out what happens are quite straightforward (Table 3.12).

Research papers can be very useful in substantiating the personal evidence collected in BEs (see, for example, van den Hout and Kindt, 2003; see Box 3.2). This can also be incorporated into BEs, getting others to check repeatedly to see the effect on the meta-memory.

For Saul, who has been struggling with trying to achieve a 'just-right' feeling, the therapist uses a specific metaphor to illustrate the idea that, whilst changing

Table 3.11 Behavioural experiment record

Complete before		Complete after		
Planned experiment	Specific predictions and how much I believe them	What happened? Did the predictions come true?	Conclusions? What do you make of this?	Does it fit best with theory A or B?

Table 3.12 Behavioural experiment record for challenging checking

Complete before		Complete after		
Planned experiment	Specific predictions and how much I believe them	What happened? Did the predictions come true?	Conclusions? What do you make of this?	Does it fit best with theory A or B?
Leave the house without checking and stay out for 1 hour	The house will burn down (80%). I will feel awful and won't be able to cope with it (90%)	The house did not burn down	It could be luck … but it might not be. I need to do it again. I did feel very anxious initially but it went down quite quickly. I was even thinking of other things after half an hour	Theory B. When I felt less anxious it felt much less convincing that something bad would happen

things is going to feel 'wrong', this is just a feeling (the 'driving on the right' metaphor):

THERAPIST: I want to think about driving—you drove here in a car with a steering wheel on the right hand side of the car, and drove on the left hand side of the road? Imagine we heard on the news that from tomorrow we are going to drive on the right hand side of the road, rather than the left. Have you ever driven on the right?

SAUL: Yes, a few times on holiday; it does feel very strange and I was quite nervous.

THERAPIST: Exactly—especially at the beginning it does feel quite wrong and it is a bit stressful. So if we switched over to driving on the right—what do you think would happen?

SAUL: People would be nervous at first, but I suppose we would all get used to it.

THERAPIST: I reckon so. So how would it work in the same way if you started doing things differently?

SAUL: I suppose I would feel nervous to begin with but then get used to it.

THERAPIST: Do you believe that?

SAUL: I don't know—if we did start driving on the right, what about all the road signs and junctions and all that?

THERAPIST: Good point—that would take a while to sort out and it probably would be a bit confusing for a while. Going back to your problem, what's the equivalent of sorting out the road signs?

SAUL: I suppose doing everything differently—as there is hardly anything that I do that isn't affected by this problem.

THERAPIST: Right, so it will take a while to even notice some of the things, but once you have decided to do things differently, you know what you need to do. If we switched to driving on the right and noticed a street sign that hadn't been changed, would we suddenly start driving on the left again?

SAUL: No, that wouldn't make sense. I get it—once I decide to do things differently, I need to do it with everything.

THERAPIST: And going back to my question, do you believe that you would get used to it?

SAUL: I'm not sure—I'm about 50/50. There is a bit of me that thinks it's not worth it; I can usually manage, it's only the odd day that I actually get in trouble.

THERAPIST: So there has to be a good reason to want to try. If the government told us that we were switching to driving on the right for no particular reason, there were no economic benefits, no real advantages—what do you think would happen?

SAUL: There would be outrage—protests and things like that—it would cost an enormous amount of money and create masses of inconvenience for no reason.

THERAPIST: Okay—so shall we remind ourselves of what this problem really costs you?

Saul and his therapist set up a BE where he did things that felt 'wrong' (Table 3.13).

Jane, who has religious concerns, was quite preoccupied with 'bad' thoughts she had had in the past. She had had a difficult time when she was 19 and could recall being bullied and condemned by her religious companions. There were several discussions concerning the nature of thoughts and normalizing the occurrence of all types of thoughts. Jane had lots of beliefs about the importance of thoughts and the occurrence of thoughts. The Responsibility Interpretations Questionnaire (RIQ; Salkovskis *et al.*, 2000; see Appendix 6) was useful in helping to identify key beliefs that are feeding into Jane's anxiety and guilt about intrusive thoughts. It is not possible to disprove theory A that she will be damned. It took a while for Jane to feel ready to contemplate a BE. She felt very

Table 3.13 Behavioural experiment record for challenging 'not just-right' feelings

Complete before		Complete after		
Planned experiment	**Specific predictions and how much I believe them**	**What happened?** **Did the predictions come true?**	**Conclusions?** **What do you make of this?**	**Does it fit best with theory A or B?**
Leave the house and do things in the opposite way to the OCD way—shut the front door by pulling it behind me, walk on the right of the path, and open the gate with my left hand. No counting or repeating	I will be 100% anxious for the whole day (0830–1800) (belief: 95%); I will not be able to have a conversation with my friends, i.e. stuttering or silent and they will leave giving me dirty looks (belief 95%)	I was 90% anxious for 20 min on the way to the station. I ran for my train and by the time I got on it I was 50% anxious. When I met my friends 30 min later, 55% anxious. Over lunch, 20%. By the time I got home, 5–10%. I did talk to my friends and on several occasions made them laugh with stories about rude customers in the café. I felt awkward at times. No one left or gave me dirty looks	I found it really difficult to tolerate the urge to do the door/path/gate like I usually do. I did feel anxious but not as much as I feared. I could tolerate the feeling and it passed. I was fine with my friends	Theory B: a problem of being tuned into urges and getting the 'just-right' feeling and this causes me anxiety. I was able to cope and no one said I was weird—so theory A doesn't fit

guilty challenging her religious OCD or even calling it OCD. This led to considerable discussion of the nature of religion and the purpose of observance. Jane was able to reflect on what makes a good person good and the importance of 'lived goodness' that she felt her religion was trying to achieve, rather than scrupulously spending every moment in prayer. She agreed to try a BE of not praying (Table 3.14).

3.7.5 Spotlight on supervision: behavioural experiments

'My client fears that treating the problem as OCD may be blasphemous.'

Check theory A/B: framing the question correctly within theory A/B is key to engaging the client in change. This is similar to people who believe that they really will die from contamination.

'I don't know anything about Islam/Sikhism/Christianity, etc. or I am also a Muslim/Sikh/ Christian, etc. and don't feel well equipped to deal with this type of OCD.'

Table 3.14 Behavioural experiment record to challenge religious concerns

Complete before		Complete after		
Planned experiment	**Specific predictions and how much I believe them**	**What happened?** Did the predictions come true?	**Conclusions?** What do you make of this?	**Does it fit best with theory A or B?**
Do not go to church or pray for a week	I will feel very guilty. The guilt will be unbearable	I felt *very* guilty at first but did not respond. After 3 days I felt better. I had more time to do things for others	I do not need to go to church all the time to be a good person	Theory B

It may be helpful to ask the therapist to reflect on his or her own belief system and how it may play into this particular issue. What fears does (s)he have about working with the problem and why? How does (s)he think this form of OCD differs from any others? This may be useful in eliciting unhelpful therapist beliefs and refocussing the therapy on processes. Obtaining help from other people who are religious leaders or from family members regarded as 'good' observers of the religion is usually helpful. However, this is so that the therapist can better understand; it is seldom helpful to enter into discussions directly with religious authorities; after all, the problem is one of being worried about religion rather than being actually 'impaired' in the religious sense. One would not, after all, take someone who had OCD about sexually abusing children to a child abuse expert!

'How do I do anti-OCD religious experiments?'

Abstaining from religious observance is anti-OCD. It may not be possible always to 'do the opposite of OCD', such as eliciting and tolerating blasphemous thoughts. However, it is possible to go against the OCD as far as the person can.

'My client is finding it difficult to do anything she feels might harm her baby. Is it better to treat her when the baby comes?'

'Surely it makes sense for her to avoid work if she might catch something when pregnant?'

These questions are similar in their implications, that OCD during pregnancy may be somehow dangerous or difficult to treat. The supervisor can give clear information in this case; there is evidence that untreated anxiety presents longitudinal risks to the unborn child, increases the risk of maternal postnatal depression and anxiety, and is clearly unpleasant and impairing in itself (Heron *et al.*, 2004). It is important to address perinatal OCD at an early stage to avoid a negative impact on the capacity to parent. Therefore early intervention is likely to be of benefit both to mother and child. Whilst there may be some modifications in BEs during pregnancy, they can still be undertaken. Gaining a good understanding of OCD and planning specific ways to fighting it once the baby is born will be useful. It might be useful to consider any specific therapist beliefs that are getting in the way of intervention during pregnancy.

Jessie felt able to attempt a BE after discussion about the importance of fighting the OCD during pregnancy and the benefits of getting a head start for when the baby was born. Having the baby is an opportunity and an imperative to do things differently (Table 3.15).

Therapy continued with further BEs, and with some observation of what other mums did. Jessie generated a list of what qualities are important in being a good mum and realized that being careful and avoiding harm was only one aspect of this multifaceted task.

Walter found the 'unwanted guest at a party' metaphor helpful to remind him to 'let thoughts go':

> Imagine that you are at an enjoyable party, drinking your drink and making conversation. Someone you really dislike comes through the door. You could run up to them and try to push them out of the door, shouting and screaming at them and trying to get other people to help you. This would ruin the evening for you and many other people. Or, after you noticed their arrival, you could ignore the unwelcome guest. Even if they brush past you or remain in your sight for a while, carry on drinking and talking.

This is like ignoring your intrusive thoughts, even if they are rattling around for a while. Another widely used metaphor is a train passing through the station—if you tried to examine every detail of the train, count the carriages, establish its speed, destination, and origin, you would not be able to do so. Instead, practise letting the train pass through the station (Table 3.16).

3.7.6 Why would anyone put their hands down the toilet? The purpose and value of anti-OCD behavioural experiments

For someone with contamination concerns, what they are aiming for in treatment is that they do not believe that they are responsible for preventing the

Table 3.15 Behavioural experiment record for challenging contamination fears

Complete before		Complete after		
Planned experiment	Specific predictions and how much I believe them	What happened? Did the predictions come true?	Conclusions? What do you make of this?	Does it fit best with theory A or B?
Use the toilet at work	I will get ill, which will harm my baby: 90%	I did not get ill	I can see it is more likely that I'm oversensitive but this may have been luck	It could fit with either. I need to do it again!

Table 3.16 Behavioural experiment for challenging beliefs about unwanted thoughts

Complete before		Complete after		
Planned experiment	**Specific predictions and how much I believe them**	**What happened? Did the predictions come true?**	**Conclusions? What do you make of this?**	**Does it fit best with theory A or B?**
Collect my grandchildren from school	I will get images of them naked: 100%. I will get an erection: 80%. I will be preoccupied with doubt throughout the day and into the night (100%) and be unbearably anxious (100%)	I did not get images of them naked; I had some fleeting images of sexual scenes but they came and went. I did not get an erection. I was aware of my genitals. I was actually very busy making sure they had all their school bags, getting them home, giving them a snack, making their dinner, and helping them with their homework (which I enjoyed ...)	I enjoyed being with my grandchildren. This is normal and lovely	I'm not a pervert. I'm a loving grandfather and father, and a trustworthy and dedicated teacher

spread of disease with catastrophic consequences, therefore they do not feel compelled to wash their hands repeatedly, nor have to avoid touching certain things, or have to take particular precautions, and do not feel anxious. To be able to do this, they will need actively to challenge their belief that something bad will happen if they 'take the risk' of doing things differently. For someone with contamination concerns, touching a stranger's hands can feel as dangerous as touching the inside of a toilet.

When faced with an intrusive thought, the person with OCD has three choices—to go with the OCD and engage in SSBs, to ignore the OCD and do nothing, or to stand up to the OCD and actively challenge the belief—anti-OCD. It is useful to draw out the choices. A metaphor is often the best way of explaining why we would want to do something that is actually more extreme than most people would do day to day. Drawing an analogy with another form of anxiety can illuminate the rationale for doing more 'extreme' experiments—if you had a friend who was afraid of heights, and they wanted to visit their granny on the sixth floor of a block of flats—would there be any value in taking them somewhere higher than the sixth floor? What if their granny moves to another, higher block? What if a friend moves to a penthouse? Would there be any value in taking the person with a height phobia to the top of the Shard—what would they learn? Would they still be bothered by their phobia?

Anti-OCD BEs are still within the realms of 'normal behaviour', even if they are not everyday behaviour. Hundreds of thousands of mobile phones are dropped in the toilet each year, as well as a similar number of items of jewellery, keys, etc. Most people attempt to retrieve them.

Sometimes it is helpful to have a discussion about the reality of BEs, linking this to the fact that the therapist will never ask the patient to do anything that (s)he would not be prepared to do first (see Section 3.7.7 on Modelling). Some kind of perspective on 'risk' is important. The authors of this book are all aware that by modelling contamination experiments they might develop a stomach upset or diarrhoea. Although it has not happened to us yet, we accept that it might, but, to help people with OCD, it seems a small price to pay. For the patient, if it were to be a choice between having a stomach bug for a few days or OCD for the rest of his or her life, it is pretty clear what choice (s)he would make. It is appropriate to have this discussion with patients who express concerns about doing 'over the top' BEs.

3.7.7 Modelling

This involves the therapist carrying out the required task first and sometimes to a greater degree than the individual with OCD. Clinical experience indicates that modelling is helpful in two important respects. First, it is the clearest way of demonstrating which behaviours are required during BEs, especially as these are often unusual (e.g. running hands over toilet seats, closing doors without looking at them). Secondly, modelling *early on in treatment* is accompanied by greater willingness to undertake further experiments during treatment sessions and with homework. Modelling should be rapidly faded out once treatment has started because it can serve as a powerful form of reassurance.

In the case of a person who feared contamination by bathroom products that could be carcinogenic, the therapist introduced exposure by asking the client to smear shampoo on the back of her hand. First, the therapist smeared a large amount of the shampoo on his own hands and face and licked his hand. The person then smeared a small amount and agreed not to wash for 3 hours and to give ratings of discomfort and urge to wash at periodic intervals. Throughout the session the person was repeatedly praised and her attention drawn to the degree of anxiety reduction and the decay of the urge to wash that occurred without any neutralizing behaviour.

For people who check, the general strategy is the same, but more emphasis is placed on the actions of the person with OCD him or herself. For example, the therapist may model putting an iron on for a while, then switching it off and leaving the room without checking. The person is invited to do the same (without the therapist watching when the iron is switched off), then both leave the house for a predetermined period.

This aspect of treatment progresses with the person carrying out homework assignments, starting with tasks practised with the therapist. Early on, it is suggested that confronting their fears should be 'a job, not a hobby'. In all sessions and homework the person with OCD rates discomfort and urges to neutralize; this improves compliance and helps to identify difficulties that arise. Changes in discomfort during the session are discussed, as well as the overall reductions from session to session.

Subsequently, self-directed response prevention for any avoidance or neutralizing is crucial. Such behaviours may not be immediately obvious to either party. Useful questions for people with OCD to ask themselves are: 'if I didn't have an obsessional problem, would I be doing this?' (identifies neutralizing and avoidance); 'what extra things *would* I be doing if I didn't have the problem?' (identifies avoidance). As treatment progresses, the intensity of self-directed BEs is built up as rapidly as possible.

To reduce responsibility should anything go wrong, the client may seek frequent reassurance from the therapist or carry out homework literally as directed. This is a form of avoidance and indicates the need for direct exposure to responsibility as part of the treatment programme, after a discussion about the role of worries about responsibility. This involves the client being given homework in which the entire assignment is self-initiated and the *details* not discussed with the therapist. The therapist says: 'I would like you to plan this week's homework yourself; it should be the normal type of assignment, but I don't want you to tell me any details of what you do. I want you to record, as usual, how uncomfortable you get and other results of your experiments. It is important that you set things up so that you become uncomfortable but don't check, avoid, or neutralize. Try not to tell or even hint to anyone what you have done. Next session we will discuss how you *felt* but you and only you will be responsible for the assignment. So, without telling me any details of what you will leave unchecked, can you outline what the homework is for this week?'

3.7.8 Reassurance

Reassurance-seeking is a prominent feature of OCD, and is usually an attempt to ensure that harm has not been caused to self or others; it also has the effect of sharing or passing on responsibility. It is tempting for the therapist to reduce the person with OCD's anxiety by providing such assurance, but the enterprise is doomed to failure; proving that harm has not and will not be caused is an impossibility. For example, someone told her therapist that she had not checked her rubbish bin to see if there were any tablets in it, and asked whether the therapist thought that was alright? Telling the therapist provided sufficient reassurance regardless of whether an answer was given; the therapist had the opportunity to suggest corrective action and the patient could gauge the therapist's reaction. The repetitive, persistent, and stereotyped way in which reassurance is sought closely resembles other forms of ritualizing. To work out a treatment rationale for this problem, the therapist should question the patient about whether the relief obtained from reassurance is persistent or transient, and compare reassurance with other forms of neutralizing.

THERAPIST: You seem to be going over your worries about HIV again and again right now; are you wanting me to respond in a particular way?

JESSIE: Yes, I suppose so. I just need to know that I won't get HIV. I don't see what's wrong with finding that out.

THERAPIST: In the last couple of sessions we discussed the way that washing hands can actually keep the problem going when feeling contaminated, and that it was likely that asking had similar effects when it came to your doubts and fears. Am I right in thinking that asking for reassurance seems different to you?

JESSIE: Well, I feel you would know about it, so why not just tell me and make me feel better?

THERAPIST: You are right, obviously I should if it will help the problem. OK, I can do it right now. How much would I have to reassure you to last the rest of this month?

JESSIE: The rest of this month?

THERAPIST: Yes, I've got at least another two hours now. If it'll solve the problem for the rest of the month I should tell you. How much would you need for that?

JESSIE: It doesn't work like that. It'll only help for a few minutes.

The therapist can go on to discuss how reassurance prevents the person from confronting the anxiety about being responsible for harm, and hence that self-imposed response prevention is required (Salkovskis and Westbrook, 1987). Involvement of other family members is helpful in extending reassurance prevention and in reminding the person about it, particularly when the patient is having difficulty.

A useful discussion to have, including both the client and their loved ones, is how others might deal with distress. They do not obsessionally seek reassurance, so what do they do? The answer being sought is that they do many things, usually intended to help them deal more effectively with their distress. This can include engaging with other important things (work, gardening, reading something exciting, going out socially) and seeking support for their distress by sharing it with others, not discussing theory B fears. Involving family members in that discussion typically helps the patient to implement this more readily. This is covered more fully in Section 4.6.

3.7.9 Safety-seeking versus approach supporting behaviours

To test things out, ideally we want the person to drop any safety behaviours so that (s)he can clearly see the difference between doing things in a theory A and theory B way. For example, bringing on an intrusive thought of wishing death on others, then neutralizing by use of a mental ritual or prayer, or tracking contamination that will then later be cleaned will be no different to what usually happens. In these cases, subtle SSBs need to be eliminated. By contrast, there has been new and increasing interest in the notion of approach supporting safety behaviours (ASBs; Salkovskis, personal communication; Levy & Radomsky, 2014). These are behaviours of which the patient's intention focusses on a wish deliberately to choose to *approach and overcome* feared stimuli rather than protect him or herself from harm or responsibility for it. An example would be the use of latex gloves to touch a toilet early on, quickly progressing to more direct exposure. The role of ASBs to enhance approach as a type of scaffolding should be *explicit* and carefully considered within the predictions and results of any BE. The ultimate goal of dropping safety behaviours should be clearly in sight.

3.7.10 Consolidation

Moving on with BEs is a crucial part of therapy and, once begun, the momentum should grow. Most people can relate to the experience of riding a bike:

> When you first learn to ride a bike, it can feel quite scary. You might think you're going to fall off and hurt yourself and it can take a lot of courage to get on the bike. When you start pedalling, you will feel a bit wobbly, and you might still fall off. What happens when you start to pedal faster? Do you still think that you are going to fall off?
>
> Getting on the bike and starting to ride is starting to live in a non-OCD way. OCD will tell you that you're going to fall off and hurt yourself, so there's no point in doing anything differently. If you get on the bike, and pedal a couple of times you might feel a bit wobbly—the OCD will continue to tell you that you are going to fall—but you keep going and you wobble less, and feel more confident and stable. What happens to the OCD if you really go for it? You pedal faster—like trying the anti-OCD ways—you find out that you don't fall, and in fact you might even enjoy it. Once you learn to ride a bike and get past this phase, it becomes second nature, something you don't even have to think about.

> (Metaphor by Salkovskis and also developed by Poole, J.
> personal communication)

Another metaphor:

How would you train soldiers in the special forces? They need to be on top form to deal with extremely challenging situations at a moment's notice. Would you send them to a beach and instruct them to lounge about drinking cocktails for a year? Or would you insist on plenty of practice dealing with difficult situations, with repeated exercises of what they would need to do? The only way to deal with difficult situations in the future is to practise now—so when the soldiers are called into action they are well prepared mentally and physically for what confronts them.

Dealing with OCD requires practise of dealing with difficult situations. 'Anti-OCD' BEs provide 'training' for the times outside therapy sessions.

Other ways of putting the idea are:

'Fake it 'till you feel it,' i.e. give it a go anyway, despite feeling anxious

'Try it on for size'

3.7.11 **Where do you 'draw the line' with behavioural experiments?**

The purpose of BEs is to trigger the same kind of thoughts that would come anyway, and allow the person to practise a non-OCD or anti-OCD stance, with the aim of building up their belief in theory B (Table 3.17).

In the examples in Table 3.17, it would not be necessary actually to pick up faeces to evoke thoughts of contamination and it would not be necessary to look at naked images of children to evoke thoughts of being a paedophile. In the fullness of time, as the person with OCD overcomes their problem, like every-one else, (s)he will be able to deal with clearing up faeces if required (from pets, children, illnesses) and not think twice about seeing a naked child on a beach. This is the purpose of the anti-OCD BEs—that you and the person with OCD are in training so (s)he they can fight this problem on his or her own, including unexpected future faeces or nakedness scenarios.

The same applies for thought–action fusion BEs of 'thinking something bad' meaning it will happen. It is not customary to actively wish something bad on someone else, but it is a crucial BE. Everyone has something that makes them feel uncomfortable or 'wrong' for cultural reasons and personal beliefs/values. For example, people do not say racist or anti-religious words owing to personal beliefs and values about equality and discrimination. If the person with OCD has intrusive racist thoughts, it will be necessary to say or write the words—under these particular circumstances of treatment.

Anti-OCD experiments can provide very clear evidence that it really is okay to live in the non-OCD (normal) zone for most of the time. It can also be

Table 3.17 Examples of where to 'draw the line' with behavioural experiments

Intrusive thought	Threat appraisal	How to trigger thoughts
Germs are everywhere	I will spread germs, contaminate my family, and they will die	Not washing hands after touching the toilet
		Touching items that others have touched
		Drinking from a cup that someone else has used
Am I attracted to that child?	I'm a pervert, a child molester	Walking past a school
		Going to the children's section in a bookshop
		Watching a film with child actors in
		Reading a newspaper article about Jimmy Savile

motivating to reflect on what would be the quickest way for the person to find out what (s)he needs to know and get his or her life back on track.

3.7.12 Spotlight on supervision: therapist beliefs

'I don't like wishing death on people; it feels wrong (therapist belief).'

What is it in particular that bothers you? If it is a squeamish unpleasantness, this will pass when you keep doing it, so keep doing it until you are not concerned. If you are actually engaging in some magical thinking, that something bad might happen, then it is important to be able to challenge yourself or you are unlikely to be able to help the person with OCD.

3.7.13 Difficulties: change feels too 'risky'

It is understandable that the prospect of giving up one's SSBs can feel daunting, particularly given the person's theory A perspective, which is focussed on danger, threat, and their responsibility for it. For example, Walter may fear that he is more likely to act on his intrusive thoughts of paedophilia if he stops avoiding children or stops trying to get rid of the thoughts. Similarly, Jessie may feel that she is more likely to become ill through contamination if she disengages from her cleaning rituals.

The insurance policy metaphor (described in Section 3.6.2) challenges the idea that the person's current theory A offers as much protection as (s)he feels it does while drawing his or her attention to the long-term costs of continuing with existing strategies. Other metaphors can also help the person to make the necessary leap of faith to start testing things out (for example, the builder's apprentice (see Box 3.5), or the elephants on the track—explained fully in Section 3.7.2. Personifying the OCD as a bully or protection racket can be another useful metaphor in helping the person to recognize that the OCD has developed its grip over time by starting out offering what seemed to be helpful suggestions (e.g. avoid being around children, double-check it is locked, if in doubt just wash or clean it) and that over time the OCD has become more like a bully making demands (e.g. 'you'll end up in prison if you're not careful', 'you have to go back to check it's locked', 'it will be your fault if you become ill'). Asking the person what advice (s)he would offer a child (s)he cared about if (s)he was being bullied can help the person to make a link with what (s)he needs to do to confront the OCD.

3.7.14 **Tolerating (some) anxiety**

It is important to acknowledge that experimenting with living according to theory B will cause greater anxiety in the short term, but that this will pay off in the longer run—short-term pain for long-term gain. Having discussed psychoeducation about anxiety and explored or challenged beliefs about anxiety adds useful context. Anxiety is aversive, but has no deeper meaning (see Section on Ex-consequentia reasoning in Section 1.8.1.2). Illustrating anxiety decay with the use of graphs can be helpful, with time running along the x axis and anxiety (rated 0–100%) along the y axis (see Figures 3.3, 3.4, 3.5).

Begin by illustrating the effects of their existing strategy; a graph that illustrates that anxiety escalates following an intrusion that is quickly brought back down to more tolerable levels by engaging in a compulsion (Figure 3.3). Ask the person how long his or her anxiety remains at this level; this is typically until the occurrence of the next intrusion. So we have a graph that looks something like a rollercoaster, illustrating the peaks of anxiety that come with an intrusion and the troughs brought about by engaging in a compulsion. It is important to illustrate an upward incline in the peaks and troughs

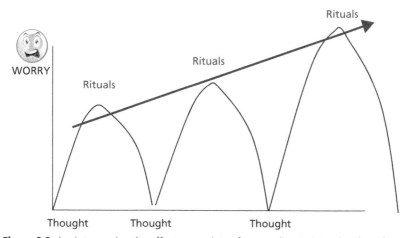

Figure 3.3 Anxiety graphs: the effect on anxiety of responding to intrusive thoughts.

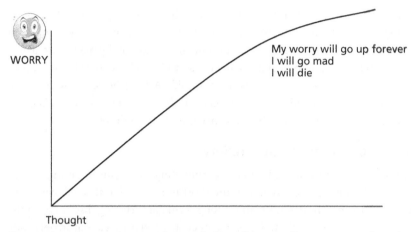

Figure 3.4 Anxiety graphs: a prediction of what will happen if no response to intrusive thoughts.

over the long term, capturing the fact that anxiety gradually increases as the problem remains and that the compulsions have less and less impact in reducing the anxiety.

Next ask the person to illustrate what (s)he thinks will happen if (s)he refrains from his or her usual compulsions. The person will typically draw a graph that shows a steep increase in anxiety towards 100%, which is maintained indefinitely if no compulsion is performed (Figure 3.4).

This offers an opportunity to provide some information about the 'spontaneous decay' of anxiety and the urge to perform compulsions based on the seminal

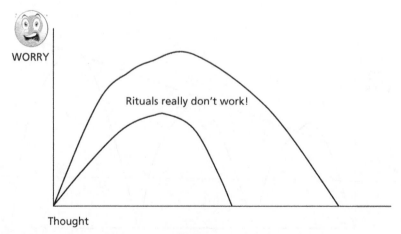

Figure 3.5 Anxiety graphs: what actually happens when no response to intrusive thoughts.

work of Jack Rachman (Likierman and Rachman, 1980). These experiments carefully demonstrated the principles of ERP—i.e. that if the person desists from ritualizing then both discomfort and the urge to ritualize decrease over time (Figure 3.5). Explanation of the body's 'fight or flight' response can also help the person to understand the physiological response to anxiety, and in particular that the body cannot maintain this level of intensity for a long time and that, if left to run its own course, the intensity of the anxiety will begin to fade with time. This can be illustrated on the graph by showing the anxiety beginning to fade eventually. Furthermore, add more lines to the graph to illustrate what happens with each subsequent episode of anxiety if the person continues to refrain from their compulsions; over the longer term, this anxiety will start to decay at an earlier stage and will take less time to come down.

It can also be helpful at this point to illustrate the effects of 'having a foot in both camps', in which the person may act according to theory A on some occasions (perform the compulsion) and theory B on other occasions (refrain from the compulsion). This graph illustrates a pattern in which anxiety escalates rapidly and remains high over the longer term.

Illustrating with the use of graphs delivers a powerful message that anxiety will indeed rise but also that it will not remain at intolerable levels and will decay if the person can stick it out. The graphs also offer some powerful images that the person can bring to mind when engaging in BEs, to help him or her recall that the anxiety will fade eventually if (s)he continues to refrain from safety-seeking. It can be helpful to explore any ideas that the symptoms of anxiety itself can be harmful; for example, by reflecting on why we all have the capacity to feel anxiety (see Box 3.3 'Threat alarm').

Using analogies with other anxiety disorders can be a useful way to consider why putting up with some anxiety in BEs is worth doing. Ask the person with OCD what (s)he would do if (s)he was helping a friend to overcome a fear of spiders—(s)he believes that the spider will jump in his or her face. If their friend saw a spider, (s)he would have a rush of anxiety and run away—and his or her anxiety would go down. The next time (s)he saw a spider (s)he would be just as scared. When the person with OCD has an intrusive thought, (s)he will feel anxious and will want to engage in SSBs or leave the situation altogether. If the spider-fearing friend stays with the spider, (s)he gets the chance to find out whether the spider does do anything to them, and to find out that anxiety goes down as (s)he stays in the situation. When the person with OCD has an intrusive thought and doesn't do anything, (s)he gets the opportunity to find out how the world really works, and to change his or her beliefs.

It is useful to consider the principle that everyone is capable of habituation to anxiety. In BEs, we can predict that anxiety will go up, and make a specific prediction about how bad it will be and for how long (see the anxiety curves in Figures 3.3, 3.4, and 3.5). Remind the person with whom you are working that (s)he is living his or her life with anxiety every day, and that OCD has stopped him or her from enjoying himself or herself, and often robbed people of important things, such as time with their family, relationships, work, having friends, being able to eat what (s)he chooses, being able to move freely around his or her own home, being able to travel … Putting up with *some* anxiety is a price worth paying to be able to overcome the problem. It is sometimes worth reflecting on the fact that (s)he is already paying that price whilst *also* keeping the problem. For many people with OCD, anxiety and/or discomfort rises as the rituals go on, so that they end up being more rather than less anxious.

Sometimes disgust is a strong component of the emotional response to confronting fears. Some individuals may be more prone to feeling disgust and may experience it as more aversive, particularly if the things they fear are disgust-type stimuli (e.g. bodily fluids or waste). It may be important to acknowledge the presence of disgust and any associated beliefs. The evidence suggests that disgust decays in the same way as anxiety, but can take longer (Adams *et al.*, 2011).

3.7.15 Tolerating (some) uncertainty

Uncertainty is a part of life—we all live with the uncertainty of death, illness, or what will happen tomorrow. We have all learned or become accustomed to living with this uncertainty. However, if we are not completely certain, it does not mean that we are completely uncertain. Being 100% certain is impossible, and any lack of certainty does not equal total uncertainty. In BEs, we can make predictions about how hard it is to tolerate uncertainty, and how long it will last. Trust of oneself is enabling, and allows you to do what you need to do. Imagine a positive relationship—if you were trying to be certain all the time about this (positive) relationship, what would you do? Text and call the person all the time just to make sure they were where they said they were? What would be the impact of this? Tolerating uncertainty is a positive thing—it is the other side of having trust and confidence.

3.7.16 Tackling feelings of hopelessness or helplessness

Feelings of loss can be common, particularly for those who have had their obsessional problem for a long time and led a very restricted life as a result. Feelings of hopelessness can make it difficult to get started on trying a new approach. Similar to working with depression, it is important to acknowledge these feelings with sensitivity, and it may be necessary for the therapist to model the optimism with which the person is struggling. It is important to challenge beliefs around it 'being too late to change' or 'being beyond help'. Validate feelings of sadness and refocus the person on how (s)he wants his or her life to progress from this point onwards. What could his or her future self be saying in 2 years' time? How different could life be if (s)he was to tackle the problem now? Again, referring back to goals, particularly those focussed on 'reclaiming your life', can be important in supporting the person in choosing to change.

3.7.17 Spotlight on supervision: active change

3.7.17.1 Where do I start?

The choice of early tasks and the order in which problems are dealt with depends considerably on the person's confidence, the degree to which each aspect of the problem is affecting them, the extent to which a given aspect occurs in the person's normal environment, and readiness to carry out the task. Success should be self-reinforcing.

'We have been doing lots of BEs but the person still has a high belief rating in theory A.'

Check the basics:

Have you identified the threat appraisal? Is there anything else 'beyond' the threat appraisal? 'I'm a bad person … and this means …'

Does theory A/B genuinely make sense to both of you? If not, do it again

Is the person engaging in subtle or covert SSBs? Is (s)he still avoiding anything?

Do a BE together and keep asking what's going on. Watch out for SSBs as the therapist or for the responsibility shifting from the person to the therapist.

3.7.17.2 Why won't (s)he do homework?

Make sure that homework is agreed, rather than 'set'.

'Every time you find homework difficult we can learn more about the problem and the way it affects you. It's important that you try your hardest with all the homework we agree, but if you are not able to manage it, then it is helpful if you write detailed notes about what happened so that we can deal better with similar problems when they arise in future. Often the problems that come up are just different aspects of the problem that we have not yet worked out.'

A foot in both camps: 'My client is willing to engage in some experiments where he's testing out theory B but also seems to be "bargaining with the OCD" at the same time. For example, he is willing to expose himself to contamination during the day but continues to engage in lots of neutralizing once he gets home.'

Design BEs where the outcome cannot be 'undone'; e.g. for a contamination BE, ensure that you touch items that cannot be easily discarded, such as mobile phones, spectacles, or contaminate everything in the whole house.

'My client is rehearsing all the evidence for theory B when he undertakes an experiment.'

In this case the evidence is now functioning as a form of self-reassurance. Check belief ratings for theory B to verify this and beliefs about uncertainty. Incorporate dropping rehearsing the evidence into the experiment.

3.7.18 **Where to stop?**

As treatment progresses and the person reclaims his or her life, a number of issues can arise. About half way to having completely overcome their OCD some people, particularly those who have a long history of being profoundly disabled by their problem, quite understandably start to feel nervous about how things are progressing. They have reached a point where they are better than they have been for years, and feel that pushing things further could be a bit 'risky'. Maybe they should just keep things at the level they have got to, and not do anything to 'rock the boat'. This is worth discussing in a range of ways, the therapist's aim being to encourage the person to continue until the OCD is completely overcome.

There are two helpful metaphors that can be used here. First is the infected wound metaphor. The person is asked to imagine that (s)he has a nasty gash on his or her arm, which has become infected and is full of dirt. That's like OCD. What you have done in treatment so far is like cleaning out the infection from about half of the wound, and it is feeling better already, although it was tough and uncomfortable doing that. There is some pretty nasty looking infection remaining, and you know that it is going to be hard to remove it. Would it be sensible to leave it there, just bandage over it, and forget it? Why not? What will happen if you do that? The aim is to conclude that remaining traces of OCD may form the basis of its resurgence. It is discussed that this is not necessarily so, but likely. Quite often, people understandably want to deal with a range of issues around the core fears, but are reluctant to confront their very worst fears. Our experience is that this is unhelpful and that people should be encouraged to have the aim of confronting their core fear. Sometimes the individual wants to consolidate the gains (s)he has made before tackling his or her worst fears. If, having not dealt with such issues, (s)he returns later, having had some return of symptoms, early discussion on dealing with core fears is recommended.

It is worth linking this to the person's long-term goals. Ask him or her 'Are there any "no-go areas" in the map of your life, dictated by your OCD?'

'Not rocking the boat', or ideas similar to this, can be dealt with using another metaphor. It is suggested to the patient that not rocking the boat was pretty much the only way (s)he could have behaved when (s)he was in the grip of OCD. It is like being in a little boat, far out to sea, with the constant risk of it capsizing, which would have been disastrous. However, as therapy has progressed, (s)he has learned how to steer the boat into shallower waters, right up to the point where (s)he is very close to shore, and the boat is in a few inches of water. That's precisely the time to rock the boat as vigorously as possible, up to and including the point where it capsizes, which means (s)he can get out of the boat entirely and walk to shore, to get on with life out of the boat that was OCD.

3.8 **Other discursive methods to promote belief change**

3.8.1 **Challenging responsibility appraisals**

As well as physical checking, Lydia checked in other ways to prevent something bad happening:

LYDIA: If I hear a noise and I'm not sure what it is, I must investigate it to be sure that it is not someone in trouble. If I don't find out, that means that I don't care about people and that I am a bad person. So I listen carefully, leave my house, and check if it is a noise in the street, then check again later if I'm still not sure. What if it was a car crash, and someone was hurt, and if I didn't help, they died?

Asking Lydia how likely it is that something bad will happen will reveal another example of a general tendency to overestimate threat—that bad things are actually quite likely (see probability × awfulness and attention and reasoning biases; Section 1.8). Discussing specific concerns can be helpful at this stage:

LYDIA: If I hear any sort of bang sound then I immediately think that it is a car accident and that I need to see if anyone is hurt.
THERAPIST: So do you live on a busy street?
LYDIA: Reasonably busy.
THERAPIST: Has there ever been a crash?
LYDIA: Not that I can remember … and I have lived there for 7 years.

This discussion with Lydia would go on to consider the cost of responding to each and every noise. She could continue to do this, but would continue to feel anxious and tired, have disrupted sleep, not be able to concentrate on her work/studies, and worry her husband, who has noticed her behaviour. It is *possible* that one day, one of these noises could be from a car crash, and that Lydia could help, but it is *extremely unlikely*. We would go on to consider that, in the event of a car crash, would Lydia be entirely responsible for responding and stopping people dying from their injures? If the worst of the worst happened, and somebody did die, would it be her fault?

Lydia is asked to come up with a list of people who would hold responsibility for someone dying in a car crash in her street:

Me

Driver of the other vehicle

Driver himself or herself

Emergency services

A&E staff

Other people in the street who could have stopped

Government for not making the roads safer.

After generating as many people as possible, we would ask Lydia to decide the size of each slice of the responsibility pie (Figure 3.6), *starting at the bottom of the list*, thus leaving her share of responsibility until last. This would demonstrate that, actually, in the worst case scenario that Lydia fears, she would not be 100% responsible for preventing someone's death.

Lydia's belief that, if she could in any way influence the outcome of events, she is 100% responsible for the outcome is an example of all-or-nothing thinking. The aim of the responsibility pie chart is not to convince her that she is 0% responsible, but to draw her attention to the fact that she is only one contributor to the (hypothetical) outcome. For past events for which people feel overly

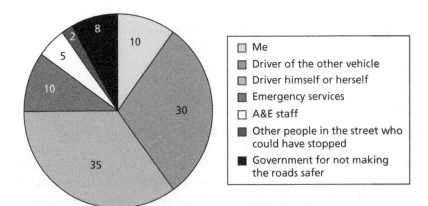

Figure 3.6 Responsibility pie chart.

responsible (such as when they have in some way been involved in an accident), this exercise can be helpful for making the point that reviewing the events in great detail is unlikely to prove that they had absolutely no influence whatsoever over an event; this reviewing will lead to an increase in doubt rather than certainty that they were not responsible.

3.8.2 Double standards/what would you advise others to do?

Following the pie chart, Lydia looked unconvinced.

LYDIA: I can see what you mean, and I do know that really it would not be my fault, but I still do think that if there is any possibility I could help, I should—a good person should always help.

THERAPIST: One hundred per cent of the time?

LYDIA: Yes, I think so.

THERAPIST: Can you think of anyone who really does that?

LYDIA: I know lots of good people; I think they would help people all the time.

THERAPIST: So these good people you know, do they jump out of bed when they hear a noise?

LYDIA: No.

THERAPIST: Do they go back and check conversations with people to make sure they haven't offended them?

LYDIA: No.

THERAPIST: Do you think that they should do these things?

LYDIA: No.

THERAPIST: Well, how come you have to? Why are you applying these strict standards to yourself when you don't expect them from other 'good' people?

The discussion would go on to explore the disparity between Lydia's standards for others and her standards for herself, and question why she holds herself to such high standards. Some of this might be related to OCD-specific beliefs identified on the RAS (Salkovskis *et al.*, 2000; see Appendix 5), such as 'For me, even slight carelessness is inexcusable when it might affect other people' or may be less specific beliefs about herself 'I need to try harder than others'. Whatever the nature of the belief, it is likely to be negative and inflexible. Some discussion of the origin of this belief may be useful—it may relate to her early experiences or to a specific experience when she felt that she didn't do something she should have done (see Section 1.8 on the origin of responsibility beliefs).

Challenging this belief comes out of this discussion—what would a new version of this belief look like? What is a fairer, more realistic version? What do some of Lydia's friends, who are 'good people', have as their version of this belief? This discussion refers back to theory A/B, added to and amending it as more information is gleaned.

3.8.3 Continua

The use of continua can be helpful in challenging dichotomous thinking; for example, the view that being less careful is equivalent to being totally careless or irresponsible.

When Lydia was struggling with the idea of ignoring her urges to check, she was still at least partly convinced that she needed to check to be a careful and responsible person. The therapist drew out a continuum:

THERAPIST: Okay, so it really seems like a fact that if you do less checking you are going to be less careful. Let's have a think about that. Let's draw up a scale of 'carefulness'. Let's think of some people who are really careless, perhaps famous people or people you know who you consider careless, and put them on the line.

LYDIA: How about a drunk driver, going too fast past a school at home time?

Drink driver going past a school	Me
Totally careless	Totally careful

THERAPIST: Yes, I see your point, that to do less will make you feel like you are more like the drink driver. However, I'm wondering where you would put some other people on this line. What about your husband, Mike?

LYDIA: Well, of course he's not like the drink driver, but he is less careful than me, so about in the middle?

Drink driver going past a school	Husband	Me
Totally careless		Totally careful

THERAPIST: Right, and what about your friend Gretchen who is having a baby soon?

LYDIA: Oh yes, well, she is pretty laid back so probably between Mike and the driver.

Drink driver going past a school	Gretchen	Husband	Me
Totally careless			Totally careful

THERAPIST: What do you think so far?

Often the person will see that (s)he is far above average in his or her behaviour and that to change will take him or her towards the 'normal' range, which is usually what (s)he wants to achieve. It is important to reinforce the idea that it is okay to be 'careful enough' to enjoy the other things life has to offer. Exploring the other qualities of people they like can also help to challenge the idea that to fight OCD is not to be careless. Further, once the damage that OCD causes is truly acknowledged, it can be very helpful to frame fighting OCD as a choice that reduces emotional harm to herself and her loved ones, whilst the converse is also true, that to stick with OCD is now an active choice that keeps life restricted and can cause suffering (Table 3.18).

Continua were helpful for Jane, who believes that she is a bad person who doesn't observe her religion properly and will be damned. It was useful for Jane to consider what she was trying to achieve by striving to be perfect in her religion. She developed a continuum for being a good Christian and put people she

Table 3.18 Lydia's summary of her learning using the theory A/B framework

Theory A	Theory B
Useful things to remember (learning points from discussion)	
Narrow focus:	**Broad focus/bigger picture:**
Only thinking about the next dangerous thing (fire-fighting), which is why it is so anxiety-/feeling-driven	There is a significant cost of buying into danger *all* the time—doing things less will help me be better in other ways
Feelings are *not* the same as evidence, especially when you are anxious!	I will actually be better able to notice danger
There is no 'real' evidence that I need to take more precautions than other people	I will be more confident in myself and trusting of myself
The more I check and try to be certain I've done my best, the more doubt and worry I feel	It is about trust not certainty
This is about all or nothing, and I can't give all	This is about doing my best, which will mean focussing on other things as well as safety and harm

knew on the line. Jane was surprised when she reflected that all the people she respected as people and Christians went to Church considerably less than she did. She repeated the continuum with a more general moral concept of 'good':

THERAPIST: So if this is a line of bad to good, where would you put the friends that you mention?

JANE: Nick would go right at the top, Paul a bit below, and David more towards the middle.

THERAPIST: So these 'good' people are not all at 100%; in fact, they cover a bit of a range. Where would you put yourself?

JANE: I'm not as good as them; I'll put myself below.

THERAPIST: Who is the 'most good' person you know? Where would you put him or her?

JANE: Mother Theresa was good, or Nelson Mandela, or Ghandi—all of them would be at 100%.

THERAPIST: Okay, do you think everyone would agree with you that they were 100% good all the time? They never had a day off being 'good', or never ever did anything that might have hurt another person?

JANE: I suppose they might have done ...

The therapist continues to challenge the idea that anyone is 100% good all the time and changes the dot on the line to a range, representing the idea that people's behaviour varies, and that even the most 'good' person in the world still has less 'good' days. Identifying 'bad' people to put at the other end of the continuum adds to the discussion about how being defined as good or bad is actually impossible, and that these concepts are multifaceted.

Continua of responsibility often illustrate the fact that people with OCD had been aspiring to be 100% responsible all the time, which is impossible. The fear is that being a bit less responsible is as bad as being totally irresponsible. Even very responsible people have days when they put their feet up or let their hair down (e.g. prime ministers, managers of nuclear power stations, child protection officers). It is useful to conclude that most people occupy a range somewhere near the middle. Most people do not take extra precautions but are far from being totally irresponsible.

3.8.4 Surveys

Surveys can be helpful to help 'recalibrate' or gain a sense of what is normal/ typical for people without OCD. For someone who has engaged in extensive handwashing or checking for many years, this information can be useful to form a 'guideline' (not a rule) for what they can do when they are overcoming the problem. Devising a short list of relevant and specific questions can be help-ful; most surveys about day-to-day behaviour such as washing or checking reveal a range of 'normal' behaviour. An important issue with surveys is that they do not become a form of reassurance. For example, if the survey revealed that most people wash their hands seven times a day, this may become a form of self-reassurance: 'I've washed seven times so I'm okay', or even become a differ-ent way of going along with theory A: 'if everyone else is washing seven times, I had better wash ten times just to be sure'.

Surveys are a useful way to normalize; for example, a mother who gets frus-trated with her child believes that this shows that she is a bad mother. A survey distributed to friends and colleagues will reveal that all parents become frus-trated at times. For Jessie, who is pregnant and very concerned about dirt and germs, a survey of other mothers/pregnant women was performed.

1. When you were pregnant, did you avoid any particular food? Why/why not?
2. Did you avoid anything else? Why/why not?
3. Did you allow people to wear shoes in the house? Why/why not?
4. Did you avoid vacuuming? Why/why not?
5. Did you avoid touching things that other people had touched, e.g. a com-puter keyboard? Why/why not?

Answers to this survey would reveal that many expectant mothers do avoid par-ticular food—based on advice that they have been given, e.g. avoiding unpas-teurized cheese. However, the restrictions are unlikely to be many. Discussing this would help with showing that the OCD has built up and 'gained more ter-ritory'. If the answers revealed no other avoidances, this can show that Jessie's behaviour is probably overcautious and is actually making her life more diffi-cult and stressful. If the answers show a little avoidance, this is helpful to nor-malize that women do feel very responsible for the wellbeing of their unborn child and that some changes in behaviour are reasonable or required. However, the OCD rules that Jessie obeys are extreme and maintain a continuous focus on threat and danger.

3.9 **Ending treatment**

CBT for OCD is typically a short-term therapy. The idea of ending needs to be present from the outset. It is a good idea to be explicit about the number of sessions you will be having with your client. Treatment trials for CBT have gen-erally been based on about 12 sessions, and 'high-intensity' treatment in IAPT (Improving Access to Psychological Therapies) is defined as consisting of more than 10 hours of input. In terms of the timing of sessions, it may be helpful to space out sessions towards the end of therapy to increase the person's autonomy and confidence in putting things into practice in 'real life'.

Follow-up sessions to check on progress are useful. The National Institute of Health and Care Excellence (NICE) guidelines recommend that a person who is successfully treated should be reviewed every 12 months, and that those in this group who are experiencing relapse should be seen more quickly (rather than being added to a routine waiting list) (NICE guideline 31; National Collaborating Centre for Mental Health [2005]). It is unclear how often this part of the guideline is followed in routine practice.

Endings can be difficult, regardless of how the person has done in this course of therapy. It is always worth reflecting on what the ending of CBT may mean for the person. As stated, CBT is about learning a set of skills that the person can put into practice in all the challenges that life will throw at him or her. Automatic thoughts that the person cannot manage alone can be dealt with explicitly using exploration and experimentation, along with other tools of cognitive therapy, such as thought records, as required. Examining and challenging automatic thoughts can also be useful for therapists (see Supervision; Section 3.9.5).

Treatment trials indicate that even with successful treatment most people with OCD do still remain above the general population in terms of symptoms at the end of treatment, so it is possible or likely that more work is required by the individual on their own or in further therapy.

3.9.1 Moving from behavioural experiments to an OCD-free life

A common question once BEs have been initiated is how often they need to continue and when 'real life' begins. The BE phase of evidence-collecting consists of careful monitoring and articulating predictions for each planned change in behaviour. While in this phase it is also crucial to think about and process the meaning of what has happened in the experiment to reinforce learning and keep building up the case for theory B. If a result is attributed to 'luck', further discussion and experiments are required until the person is convinced 'enough' that (s)he needs to treat the problem as 'theory B'. At a certain point, it will be important to lose the scaffolding of careful experiments and data collection and commit to living life 'according to theory B'. If, in the therapist's clinical judgement, a significant enough amount of evidence has already been accrued, it can be useful to reflect back to the person as to when (s)he thinks his or her real life should resume or begin, and what (s)he is waiting for now. Sometimes people reply that they need to be more convinced that theory B is true just in case. This can lead to further useful discussion on the nature of certainty. It may be important to reflect back on how much time has already been wasted in striving for certainty, and that to live according to theory A is now a definite and active choice.

In some cases people have been caught in their OCD for so long or so deeply that they have lost touch with what is 'normal'. Losing touch in this way can also reinforce the fear that they are not 'normal'. Surveys can be helpful in some instances, but care should be taken that these do not become an exercise in reassurance-seeking. These usually identify a range of behaviour/approaches to any given problem. Thinking what version of the guidelines a person would like for himself or herself or a child if (s)he could start again might be helpful. Why would (s)he need flexibility? And what would (s)he need to do if (s)he found him/herself playing 'better safe than sorry' with the OCD creeping up again? It is helpful to discuss with the person that, as they are vulnerable, the most helpful strategy is to adopt something systematically less careful than 'the average'. Many of those who have recovered from OCD find a simple guide helpful; it they find themselves wondering whether or not something is OCD, it probably is. OCD feeds on doubt and the unhelpful and unobtainable need for certainty, and that should be recognized both when the person has OCD and when they have overcome it.

We have referred previously to the 'empty life' problem; that is, when someone has spent many hours (or even most of) each day engaging with and focussed on their obsessional fears and compulsive behaviours, then eliminating these often leaves a vacuum. This is where long-term goals are so important; although these will to some extent have steered the progression of treatment, particularly the BEs and subsequent lifestyle changes, more is needed towards the end of therapy and afterwards. Asking the person to come up with a plan of action to reclaim his or her life and life plans, and thinking about how these plans can be realized beyond the end of the sessions should form part of the discussion towards the end of therapy. Helping the patient to identify barriers and enablers for these plans can be very helpful.

3.9.2 **Staying well**

CBT is usually a short-term therapy and the aim is for the person to develop a set of tools (s)he can use generally. Therefore CBT can be described as a form of guided self-help. Notes and recordings from therapy, as well as a 'blueprint' (summary document) that is completed along the way with key points, can be very helpful in facilitating this process. Part of the thinking that must be done is anticipating any difficult situations that may be stressful in the future, and problem-solving what the person would do should obsessive symptoms arise again. Ideally, by the end of treatment, this should be a self-directed part of the work. The aim is for the person to have the tools to deal with OCD in whatever form or situation it may rear its head. The more this is done, the less likely this is to happen in the first place, as some of the vulnerability factors (e.g. beliefs regarding the importance of thoughts) have already been challenged.

3.9.3 Therapy blueprints

A blueprint is an individualized summary of the salient points of therapy, the key ideas that laid the foundation for change, and the key experiments or experiences that enabled it. It is more than just a relapse prevention plan. It can be helpful for clients to take notes of key points throughout therapy, and completing a blueprint towards the end of therapy can help check ideas and understanding as well as reinforce them. It will also serve as an important summary should the person ever need to re-engage with the therapy skills in the face of a lapse or relapse of the problem. It is therefore important that the client completes the blueprint himself or herself and uses his or her own words as far as possible.

Key headings for a therapy blueprint may include:

Development and understanding of the problem

- What sort of background factors made me more likely to develop OCD?
- How did the problem develop (what was going on in my life)?
- What were the intrusive thoughts/images/urges/doubts and what did I think they meant when they were bothering me?
- What were the underlying ideas about myself, responsibility, or how the world works that kept the problem going?
- Once the problem took hold, what was it that I was doing, thinking, and paying attention to that kept the problem going? (Draw a vicious flower if you can)

Change

- *Intrusive thoughts*: what do I know now about intrusive thoughts? Who gets them and when do they feel important?
- What did they mean to me at the start of treatment?
- *Beliefs about the world/others/myself*: how did I challenge these and what did I learn? (Describe the most useful BEs and metaphors, and any other ways you identified or challenged the processes):

- What are more helpful versions of these ideas?

Costs of OCD and benefits of changing

- What can I do now that the OCD was stopping me from doing previously?
- What can I continue to do to reclaim my life from OCD and beyond?
- What is the best thing about me standing up to OCD?

Future planning

- What sort of situations might I find difficult in the future and why? What would I do?
  - Possible difficult situations
  - What OCD might say
  - What I need to remember and do

3.9.4 **When more work is needed**

The time and financial constraints of the service you work in, or other factors beyond your control, may mean that you are limited to a certain number of sessions from the outset, regardless of the severity of the person's OCD or any other factors that might mean that engagement and therapy takes longer than the time allowed. The fact that sessions are time-limited can be both helpful in motivating people to commit to the therapy, but can also be a daunting prospect for therapist and patient if change is taking longer than hoped. Of course, all therapists hope that they will make significant inroads into tackling the problem in front of them during therapy. Breaking this down, 'tackling' it, encompasses the following: developing a clear understanding of what OCD is and how it works; being open to and testing out the alternative notion that the problem really is one of too much worry; and acting on that knowledge to gain enough information to 'live theory B'. It may be, for a number of possible reasons, that a single course of therapy is not able to complete all of these components, but it may also be the case that you have done enough work together for parts of this message to percolate through. Whatever point you get to, it will always be helpful to show empathy and patience, and to keep reinforcing the cognitive understanding of OCD. Self-efficacy is most likely to be enhanced by using socratic questions (guided discovery) and self-directed tasks such as formulating specific instances of the problem and homework-setting. If it has been very difficult for the person to take the reins in therapy in this way, it may be useful to reflect on that with the person and include relevant ideas and blocks in a therapy blueprint. Failing that, a compassionate letter to the client can help convey empathy and understanding of what might have been difficult this time in a way that can be reflected on after the end of therapy.

OCD has historically been considered a 'difficult-to-treat' problem—this generated advances in behaviour therapy and CBT that transformed the lives of many people with OCD and have now become standard practice in treating OCD. The example of recent advances in the understanding of mental contamination shows that people previously considered 'treatment-resistant' could be treated (Coughtrey *et al.*, 2013). Therefore it is reasonable to assume that our understanding of OCD remains partial and will improve to enhance treatment outcomes. There is no such thing as a 'last chance' with therapy, which will always be delivered slightly differently in a slightly different context by each therapist. If little change has occurred it will be useful to convey this message explicitly to the client to encourage them to seek further help in the future.

Discharge usually involves writing a summary of treatment, with any recommendations for future treatment, if identified, or making a referral on for further treatment. This may be the case if other comorbidities have become apparent during therapy, such as post-traumatic stress disorder or social phobia, that now need treating in their own right, or it is felt that the person could benefit from CBT for OCD in a different setting, e.g. inpatient/residential. It may be that you have flexibility in your particular setting and are able to continue to see a particular client for comorbid problems. It might be important to reflect on what would make a suitable endpoint for therapy should the client have many interlocking issues. Alternatively, there may be other services available to provide help with underlying problems such as low self-esteem.

3.9.5 **Spotlight on supervision: endings**

3.9.5.1 No-one I treat for OCD ever gets better

Firstly, is this true? Have you done a mini-audit of your cases and examined the Yale-Brown Obsessive Compulsive Scale (YBOCS; see Section 2.8) and Obsessive-Compulsive Inventory-Revised (OCI-R; see Appendix 4) for each? Even if there is one counterexample we know that this statement is not a helpful version of reality. Are they not changing on all variables? Is there a particular type of OCD that you find more difficult to treat? Does this play into any of your own concerns about therapy, e.g. contamination, etc.? Or beliefs about OCD (that it really is a brain disease, or an intractable problem).

What factors enable change in OCD? Are there things you can work on in your own practice to enhance these? See Section 4.7 for structured advice on continuing to develop as a therapist.

If there is very little or no change in symptoms, has the person benefitted from an experience of empathic understanding, had some insight into an alternative perspective of the problem, or understood that other people have similar concerns and have overcome them? This may be sowing the seeds for future work that leads to more pronounced change in beliefs and behaviour.

3.9.5.2 My client has the potential to do well but nothing has changed yet and we have already had 12 sessions. I think I need twelve more

Explore perceptions of change: is the client's view the same? What has prevented any change so far? What is it that makes you and the client feel that change is possible now? What are the specific barriers to starting behavioural change? CBT is a form of self-help. What is the most likely course of action that will enable the client to use it as such—is it staying in therapy, or leaving it?

Are there indices of change that are not captured by the measures you are using? For example, the client has a very entrenched problem, but is, however, able to do more than (s)he was at the start of therapy—is this captured in idiosyncratic belief ratings? If there is no measurable change, is there a change in his or her openness to discussing the problem or a change in his or her overall insight into OCD?

If you are planning further sessions it may be useful to suggest these in small bursts (e.g. groups of three sessions), setting a clear rationale and expectations for each block from the client. Ending should be an integral part of the discussion at each of these review points.

Recommended reading

Bennett-Levy, J., Butler, G., Fennell, M., Hackman, A., Mueller, M., & Westbrook, D. (2011). *Oxford Guide to Behavioural Experiments in Cognitive Therapy*. Oxford: Oxford University Press.

References

Abramowitz, J. S., Foa, E. B., & Franklin, M. E. (2003). Exposure and ritual prevention for obsessive-compulsive disorder: Effects of intensive versus twice-weekly sessions. *Journal of Consulting and Clinical Psychology, 71*(2), 394–8.

Abramowitz, J. S., Taylor, S., & McKay, D. (2005). Potentials and limitations of cognitive treatments for obsessive-compulsive disorder. *Cognitive Behaviour Therapy, 34*(3), 140–7.

Adams, T. G., Willems, J. L., & Bridges, A. J. (2011). Contamination aversion and repeated exposure to disgusting stimuli. *Anxiety, Stress & Coping: An International Journal, 24*(2), 157–65.

Beck, J. (2011). *Cognitive Behavior Therapy: Basics and beyond* (2nd ed.). New York: Guilford Press.

Bennett-Levy, J., Butler, G., Fennell, M., Hackmann, A., Mueller, M., & Westbrook, D. (2004). *Oxford Guide to Behavioural Experiments in Cognitive Therapy*. Oxford: Oxford University Press.

Coughtrey, A. E., Shafran, R., Lee, M. & Rachman, S. (2013). The treatment of mental contamination: A case series. *Cognitive and Behavioral Practice, 20*(2), 221–31.

Gilbert, P. (2010). *Compassion Focused Therapy*. London: Routledge.

Heron, J., O'Connor, T. G., Evans, J., Golding, J., Glover, V. & ALSPAC Study Team. (2004). The course of anxiety and depression through pregnancy and the postpartum in a community sample. *Journal of Affective Disorders, 80*(1), 65–73.

Kazantzis., N. & L'Abate, L. (eds)(2006). *Handbook of Homework Assignments in Psychotherapy: Research, Practice, and Prevention*. New York, Springer Science + Business Media.

Levy, H. C. & Radomsky, A. S. (2014). Safety behaviour enhances the acceptability of exposure. *Cognitive Behaviour Therapy, 43*(1), 83–92.

Likierman, H. & Rachman, S. (1980). Spontaneous decay of compulsive urges: Cumulative effects. *Behaviour Research and Therapy, 18*(5), 387–94.

National Collaborating Centre for Mental Health (2005): *CG31. NICE Guidance on OCD*. London: The British Psychological Society and the Royal College of Psychiatrists.

Prochaska, J. O. & DiClemente, C. C. (1982). Transtheoretical therapy: Toward a more integrative model of change. *Psychotherapy: Theory, Research and Practice, 19*, 276–88.

Rachman, S. & de Silva, P. (1978). Abnormal and normal obsessions. *Behaviour Research and Therapy, 16*(4), 233–48.

Radomsky, A. S. & Alcolado, G. M. (2010). Don't even think about checking: Mental checking causes memory distrust. *Journal of Behavior Therapy and Experimental Psychiatry, 41*(4), 345–51.

Radomsky, A. S., Dugas, M. J., Alcolado, G. M., & Lavoie, S.L. (2014). When more is less: Doubt, repetition, memory, metamemory, and compulsive checking in OCD. *Behaviour Research and Therapy, 59*, 30–9.

Roth, A.D. & Pilling, S. (2007) *The Competences Required to Deliver Effective Cognitive and Behavioural Therapy for People with Depression and with Anxiety Disorders*. London: Department of Health.

Salkovskis, P. M. (1996). The cognitive approach to anxiety: Threat beliefs, safety-seeking behavior, and the special case of health anxiety and obsessions. In: P. M. Salkovskis (ed.), *Frontiers of Cognitive Therapy* (pp. 48–74). New York, NY: Guilford Press.

Salkovskis, P. M. (1997). Obsessional-compulsive problems: A cognitive-behavioral analysis. In: S. Rachman (ed.), *Best of Behavior Research and Therapy* (pp. 29–41). Amsterdam, Netherlands: Pergamon/Elsevier Science Inc.

Salkovskis, P. M. (2010). Cognitive behavioural therapy. In: M. Barker, A. Vossler, & D. Langdridge (eds.) *Understanding Counselling and Psychotherapy*. Milton Keynes, SAGE Publications/Open University.

Salkovskis, P. M. & Harrison, J. (1984). Abnormal and normal obsessions: A replication. *Behaviour Research and Therapy, 22*(5), 549–52.

Salkovskis, P. M., & Westbrook, D. (1987). Obsessive-compulsive disorder: Clinical strategies for improving behavioural treatments. In: H. Dent (ed.), *Clinical Psychology: Research and Developments* (pp. 200–13). New York, NY: Croom Helm.

Salkovskis, P. M., Wroe, A. L., Gledhill, A., Morrison, N., Forrester, E., Richards, C. *et al.* (2000). Responsibility attitudes and interpretations are characteristic of obsessive compulsive disorder. *Behaviour Research and Therapy, 38*(4), 347–72.

Shepherd, L., Salkovskis, P. M., & Morris, M. (2009). Recording therapy sessions: An evaluation of patient and therapist reported behaviours, attitudes and preferences. *Behavioural and Cognitive Psychotherapy, 37*(2), 141–50. doi: http://dx.doi.org/10.1017/ S1352465809005190

Steketee, G. (ed.)(2012). *Oxford Handbook of Obsessive Compulsive and Spectrum Disorders*. New York: Oxford University Press.

Stott, R., Mansell, W., Salkovskis, P., Lavender, A., & Cartwright-Hatton, S. (2010). *Oxford Guide to Metaphors in CBT*. Oxford: Oxford University Press.

van den Hout, M. & Kindt, M. (2003). Repeated checking causes memory distrust. *Behaviour Research and Therapy, 41*(3), 301–16.

Whittal, M. L., Robichaud, M., *et al.* (2008). Group and individual treatment of obsessive-compulsive disorder using cognitive therapy and exposure plus response prevention: A 2-year follow-up of two randomized trials. *Journal of Consulting and Clinical Psychology, 76*(6), 1003–14.

Chapter 4

Beyond the fundamentals

Obsessive-compulsive disorder (OCD) can occur with other problems that can present a challenge in treatment. This chapter discusses a number of examples of other co-occurring problems: obsessive-compulsive personality disorder (OCPD), with particular emphasis on perfectionism, post-traumatic stress disorder (PTSD) and mental contamination, and working with guilt, shame, and self-criticism. We go on to consider flexibility in applying cognitive-behaviour therapy (CBT) for OCD, including discussion of intensive treatment, internet delivery, and group work. Finally, we discuss continuing to develop as a therapist and supervisor, with specific references to OCD-specific competences and metacompetences.

There is an infinite number of variables in the ever-changing equation of what makes a person with OCD's problems 'complex' and what makes treatment more or less effective. Variables that can be kept constant include the therapist's diligent focus on a shared understanding of the problem that guides focussed intervention. The therapist must skilfully enhance the 'standard' treatment to work with more 'complex' presentations of OCD. The message throughout this section on comorbid problems is not to 'throw the baby out with the bath water'—the treatment described in Chapter 3 should still be used, but adapted to the formulation, taking account of the other issues agreed to be important in the assessment. It is essential to include all relevant elements in treatment with individuals with complex difficulties and to use complementary (rather than alternative) formulations and methods to promote change in the face of difficulties. The key is always a shared understanding that evolves over time with treatment.

4.1 Obsessive-compulsive personality disorder

OCPD is a pervasive pattern of preoccupation with orderliness, perfectionism, and mental and interpersonal control at the expense of flexibility, openness, and efficiency. There is a relatively high prevalence rate of 1–2% in community samples (Torgersen *et al.*, 2001) and up to 26% in clinical samples (Ansell *et al.*, 2010). However, there is controversy over the categorical diagnosis—see Fineberg *et al.* (2014) for a detailed discussion.

Although there is an obvious similarity in terms of the terminology (OCPD/ OCD), this may represent only a superficial similarity. The diagnosis remains in *DSM-5* (American Psychiatric Association, 2013), including a range of possible characteristics, such as being overly focussed on detail, unhelpful perfectionism, being inflexible in terms of decision-making and moral matters, hoarding behaviour, excessive working at the expense of other life activities, and miserliness.

The major difference between this and OCD lies in the fact that anxiety and discomfort are not necessary features of the diagnosis of OCPD. OCPD has nevertheless been found to co-occur with OCD, but the majority of people (75–80%) with OCD do not meet the diagnostic criteria for OCPD (e.g. Mancebo *et al.*, 2005). OCPD is found at a similar prevalence rate in those with panic disorder, so a specific relationship between OCD and OCPD is unlikely (Albert *et al.*, 2004). A rigid/inflexible style may be a feature of OCD, but in OCD these behavioural responses are more likely to be a means of preventing something bad happening rather than an actual desire to do things in a set way. People with OCPD do not tend to have upsetting intrusive thoughts; the thoughts or urges are more likely to be considered as appropriate and correct (the 'ego-dystonic versus ego-syntonic distinction'). Coles *et al.* (2008) looked specifically at people who had both OCD and OCPD compared to those with OCD alone. The group with OCD and OCPD was more likely to have more comorbid anxiety disorders, more likely to have hoarding symptoms, and more likely to report incompleteness symptoms, i.e. a more complex clinical picture. However, it is important not to assume that this means treatment will always be less potent. In a study of the prevalence of OCPD in a specialist anxiety disorders clinic, Gordon *et al.* (2013a) found that a comorbid OCPD diagnosis was associated with a greater degree of depression, greater self-reported OCD severity, along with more doubting, ordering, and hoarding symptoms, relative to those without OCPD. However, those with comorbid OCD and OCPD demonstrated greater treatment gains in terms of OCD severity, checking, and ordering than those without OCPD. Individuals with OCD and OCPD had higher levels of checking, ordering, and overall OCD severity at initial assessment; however, at post-treatment they had similar scores to those without OCPD (Gordon *et al.*, 2016).

When working with someone with OCD and OCPD, asking the person what features of either diagnosis cause them the greatest problems is the best place to start, as the different features may require quite different treatment plans. For example, hoarding behaviour (of possessions or money or both) requires a consideration of the beliefs associated with hoarding and exploration of positive emotions associated with acquiring or retaining possessions (Frost *et al.*, 2015). If the person has no inclination to hoard possessions but does acknowledge perfectionism, focussing on perfectionism would be required using, as ever, a formulation-driven approach and evidence-based, empirically grounded interventions.

A note on hoarding: although hoarding was considered as a part of OCD (Pertusa *et al.*, 2010; Seaman *et al.*, 2010), in general it has been found to differ on a number of phenomenological and outcome variables, leading to its new status as a stand-alone disorder in *DSM-5* (Mataix-Cols *et al.*, 2010; see Rachman *et al.* (2009) and Pertusa *et al.* (2008) for detailed discussions). 'Threat-related hoarding' (Seaman *et al.*, 2010) is probably where OCD and hoarding overlap. Gordon *et al.* (2013b) investigated beliefs in individuals with hoarding with and without coexisting OCD; those with hoarding and OCD reported greater harm avoidance beliefs in relation to possessions compared with the group of people with hoarding without OCD.

An example of threat-related hoarding would be someone who picked up broken glass from the street and took it home for proper disposal so that no-one would get hurt (an inflated sense of responsibility for preventing harm to others). The glass would accumulate and take up space in the person's home. However, the glass is not associated with beliefs about its usefulness or beauty (beliefs that are common in hoarding disorder). A vicious flower formulation would help to show that looking out for glass (attentional bias) and keeping it (safety-seeking behaviour; SSB) keep the threat-related belief going. Gordon *et al.* (2013b) suggest their findings indicate that there is a 'malignant interaction' between hoarding and OCD.

When hoarding is not related to threat and scores on OCD-specific questionnaires are low, treatment should follow the detailed assessment and treatment guides for hoarding (e.g. Steketee and Frost, 2013).

4.1.1 **OCD and perfectionism**

Media stories on OCD often focus on meticulousness and inflexibility—stories of celebrities lining up the contents of their fridge, insisting their cocktails are made with exactly four cubes of ice ... the reality of perfectionism-related OCD is that it is more likely to include paralysing procrastination.

Perfectionism was recognized by the Obsessive-Compulsive Cognitions Working Group (OCCWG) in 1997 as an important cognitive feature of OCD. Several studies show a correlation between perfectionism and OCD; experts in the field argue that perfectionism interferes with treatment response, thus should be a specific target in treatment (see Egan *et al.* (2011) for a clinical review).

Shafran *et al.* (2002) reviewed definitions of perfectionism and provide a definition of clinical perfectionism as:

> 'The overdependence of self-evaluation on the determined pursuit of personally demanding, self-imposed standards in at least one highly salient domain, despite adverse consequences.'
>
> (Shafran *et al.*, 2002, page 778)

Shafran *et al.* (2010) devised a cognitive-behavioural model of perfectionism where self-worth is highly dependent on striving and achievement, resulting in inflexible high standards. Performance is evaluated using black-and-white thinking; in the event of doing well, the standards are re-set to be higher the next time. If performance was evaluated as not good enough, the person with perfectionism is highly self-critical and re-sets their standards higher. Alternatively, the person engages in avoidance and procrastination.

A fundamental point in treating clinical perfectionism is that it is not about lowering standards. Egan *et al.* (2014) note that, if people with perfectionism think that treatment will involve lowering their standards, then it is unlikely that they will engage. Instead, it is important to emphasize that CBT for perfectionism focusses on broadening the basis for self-evaluation away from striving and achievement, and adopting different ways of achieving standards.

Notably, Egan *et al.* (2014) suggest that, whilst the definition of OCPD includes perfectionism, OCPD is not necessarily an issue of excessively *high* standards, rather it is characterized by *arbitrary* standards that are excessively rigid. However, many of the techniques used for challenging clinical perfectionism are still helpful for OCD and perfectionism; for example, identifying 'thinking errors', cost–benefit analysis, use of continua to challenge all-or-nothing thinking, and behavioural experiments to challenge beliefs.

Procrastination occurs in clinical perfectionism when tasks are avoided due to fear of not doing them well enough because of high standards. In clinical perfectionism, people tend to oscillate between episodes of intense striving and achievement and avoidance and procrastination (Egan *et al.*, 2014). In OCD, when people have set high and/or particular standards for doing a task to prevent something bad happening, it is often the case that they avoid the activity almost totally. For example, someone with very high standards on how clean (s) he should be may take 8 hours to have a bath, and will need to start again if (s) he does not 'get it right' during this process. This can result in avoiding bathing, going for weeks on end without washing rather than put themselves through the ordeal of the ritual.

An example of where OCD, OCPD, and perfectionism can collide is when there is a clear threat appraisal ('if I don't get this right then something bad will happen'), a reliance on 'just-right' criteria to complete a task,

avoidance/procrastination owing to the overwhelming nature of the particular standards set to complete a task, all resulting in high levels of anxiety. This
is illustrated with the case example of Marie:

> Marie is in her mid thirties and is off work due to anxiety. She can still return to her job but
> she is under disciplinary review because of persistent lateness. She works in IT; mainly she
> works alone but when she does have to work as part of a team she runs into problems as
> she is reluctant to delegate tasks and will re-do work completed by others.

She is frustrated and depressed as she is finding it difficult to leave the house—
this is making her feel very pessimistic about ever returning to work, which
in turn makes her think that her life is 'stuck' and that she will never get into a
relationship, have a family, or own a home.

Her lateness is due to being caught up in making 'perfect' decisions when she
leaves the house:

> 'When I am in the bathroom I have to wash my face in a particular way to make sure that my
> face is completely clean so that I have the perfect base to my make-up. I wash with particular
> products that have the best reviews. I wash my face until I feel really clean, then I check in the
> magnifying mirror to be sure that I haven't missed anywhere. This takes about half an hour.
> Once I am completely clean I can apply my make-up—I need to make sure that my skin is
> completely even and my eye make-up and lipstick is totally symmetrical. If I'm not sure that
> it is, I have to start again. This usually takes another hour. It's not that I think I will look ugly
> without make-up, just that if I'm going to do it, I should do it properly.
>   I have to select the right outfit—I need the perfect dress for that day, depending on
> what I am doing and where I will be. This can take a long time if I don't get it right first
> time—I then get tied up in doubt about whether it is the right outfit and whether I will feel
> comfortable enough, and feel smart enough, or casual enough. If I don't look right, then
> I would be uncomfortable and anxious all day.
> When I was working I got up every day at 05:00 to make sure that I had enough time—this
> didn't go very well as I struggled to get out of bed as I was so tired, then when I did get up
> I still got stuck on every aspect of getting ready. I would always leave the house late and in
> a big panic, and arrive at work after everyone else. In fact, running out of the house at the
> last minute meant that I looked like a mess as I would be sweaty and dishevelled by the
> time I got to the office. In the end I started calling in sick as I just couldn't face the long
> process of getting ready. It was easier to avoid going in than endure the stress of getting
> ready and still being late.'

Marie's need to do things perfectly actually led to one of her worst fears coming true—she couldn't do her job at all. This had a serious impact on her mood,
which had its own effect on her motivation, and led to ruminating about how
bad her life was. Her own efforts to get up and get out were subsumed into 'trying to do it perfectly' and the problem is further compounded:

> 'The problem is at home now I am feeling miserable as I can't believe I'm not working, so
> I'm trying to get the most out of each day. I try to go out and do something worthwhile
> every day but this is getting harder. I look up exhibitions and lectures and plan which ones
> to attend—but I rarely get there. I get caught up in which one would be the very best one

to go to and end up trying to decide at the last minute. I spend ages researching the best route on public transport to where I need to go, to make sure that I am taking the most direct and efficient route, and I get stuck checking over and over, refreshing the page on the website to see if there are any last minute problems. Then I look at the weather forecast and see what I need to take with me; I try to think through any possible scenarios and make sure I have a rain coat, sunblock, an extra layer, an extra bag … If I make plans with other people I worry about what route they will take and whether they will get delayed. But every single time it is me that is late to meet friends and they tease me about it—I try to play along but I feel crushed and humiliated. It is easier not to make plans rather than risk it all going wrong. I really miss my friends and I feel even more like I have dropped out of mainstream life and that I am an outsider. But the harder I try to get things right, the more difficult it becomes.'

The perfectionist rules start to affect everything, and doubt creeps in to every decision:

'Even simple things like going to the supermarket have become impossible. I write a list of things I need but I get stuck doing this as I try to write the list in categories to make sure I remember everything I could need. I get distracted writing the list as I stop to look up recipes that I plan to cook that week so that I can keep to a tight budget and eat really healthily. Usually it takes me so long to write this all down that the supermarket is shut and I end up buying food at the local shop—this is more expensive and there is less healthy food available, so yet again I find myself doing the opposite of what I really want to do. I need to replace my car but this is so difficult as I can't make the decision. I have put off deciding which car to buy as I got so stuck researching all the details. I found that I couldn't research it 'properly' so I put it off—but in the meantime my car needs repairs so I am wasting more money.'

A good place to start with Marie is to acknowledge that she is someone with high standards who wants to do well in life, and there is nothing wrong with high standards per se. Where she has been caught out is by trying too hard, and 'the solution has become the problem'. Looking at the pros and cons of staying the same and change will illuminate the high cost of her procrastination (Table 4.1). Looking at a list of 'thinking errors' (common biases in thinking, such as overgeneralization, personalization, minimization/magnification) will help to show that a lot of her thinking at present is 'quick and dirty'—black-and-white thinking about things being done properly, catastrophizing about not getting a job—this is understandable as she is depressed and anxious—but it doesn't mean these thoughts are true. Egan *et al.* (2014) go through the classic 'thinking errors' and give specific examples of how they contribute to perfectionism and provide handouts to challenge this thinking.

A vicious flower formulation (Figure 4.1) reinforces the idea that the procrastination behaviour fuels the threat appraisal that bad things will happen if Marie does not make the perfect decision.

Table 4.1 Theory A/B

Theory A	Theory B
The problem is I must do everything perfectly or I will mess things up and this will have catastrophic consequences for me—losing my job, disappointing my friends and family	The problem is I have thought that I must do things perfectly in order not to mess things up but 'the solution has become the problem' and this has caused me a lot of stress and anxiety
Belief at the start of treatment: 50%	Belief at the start of treatment: 50%
What is the evidence?	
Why do I believe this?	
Many people who are successful have high standards	The more perfectly I tried to do things, the more unachievable it became
	I have started to avoid work and seeing friends as I cannot face trying to obey my perfectionist rules, which has made me feel worse
What are the implications?	
What do I need to do if this is true?	
Get everything right from the start to the finish of the day, including what I wear/what I look like, making the most effective journeys, being productive every day, having everything organized at home, everything clean and put away at all times, getting the right amount of sleep, eating the right food	Work on being less self-critical—watch out for selective attention to things I am unhappy with, get better at recognizing my successes
	Watch out for double standards (unachievably high standards for me, easy-going standards for others)
	Watch out for 'overgeneralizing' from one disappointment/problem
	Watch out for catastrophizing
	Do not take 100% of the responsibiiity for mistakes at work
	Use continua if I spot myself doing black-and-white thinking
	Revise my rules for getting ready/leaving the house, how to get work done, how to make decisions, etc. to be more flexible
	Experiment with doing things differently and see what happens
	Tolerate feeling anxious and uncomfortable (to begin with)
	Do more enjoyable and relaxing things to get my mood up
What does this say about me as a person?	
Right now, I'm a failure	I'm an interesting person, I'm a capable person, I'm a good friend to people

(continued)

Table 4.1 Continued

What will my life be like if I carry on acting in this way?	
What does this say about the future if I keep perfectionism?	**What does this say about the future if I no longer have perfectionism?**
I will be sacked for lateness/absence	I will see my friends and enjoy my time with them
I will get more depressed, more anxious	
My friends will put up with me for a while then things will become strained	I will actually turn up to work, do okay, might make the odd mistake but probably no more or less than everyone else
I will never have a partner	
I will avoid seeing my family as I feel so ashamed	I will go out dating
	I will see my family and tell them what is going on in my life
	As I tackle this problem I will be less stressed

Perfectionist ideas may arise from early experiences of being under pressure to achieve academically or at sport (Egan *et al.*, 2014). These ideas are likely to have been reinforced by success in these domains. This would lead to an over-evaluation of self-worth based on achievement and 'getting things right'. Beliefs about the self as a failure or worthless person may need to be challenged. Rules and assumptions that arise in perfectionism are a clear target in treatment.

It is obvious to Marie that her rules are not working. Finding alternatives to these rules follows the same pattern as challenging any unhelpful, rigid, and negative belief. Useful questions include:

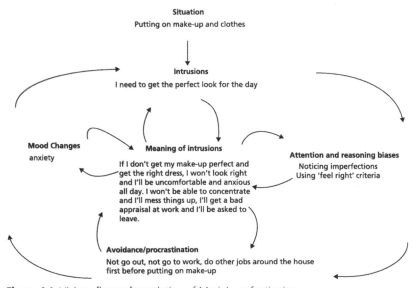

Figure 4.1 Vicious flower formulation of Marie's perfectionism.

If you could start again, would you have these rules? Why not?

Do you wish everyone had these rules? Who do you think has a good version of these rules?

Does anyone else you know have high standards? Do they ever relax them? Do you know someone who has high standards in some areas but is really relaxed in other ways? What makes this okay?

A key situation for Marie was leaving the house and trying to cut out the repeated and extended getting-ready. She undertook to get up *later* than usual and get ready in a shorter period of time, putting on her make-up in a few minutes, and wearing an outfit that was deliberately 'imperfect' (Table 4.2).

Marie started to use self-help materials to challenge procrastination-related thoughts, flashcards/reminders to help her remember to decrease procrastination, daily scheduling sheets, task breakdown, and thought records to challenge self-critical thoughts. There are excellent handouts available in Egan *et al.* (2014) and Shafran *et al.* (2010).

4.1.2 Spotlight on supervision: too much talking, too little action

'My client spends most of the time in our sessions going into detailed descriptive accounts of his problem. We spend so much time reviewing examples, at the expense of him practising challenging the problem.'

Engage in behavioural experiments together—do a home visit or a field trip to do something active that demonstrates that behaving differently is an effective way to challenge this problem. Agree to do this first, then have time for reviewing/more general discussion later in the session.

'We have spent four sessions on developing a formulation and my client is overly focussed on getting it 'just-right'/eliciting the exact meaning. I'm worried that we could easily spend more sessions continuing to tweak our formulation. Should I continue until she's happy with our formulation or is it more important to move on? If so, how do I get her to agree that it's okay to move on?'

Formulate this problem: the belief 'unless I get the right formulation, treatment won't work and …'.

If the problem is going into too much detail about every aspect of the problem, use the 'plague' metaphor—'if you had the plague, I wouldn't need to look at every boil; I just need to know you have the plague'.

4.2 OCD and PTSD

Clinically, it is often considered that traumatic events, either single incident or multiple, can contribute to the origins of OCD as one of several pathways

Table 4.2 Behavioural experiment record for challenging perfectionism

Complete before		Complete after		
Planned experiment	**Specific predictions and how much I believe them**	**What happened? Did the predictions come true?**	**Conclusions? What do you make of this?**	**Does it fit best with theory A or B?**
Set alarm for 7 am Get up after 10 minutes in bed 10-minute shower 5 minutes make up 5 minutes dressing—outfit that feels not quite right 10 minutes breakfast 10 minutes clearing up 2 minutes brushing teeth 5 minutes getting bag, shoes Out of the door at 8 am	I won't be able to get ready in this time	I did manage to get ready by 8.15	Allowing myself more time slowed me down—doing it quicker meant I actually got ready quicker	It shows how 'the solution had become the problem' in theory A— so fits best with theory B
Wearing an outfit that doesn't feel quite right	I will feel uncomfortable all day—100% Anxious all day 50% Upset all day (crying/tearful) 80%	I felt very uncomfortable when I left the house— 95% and I was crying (upset 80%). I felt like this for about 20 minutes, then I started paying more attention to what was going on around me and I only felt 20% uncomfortable and not upset at all. Throughout the day I had the occasional 'uncomfortable' minute—10%, but I didn't feel upset or anxious at all	I did feel a bit uncomfortable leaving the house but actually the feeling faded. Getting on with what I needed to do did help—I forgot to think about it	Fits with theory B—I didn't use my usual rules and 'feeling right' for getting ready and actually I was okay most of the time

(Salkovskis *et al.*, 1999). Note, however, that this relationship may not be specific to OCD, and is likely to be true of other anxiety disorders and depression. The development of a new understanding of mental contamination by Rachman and colleagues (2015) has highlighted the potential importance of trauma, neglect, and particularly, betrayal (see Section 4.3). Diagnostically identified PTSD as a disorder in its own right presenting with OCD is seen in a number of ways; a careful and collaborative formulation will elucidate the relationship. Some individuals diagnosed with OCD may have experienced a functionally related traumatic event (de Silva and Marks, 1999; Gershuny *et al.*, 2008; Gershuny *et al.*, 2003). That is, people who have experienced trauma may develop OCD-relevant ideas and behaviours; rates of OCD of 40% in people with PTSD have been reported (Nacasch *et al.*, 2011). When comparing lifetime rates of severe traumatic events in people with and without OCD, no differences were found by Grabe *et al.* (2008), suggesting that for most people traumatic events are not the main trigger for obsessional difficulties. However, the relationship between the two disorders remains unclear; a study by Huppert *et al.* (2005) suggested that the presence of a relationship between symptoms of OCD and PTSD may be largely accounted for by a combination of symptom overlap and depression. Nonetheless, traumatic events do influence some individuals and can and should be a target for treatment. In a noteworthy study, Veale *et al.* (2015b) used imagery rescripting for individuals with OCD who reported distressing images that may have been linked to past aversive memories and found symptom improvement, concluding that the imagery rescripting gave an alternative understanding of the intrusive image—similar to the Ehlers and Clark (2000) model of PTSD.

An example of OCD as a secondary problem following PTSD is described for Vince:

> 'I was an ordinary guy, doing alright in life, feeling happy and lucky when everything was shattered. I was mugged in the street by some young people; they took my watch, my wedding ring, and my wallet. They hurt me and threatened me. At the time I thought I was going to die as they were so aggressive and rough with me. From that day I have felt like I am vulnerable and weak and that I don't have a way to get through the rest of my life without something else bad happening. I felt depressed and I went off work sick, and stopped going out unless my family made me. I became increasingly fastidious about germs and things being clean—I thought that if I got physically ill that would be "the final straw". I'm already "mentally ill" and I can't control that; being physically ill is in my control and I can at least try to avert that. I also became very superstitious as I felt that, if only I had done something slightly different that day, I wouldn't have been mugged. So now I am always trying to be lucky and avoid bad luck. I won't go out on Friday 13th, I touch wood all the time, and I'm even genuinely happy if a bird craps on me.'

Vince had some cardinal features of PTSD; he was having flashbacks about the mugging, including the masked faces of the muggers being extremely close to him. When he was experiencing these intrusive memories or if he was reminded of the incident in other ways (for example, a news report of a similar crime), then he would feel extremely anxious and that he was in current danger (as at the time he did think he was going to die). He had appraised himself after the trauma as weak and vulnerable as he had not fought back. Every time he looked at his left hand he missed his wedding ring and watch, and was reminded of how his life had been turned upside down. His OCD beliefs mirrored his PTSD beliefs of being weak, vulnerable, and unlucky. When formulating with Vince, the therapist used the Ehlers and Clark (2000) cognitive model of PTSD and drew out these explicit links between OCD and PTSD (Figure 4.2).

Acknowledging that the OCD made him more likely to feel that he was under threat was very helpful for Vince as he knew that in some way the hypersensitivity to germs and the increase in his superstitions were unhelpful, but had not quite realized the very direct effect his OCD beliefs and behaviours were having on his overall sense of current threat.

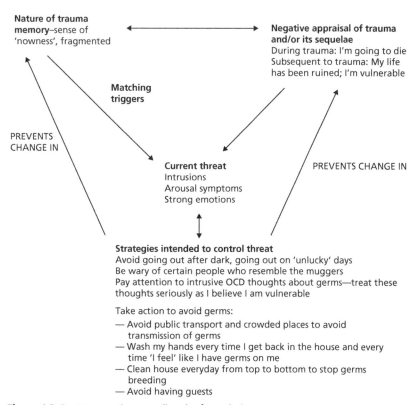

Figure 4.2 Post-traumatic stress disorder formulation.

Once you have established a coherent and useful formulation, treatment will be guided by the most troubling symptoms (with reference to assessment tools, including self-report measures such as the Revised Impact of Events Scale (IES-R; Weiss and Marmar, 1997), Posttraumatic Diagnostic Scale (PDS; Foa *et al.*, 1997); Posttraumatic Cognitions Inventory (PTCI; Foa *et al.*, 1999)) and the most achievable and helpful goals. The formulation should show how aspects of PTSD and OCD maintain the problem, and should identify where they could be distinct. There may be an indication to have an initial focus on memory reprocessing, or the behaviours that are interfering with the person's ability to do reprocessing, i.e. their strategies to decrease the sense of current threat, such as thought suppression and SSBs.

The threat appraisal can be targeted in a number of ways. Well established and powerful methods of treating PTSD such as reliving, updating hotspots, and reclaiming your life are likely to be essential (Ehlers and Clark, 2000; Grey, 2009; Grey *et al.*, 2002). The treatment described in Chapter 3 is undertaken in the same way—until the person with PTSD and OCD has a credible, alternative, less-threatening belief about what (s)he has experienced and why (s)he feels the way (s)he does, (s)he is unlikely to want to change the way that (s)he is behaving as it will feel too dangerous, and therefore anxiety-provoking. If (s)he has already tried to stop his or her OCD behaviour, without a good rationale, (s)he may have experienced an upsurge in PTSD symptoms.

It was useful for Vince to use theory A/B to see that there was a credible, less-threatening alternative to his belief that he was weak, vulnerable, and unlucky. His theory A/B (Table 4.3) provides an idiosyncratic summary of the key features of PTSD that are a target for treatment:

The nature of trauma memories

Sense of current threat

Matching triggers/stimulus discrimination

High levels of arousal and intrusions

Hypervigilance

Attentional bias

Strategies intended to decrease threat and appraisals of the trauma.

After this initial formulation phase, a combination of PTSD and OCD techniques helped Vince to overcome his problems:

• Explaining the nature of trauma memories, including the sense of 'nowness'
• Rationale for reprocessing the memory of the trauma, carrying out reliving and cognitive structuring, leading to a change in the sense of current threat and a decline in flashbacks

Table 4.3 Theory A/B for PTSD and OCD

Which is the best description of the problem I have?
Which problem do I need to solve?

Theory A	Theory B
I am weak, vulnerable, and unlucky	I have felt weak and vulnerable because a bad thing happened to me and I was very affected by it, developing PTSD, which has made me feel more in danger than I really am. I am no more vulnerable or not, or lucky or unlucky than everybody else, and being focussed on germs and luck has made me preoccupied with risk and danger

What is the evidence for this?

Why do I believe this?

No real evidence—it is unlucky to be mugged but I am actually very 'lucky' in other ways—my family are happy and healthy, I don't have money worries	I understand now that I have PTSD, which means my memories of the mugging are not 'filed away' as they should be [nature of trauma memories]—they are easily triggered by all sorts of things and make me feel frightened as if it is all happening again [high levels of arousal and intrusions], which feeds the sense of being vulnerable [appraisal of trauma], including being vulnerable to disease. As I became more worried about germs I started to see the danger in everything and everyone [hypervigilance and attentional bias]—actually before the mugging I didn't think about whether I was going to get ill, and I wasn't that likely to get ill.
	I started thinking about luck, as it was such 'bad luck' to be in the wrong place at the wrong time and to be victim of this crime. I have been so unhappy and frightened that I clung on to anything that made me feel a bit safer or better protected [strategies intended to decrease threat]—a bit of luck and superstition started off being helpful but soon I became even more fearful and preoccupied

What do I need to do if this is true?
What are the implications of this theory?

Not go out except when absolutely necessary—then be very wary and on the lookout for dodgy looking people	I need to work on getting a better sense of 'then and now'—going through the memories to get a 'time stamp' on them
Never go out after dark	Watch out for my attention being drawn to certain people and then making assumptions about whether they are a threat to me
Never go out on an 'unlucky' day	I need to come to terms with the mugging and accept that bad things do happen sometimes, but that I am not at particularly high risk of anything else bad happening again. Being mugged doesn't mean that I am weak and vulnerable; if I had fought back I might have been seriously injured or worse—in fact, I made a good decision at the time
Avoid public transport and places that are crowded to avoid transmission of germs	

Table 4.3 Continued

Wash my hands every time I get back in the house, and every time I 'feel' like there are germs on me	I need to go out and do things even on 'unlucky' days—like I used to
	I will clean my house every week or two, have guests when I feel like it, use public transport, and go to busy places
Clean the house every day from top to bottom to stop germs breeding	
Avoid having guests	

What does this say about the future?

I will never get over it—the muggers will have taken more than my ring and watch, they will have taken my life away	In the fullness of time, I will get back to normal and carry on doing what I have always done, with occasional reminders or memories of the mugging
	Enjoy my time with family and friends

- Socratic method, metaphors, and behavioural experiments to challenge his OCD beliefs that he was vulnerable to picking up germs, and that a physical illness would be the 'last straw', including the counterproductive effect of not cleaning his house and avoiding people—in fact this had been making him feel a lot worse, and had been very concerning to his family

- Rediscovering how the world really works—resuming his previous beliefs about luck—the odd family superstition or touching wood/crossing his fingers was okay, but that making decisions about whether to leave the house or not based on superstitious beliefs was actually stopping him from reclaiming his life, and was refocussing him on his threat and danger-related ideas.

4.3 **Mental contamination**

'It looks clean but it feels dirty' (Rachman, 1994)

'Mental contamination' is a feature of OCD that has recently been identified and clarified by Professor Jack Rachman (a pioneer in the field of OCD) and colleagues (Rachman *et al.*, 2015).

Fear of contamination through direct contact with dirty or diseased objects is a familiar feature of OCD. Mental contamination is contamination from a person, through an act of psychological or physical violation such as betrayal, assault, or abuse. The interpretation of the significance of this violation usually includes an idea that the victim is weak, insignificant, and worthless. This can manifest as 'relationship OCD'; for example, a betrayal by a partner can fuel an obsessional fear in subsequent relationships that the partner will cheat on him or her, or doesn't really like or love him or her, leading to potentially destructive levels of reassurance-seeking and checking.

'Self-contamination' is a sense of contamination from one's own thoughts, or personally unacceptable actions such as inflicting betrayal or harm, or doing something 'deviant' such as watching hard core pornography. Self-contamination is often accompanied by shame, guilt, and self-critical/moral judgements of the self, e.g. 'I'm immoral' (Rachman *et al.*, 2015).

'Morphing' is a belief that undesirable characteristics of people can be transferred by proximity or physical contact—that the person with OCD will be transformed into this undesirable person (Rachman *et al.*, 2015). An example would be a high achieving university student who did not want to associate with less academically able peers for fear of them 'rubbing off on him'. Rachman postulates that people are prone to beliefs about morphing if they have beliefs about the contagiousness of mental instability, disgust, or distaste associated with unusual/odd strangers, or a history of being undermined/told that they were failures. Contact with unfortunate or strange people may trigger these fears and the idea that this could happen to them. This fear is seen as irrational and as a product of their own mind.

Specific assessment tools have been developed: the Vancouver Obsessive Compulsive Inventory (VOCI; Thordarson *et al.*, 2004) includes contamination questions that cover contact and mental contamination. Other specific measures are the Contamination Thought–Action Fusion Scale and the Contamination Sensitivity Scale (Radomsky *et al.*, 2014; Box 4.1).

Rachman *et al.* (2015) note that the sense of mental contamination can be triggered by memories, images, and thoughts, or internal scanning of the body to try to detect signs of contamination. Feelings of mental contamination are particularly likely to worsen over time owing to changes in the person's perception, memories, and thoughts about the contaminating person. People may experience temporary relief from physical washing; other neutralizing behaviour is almost inevitable, including mental rituals, drinking water, or drinking cleaning products to remove internal dirt, as is avoiding people or places associated with mental contamination.

Common OCD-related beliefs, such as 'I should control my thoughts', are reinforced by the uncontrollability of the thoughts and can reinforce a feeling of being mentally unstable or damaged in some way. Furthermore, thought–action fusion (TAF) biases can add further weight to the negative appraisal of the thoughts:

Box 4.1 Research note: evoking mental contamination in the lab—simulating violations

Radomsky and Elliott (2009) asked 148 female undergraduates to listen to an audio recording and imagine either a consensual or a forced kiss from a man described as moral or immoral. More feelings of mental contamination were evoked by a non-consensual kiss than a consensual kiss (whether the man was described as moral or immoral). The fewest feelings of mental contamination occurred in participants who imagined a consensual kiss from a man described as moral. Millar *et al.* (2016) suggest that the effects obtained were caused by the visualization of the kiss (bodily fluids) rather than ideas of betrayal; scenarios involving theft show no effect on mental contamination in students. However, Pagdin *et al.* (2016) found evidence in clinical samples that a measure of betrayal experiences and betrayal sensitivity may link to OCD in general and mental contamination in particular, and that this was not so for other anxiety disorders.

'Having these repugnant thoughts about bestiality is as immoral as actually having sex with my dog'

'Having images of being a homeless nutcase increases the probability that I will become homeless and a nutcase'

After experiences of sexual assault it is common to feel physically and mentally contaminated. Rachman *et al.* (2015) note the similarities with cognitions associated with PTSD—that they are permanently damaged.

An example of mental contamination following a violation experience:

> Farah is ashamed to admit her difficulties—she has been avoiding gay people as she is worried that she will 'turn gay'. She is not homophobic and has very liberal views on sexuality and she finds her own thoughts offensive. She was chatted up at a bar by a woman who unexpectedly kissed her and touched her; Farah did not want these advances and felt angry and ashamed afterwards. She is also starting to worry that she is becoming dangerously mentally ill as she knows that being gay cannot be 'transmitted', but she feels increasingly preoccupied with the idea.
>
> 'I don't like thinking about what happened; I want to wash myself all over when it comes to mind. I am really angry that someone kissed me and touched me against my will; I don't see how I am going to get over that. When I feel anxious I feel like I am turning gay and this frightens me as I am not gay, and my life would fall apart if I was—everyone I know would think that I had been living a lie, and I would feel that I am not who I thought I was. I have been avoiding my neighbours [a gay couple], which is making me sad and ashamed as they are nice people.'

After her experience of violation, Farah had a long hot shower and experienced some relief from the feelings of mental dirtiness. She threw away the clothes that she wore that evening as they felt tainted, and because they reminded her of the event. She threw away similar looking clothes as she wondered if this type of clothing made it more likely that people would think that she was gay. She started washing her hands whenever she had a recollection of the event; this washing became more frequent and more thorough. Over time she had a raised criterion for a feeling of cleanliness (see Section 1.8.7 on Internally referenced criteria).

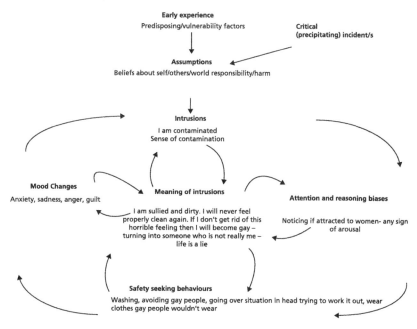

The experience of intense negative emotion was seen by Farah as proof that she was permanently damaged by these experiences. Rachman *et al.* (2015) suggest as part of treatment explaining the 'ex-consequentia' bias (concluding danger is present based on the experience of fear) in mental contamination as follows:

> Some people reason that if they feel guilty, they must have done something wrong and therefore they think 'I am contaminated'. Sometimes when people think they are feeling dirty or polluted they are actually also feeling sad or angry or disgusted but have mislabelled the emotion, that's why washing doesn't help you feel better.
>
> Rachman *et al.* (2015), page 98

This explanation helped Farah to see that these intense emotions were evidence for theory B rather than confirmation of theory A (Table 4.4).

Table 4.4 Theory A/B for mental contamination concerns

Which is the best description of the problem I have? **Which problem do I need to solve?**	
Theory A	Theory B
I have been physically and mentally contaminated by that woman and now I am permanently changed for the worse	Mental contamination is a psychological problem that I can work on
What is the evidence? **Why do I believe this?**	
No evidence	I feel anxious, upset, and angry all the time, which I have 'mislabelled' as mental contamination
What do I need to do if this is true? **What are the implications of buying into this idea?**	
Wash myself as thoroughly as possible when I am reminded of the event	Go anywhere, speak to anyone Work on not blaming myself for what happened
Avoid gay people—in person or in the media	Find out more about why this experience bothered me so much and come to terms with it
Interrogate myself about why this happened and what I could have done to stop it	
Try to remember all the men I have had relationships with to bring on heterosexual feelings	Wash myself once a day, wash my hands a few times a day (based on 'normal' rules rather than on feelings of dirtiness)
What will my life be like if I carry on acting in this way?	
I will become increasingly isolated and miserable	I will get back to how I was before— someone who is fun-loving, friendly, accepting of others

Helping Farah to come to terms with the impact of the event on her included going through what happened and finding out what the event meant to her at the time, and how she appraised it afterwards. This revealed a sense of danger at the time as she felt very vulnerable in the bar as her friends had left and she was under the influence of alcohol. Afterwards she blamed herself for allowing herself to be vulnerable and felt guilty for having allowed herself to have a casual intimate encounter with someone. Using a 'reliving' method (Ehlers and Clark, 2000; Grey *et al.*, 2002), going over the event in detail helped Farah to see that she was less vulnerable at the time than she initially recalled— she did know some people in the bar, and she was sitting by the bar itself so was near the staff. This helped her to update her belief that she had been irresponsible and allowed herself to be vulnerable—she had been in similar situations before and nothing bad had happened; she also recognized that most people put themselves in these situations regularly. She also recalled times when she had thought that men had been interested in her and had made some advances to them, to find out that they did not wish to reciprocate. She acknowledged some similarities and this decreased the threat associated with the woman who kissed her.

Farah continued to be troubled by her residual belief that homosexuality could be transmitted, and still believed that this was a sign of incipient madness. The 'Jimmy Savile' metaphor helped.

THERAPIST: Recently in the news there was a story that someone had paid thousands of pounds for a pair of Usain Bolt's shorts that he wore at the Olympics, and even more money for a pair of Muhammed Ali's boxing gloves—any idea why someone would have done that?

FARAH: People like to have a bit of history? Some kind of connection to a famous person or a memorable event?

THERAPIST: I think so—if we had the shorts here, would you want to pick them up and touch them? Would you then tell other people about it?

FARAH: I suppose I would—there would be something a bit exciting about it.

THERAPIST: But thinking about it, it wasn't the shorts that made history—it was the man himself. Do the shorts carry an essence of Usain? Is that why we would want to touch them?

FARAH: Something like that, I suppose.

THERAPIST: Would it actually make us run faster?

FARAH: No.

THERAPIST: How about if we had a pair of Jimmy Savile's shorts? Would you touch them?

FARAH: No way, it would be disgusting.

THERAPIST: Do you think anyone would want to touch them?

FARAH: No, I think everyone would want to burn them.

THERAPIST: But it wasn't the shorts that perpetrated acts of abuse—it was the man himself. What does this show us about what most people believe about characteristics of a person being transferrable?

FARAH: Most people do believe it a bit?

THERAPIST: Looks that way—so it's not that you are doing anything radically different than what most people do—we can all have this sense of something about a person being transferred.

This idea of objects taking on the properties of a person is widely described in hoarding (e.g. Steketee and Frost, 2013).

A survey of what other people would think after such an event showed that it is common to feel some sense of pollution after an unwanted advance—showing Farah the research in Box 4.1 also helped her to see that this was a normal feeling and helped to further challenge theory A.

In summary, treatment for mental contamination contains the same elements as other concerns—a clear formulation, theory A/B, building up evidence for theory B, including information and discussion on mental contamination, the role of SSBs and avoidance, and finding out how the world really works (e.g. behavioural experiments to find out if we really can transmit properties of ourselves).

4.4 **Working with shame in OCD**

Shame is a relevant issue to keep in mind when treating OCD, with respect to symptom-based shame, TAF beliefs, and shame as a treatment barrier (Weingarden and Renshaw, 2015). Symptom-based shame involves the person judging himself or herself for his or her symptoms, which could be with respect to more general shame about struggling with a mental health difficulty or in relation to symptoms specific to the OCD. As discussed previously, the content of a person's obsessional thoughts usually revolve around themes considered most abhorrent by the person; for example, the religious person with blasphemous thoughts, the new mother with thoughts of harming her baby, or the caring person concerned about being a paedophile. It is understandable that individuals with obsessional thoughts may judge themselves harshly or even fear themselves because of these inner experiences (intrusive thoughts and images), leaving them vulnerable to feelings of shame about their intrusions. They may also feel ashamed of performing compulsions that are visible to others; for example, excessive handwashing or repeated checking that may be difficult to hide from others. TAF beliefs (i.e. having a thought is morally equivalent to acting on the thought) can interact with symptom-based shame; for example, shame about the content of one's obsessions may be compounded by TAF beliefs such as 'having this thought means I am bad/evil/immoral'. Social withdrawal and avoidance of seeking treatment, as a result of shame, may also maintain and exacerbate shame in OCD. Where treatment is sought, shame may lead to non-disclosure of symptoms that evoke shame, not just with the therapist but also with loved ones.

As discussed in Chapter 3, an important aspect of working with anyone with OCD involves psychoeducation about intrusive thoughts being a common experience, typically by providing examples of the wide variety of intrusions we experience, particularly those that are 'taboo', to normalize the person's experience of intrusive thoughts. With many people this may be sufficient to assuage feelings of shame about the *content* of their thoughts and difficulties in being able to accept oneself for having these thoughts. For others, feelings of shame can be at the core of their distress and may block progress to working with OCD using the approach outlined in Chapter 3. In these cases, it will be important to include shame (in addition to anxiety) as an emotional response, and its associated behaviours, as part of formulation, and for the intervention to address shame directly.

Preoccupation with harm being done to self and/or others is a central theme in OCD. A fear of being responsible for future harm is commonly seen in fears of inadvertently causing harm through one's actions or inactions; for example, a fear of being responsible for causing a fire or a fear of making self/others ill through contamination. The common emotional response is one of anxiety, leading to attempts at verification (actual or mental checking to prevent future harm) or restitution/'putting right' (e.g. washing away contamination). Feelings of guilt may often accompany feelings of anxiety; for example, anticipating the consequences of not preventing harm to self or others. In this case, following the treatment approach outlined in Chapter 3 should be sufficient to help the person overcome his or her OCD. However, whenever the person with OCD mentions feelings of guilt it is important to explore further the nature of these feelings to clarify whether the feelings of guilt (s)he describes may be better understood as shame.

4.4.1 Distinguishing shame from other emotions

Before addressing how to work with feelings of shame, it is important to consider what is meant by shame and to distinguish shame from other self-conscious emotions. In particular, guilt and shame are terms that are often used interchangeably, by clients and therapists alike, but this lack of specificity can lead to conceptual, formulatory, and intervention difficulties. Guilt is felt when a person judges their *behaviour* negatively, while shame is felt when a person judges themselves negatively (Tangney and Dearing, 2002).

Shame is not a single emotion, like anxiety, but involves complex dynamic processes between externally focussed fears of what others may think/feel/do and internally focussed fears of what will be activated within oneself (Gilbert, 2010). Gilbert differentiates between shame, humiliation, and guilt by focussing on how these emotions differ in their impact on focus of attention, thinking, and what motivates behaviour. When experiencing *shame*, the focus is on the *damage to self and reputation*, with associated anxiety, defeat, emptiness, and self-directed anger. We may perceive that others are judging us negatively and also make global negative judgements of ourselves, and we will be motivated to defend ourselves from rejection or attack by others; we may do this by attempting to hide those aspects of ourselves about which we feel ashamed. When experiencing *humiliation*, our focus is on *harm done by other to self* and we are likely to have feelings of anger, injustice, and vengeance. Our thoughts will be focussed on the unfairness of negative evaluation by others and we will be motivated to seek revenge and to silence others. When experiencing *guilt*, our focus is on the *hurt caused to the other by our own behaviour*, which can lead to feelings of sadness, sorrow, and remorse. We are likely to have sympathy and empathy for the other, and are motivated to make reparation for harm done to the other. Whilst higher levels of shame and humiliation are commonly unhelpful and associated with higher symptomatology (Kim *et al.*, 2011), a healthy connection with guilt can be potentially helpful as it can lead to taking responsibility for harm done and making amends. With shame, we can become self-attacking and isolated; with humiliation we can become other-attacking and seek to gain power over others; in contrast, learning to tolerate feelings of guilt can help us to take necessary steps in strengthening our relationships with others. While shame motivates us to engage in damage limitation, guilt motivates us towards reconciliation and reconnection following disruption of interpersonal relationships (Gilbert, 2010).

It is also worth noting that these feelings do not necessarily occur in isolation, but that an individual may experience a blend of these emotions. Feelings of guilt may also be blended with feelings of shame for the person who feels guilty about the harm (s)he may have caused to others but who may also feel a deep sense of shame related to self-identity ('what kind of person does this make me?'). Similarly, the person who feels humiliated at the hands of others may also struggle with feelings of shame when recalling or disclosing the humiliating experience.

4.4.2 **Internal and external shame**

Gilbert (2010) also distinguishes between fears about the external (social) world and the internal world. Our external fears relate to our fears about how we are perceived and could be treated by others, while our internal fears reflect our own perception of ourselves, including fears of inadequacy and failure. Thus, when working with shame, it is important to make a distinction between external and internal shame. There is often overlap between external and internal shame, whereby our fears of how we are perceived by others often reflect our innermost fears about ourselves.

Although shame and guilt are quite different emotions, they can often be confused when people describe their experiences. For example, the new mum who has intrusive thoughts of hurting her baby may become fearful of her own desires and potential actions if she interprets these thoughts as reflecting her inner wishes. Although she describes 'feeling guilty' it may be that this can be more accurately understood as feelings of shame for having these thoughts, which clash with her own values and expectations of herself; she may feel both *internal* shame (*I* am evil for having these thoughts) and *external* shame (if *other people* knew I had these thoughts *they would think I am a monster and take my baby away from me*). In contrast, a mother may describe feeling bad for not being able to be the kind of mum she would like to be as a consequence of the effects of the OCD; for example, she may avoid interacting with her baby due to a fear of inadvertently making her baby ill through contamination. These 'bad' feelings can be understood as feelings of guilt, as reflected in her focus on harm caused to her baby by her own behaviour (i.e. how her baby is missing out on nurturing interactions owing to her obsessional fear of making the baby ill), which is likely to lead to feelings of remorse and sorrow that motivate her to make reparation by addressing her OCD so that she can interact with her baby in the ways in which she would like. This distinction is also important in relation to the therapeutic process, as the person will find it easier to disclose feelings of guilt, while shame is much more difficult to disclose as it urges us to hide rather than disclose those aspects of ourselves.

4.4.3 Understanding the impact of shame from an evolutionary perspective

Gilbert and McGuire (1998) offer a means of understanding shame from an evolutionary perspective. As humans, we are social animals who have evolved to live in groups. In our interactions with others, through observation and experiencing rewards and punishments, we learn what is attractive and unattractive about ourselves and thus what is acceptable to display and what should be hidden. As social beings, our survival within the group depends upon enhancing and avoiding damage to how we are perceived by others.

Our brains have evolved not only to detect and respond to physical threats, such as potential attack by others, but also to social threats, such as rejection by others (for example, being ignored, excluded, disliked, criticized). These social threats activate affective arousal, stimulating a primitive involuntary defensive strategy. Submission and appeasement can be adaptive 'damage limitation' strategies in response to feelings of shame, aimed at reparation and avoiding rejection; in contrast, continuing in a shameless, non-submissive way, may lead to attack or rejection by others. Gilbert and McGuire (1998) highlight the influence of social rank, which can influence our threat defence strategy. For example, rejection by someone of higher social rank may stimulate submissive strategies aimed at reparation, while rejection by someone of lower rank may stimulate retaliation and defensive strategies in efforts to preserve one's place in the social hierarchy.

4.4.4 Impact of shame on the therapeutic process

The classification of OCD as an anxiety disorder has led much of the research on emotions in OCD to focus on anxiety, with relatively little focus on other emotions. Weingarden and Renshaw's (2015) review of shame across obsessive-compulsive and related disorders (OCRDs) highlights that behavioural responses to shame, such as avoidance and social withdrawal, could easily be attributed to anxiety when they may actually arise in response to feelings of shame. This has important implications for treatment. Weingarden and Renshaw highlight that, while research supports the effectiveness of exposure and response prevention (ERP) in reducing anxiety, it is important to consider what impact ERP may have on feelings of shame (see the case study of Stewart). Weingarden and Renshaw suggest that treatment of shame can be improved by incorporating aspects of third-wave approaches that directly target shame, such as acceptance and commitment therapy (ACT), dialectical behaviour therapy (DBT), and compassion-focussed therapy (CFT).

Stewart was a 38-year-old married man who presented with contamination concerns, that involved keeping certain items of clothing separate from others. He disclosed that the 'contaminated' items were those he had worn to strip clubs.

Keeping these clothes separate was aimed at keeping aspects of his identity associated with visits to strip clubs separate to aspects of his identity associated with being a husband, father, and well respected member of the community.

Stewart's formulation made reference to shame as the primary problem (theory B: this is a shame problem; I judge myself as immoral and feel ashamed about visits to strip clubs). Stewart was encouraged to engage in ERP tasks that involved him wearing his usual clothes when visiting strip clubs, to refrain from changing out of these clothes when returning home, and gradually to wear the 'contaminated' clothes in situations that he would normally avoid (e.g. when taking his children out). Despite agreeing to engage in these tasks, Stewart repeatedly returned to therapy sessions reporting that he had struggled to do so. One means of understanding this is that ERP tasks were actually activating shame rather than anxiety. The act of changing out of clothes worn to the strip club enabled Stewart to dissociate/cut off from his feelings of shame (rather than anxiety); in contrast, engaging in ERP tasks activated feelings of shame (rather than anxiety, as intended). An intervention directly targeting Stewart's feelings of shame about his visits to the strip club was necessary to support Stewart to disengage from these behaviours. Encouraging Stewart to engage in compassion focused therapy (CFT) offers one means of directly addressing his feelings of shame.

Shame is experienced as an aspect of ourselves that we wish to avoid, with a fear that, if others knew about these aspects of ourselves, they would reject us, which makes shame particularly difficult to talk about and face. Hiding and concealment are intrinsic to feelings of shame, urging us to hide parts of ourselves from others due to fear of being judged and condemned, which understandably makes it difficult to disclose these aspects of ourselves in therapy. This can lead to non-disclosure of shame experiences and further shame for one's feelings of inadequacy, inferiority, or 'badness'. Many other different emotions may also be associated with shame, including sadness, anxiety, disgust, and anger. This can make it difficult to spot shame if the dominant emotion expressed by the person is another emotion. Additionally, the person's level of awareness of shame can vary, so that it may even be difficult to acknowledge and articulate for the person, who may describe emotions such as guilt, embarrassment, or humiliation when they are actually experiencing shame (Macdonald, 1998). As therapists, it is important to distinguish between these different emotional states so that we do not fall into the same trap of mislabelling shame experiences.

Shame experiences are difficult to talk about because of fear of judgement by others and also emotional avoidance. The person will be wary about to whom they feel safe to disclose. Anticipatory shame can inhibit disclosure if the person is avoiding further feelings of shame arising from disclosure of their shame experience. Non-verbal signals that may alert the therapist to feelings of shame are avoidance of eye gaze and keeping one's head down. If we are to support disclosure of shame experiences, it is important to create a safe therapeutic environment, in which the person experiences the therapist as non-judgemental and motivated to understand. Microskills are of particular importance; for example, slowing down to allow space and silence for reflection and experiencing within a therapy session, using voice tone and non-verbal communication, particularly facial expression, to promote safeness (Gilbert, 2010). Using the therapeutic relationship as a relationship in which the person can experience non-judgemental acceptance of the self provides an important foundation for supporting the person to adopt a similar stance towards himself or herslef.

4.4.5 Punishment beliefs, self-blame, and shame

When the person's maintenance formulation contains responsibility appraisals that reflect beliefs about deserving to be punished or the OCD itself being a form of punishment, it is important to understand the roots of these ideas. Socratic questioning to explore the origins of the person's responsibility beliefs can lead to disclosure of memories of being responsible for past harm; while the person may experience anxiety about future events, (s)he may also carry a sense of being to blame for past events, with feelings of shame and a belief that 'it was my fault'. Drawing out a developmental formulation with the person that links critical events with responsibility appraisals can help him or her to understand how (s)he came to develop an inflated sense of responsibility and how this has influenced the development of and maintains their obsessional problem. Engaging the person in a process of reappraisal of past events can help to unlock feelings of shame.

Section 1.1 describes a fuller description of Jessie's OCD, which is fear of contamination in pregnancy. Jessie's maintenance formulation is illustrated.

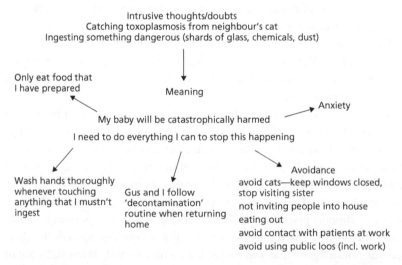

Jessie expressed some relief at the alternative explanation offered by theory B; however, she experienced great difficulty putting this into practice. During the process of exploring what was making this difficult, Jessie broke down, reporting that she knew it was only a matter of time before her baby would be taken away from her and that she had to do whatever she could to stop this happening. Socratic questioning to explore her conviction in this belief led to the disclosure of important historical information that was relevant in identifying key beliefs that maintained her OCD. Jessie disclosed that she had become pregnant at the age of 14 years. Her mother arranged a termination quite quickly without much discussion. Jessie felt that her parents were ashamed of her and that God was angry with her. Over the years she had ruminated on the termination and became convinced that God would punish her in some way, and that her ultimate punishment would be to be denied the opportunity of having a baby. Her experience of struggling to become pregnant and requiring several attempts at in vitro fertilization (IVF) reinforced her belief that God was punishing her for the termination by preventing her from becoming a mother. Having managed to become pregnant, Jessie experienced some initial relief and felt that perhaps God had punished her enough and that maybe she had been forgiven. She vowed to be the best mum that she could to prove her worthiness. However, her intrusions about her baby coming to harm led her to believe that God remained angry with her and would punish her by taking away the baby she had struggled to conceive.

It is important to consider whether shame, rather than anxiety, is the dominant emotion that is maintaining Jessie's OCD. Reviewing her emotional memories as a teenager revealed that she felt judged by her parents at the time of the termination ('they're disgusted that I've had sex at 14—I'm not the sweet little girl that they thought I was'; 'they think I'm stupid for getting pregnant at 14') and also by God ('God is angry with me for destroying my baby'), both of which maintained external shame. Judging herself currently ('I don't deserve to be a mum because I destroyed my baby'; 'not being able to get pregnant is God's punishment') maintained internal shame, self-blame, and self-criticism ('it's my own fault that I couldn't get pregnant/I will lose this baby').

This new information (highlighted in bold) can be added to the existing maintenance formulation, as illustrated. The updated formulation encapsulates all the relevant information provided by Jessie, including additional information about the historical context that helps us to understand where her beliefs about punishment and not being worthy of being a mother originate. This also led to the identification of additional SSBs (praying to God for forgiveness) and additional feelings of shame that were not identified in her original formulation.

Below is the formulation of shame beliefs underpinning contamination concerns.

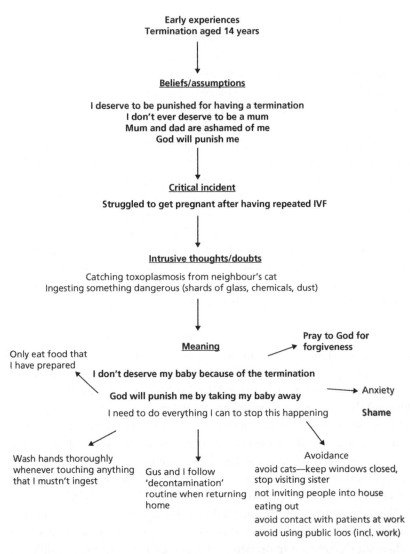

Building a developmental formulation may be sufficient to help the person to understand where his or her fears come from. Reappraising historical events using standard cognitive strategies (e.g. responsibility pie charts) may enable the person to come to new conclusions that help him or her to recognize that (s)he is not to blame for past events, allowing him or her to let go of feelings of shame.

Jessie's theory A and theory B were also amended in light of the new information (Table 4.5).

Table 4.5 Jessie's updated theory A/theory B

Which is the best description of the problem I have? **Which problem do I need to solve?**	
Theory A	Theory B
I don't deserve to be a mum because I terminated my first pregnancy	I have always felt ashamed about the termination and believed that God is angry with me and will punish me by stopping me from having a baby.
God is angry with me for the termination and will punish me by taking my baby away from me	Since getting pregnant I am terrified that God will punish me by taking my baby away
Belief: 100%	Belief: 0%

What is the evidence? **Why do I believe this?**	
I had a termination at 14 and have struggled to get pregnant once I was desperate to have a baby	Feeling ashamed about the termination and believing that God is angry with me made me feel that my struggle to get pregnant was a punishment from God that I deserved
I only managed to get pregnant after lots of IVF	
This feels like God's punishment for the termination	Despite becoming pregnant through IVF, I still believe that God is angry with me and I struggle to accept that I deserve to be a mum

What do I need to do if this is true (implications of buying this)?	
Seek God's forgiveness so that he won't punish me	Address my feelings of shame about the termination that keep me feeling like I do not deserve to be a mum
Prove to God that I deserve to be a mum and do not deserve his punishment	Have faith in a compassionate God that understands how painful the termination was for me and would not want to punish me in this way
Do everything I can in my power to stop God taking my baby away during this pregnancy or after (s)he is born	→ see my pregnancy as a blessing and go about things the way I used to

What will my life be like if I carry on acting this way (longer term implications of buying this)?	
I will constantly be waiting for something to go wrong	I will be able to stop blaming myself about the termination and will be able to let go of the feeling that I deserve to be punished
I won't be able to enjoy my pregnancy and if I get through the pregnancy I will continue to be walking on eggshells once my baby is born—always waiting for him or her to be taken away from me	I can relax more during my pregnancy and look forward to being a mum the way other women do

Socratic questioning during this process can help Jessie to re-evaluate punishment beliefs that previously made it so difficult to live according to theory B and can support the development of a new perspective on what living according to theory B would involve.

4.4.6 Bridging the 'head–heart lag'

Updating Jessie's formulation and revising her theory A/theory B is an important initial step in acknowledging what is really keeping her OCD going. However, we may still encounter difficulty in getting Jessie to live according to theory B. Despite buying into theory B in the therapy room, she may struggle to act according to theory B when she is at home between sessions. When reviewing the obstacles at the next therapy session, Jessie confides that she still feels ashamed about her teenage pregnancy and termination, and that she deserves to be punished; this feels like an unquestionable fact. Standard verbal reattribution strategies can be used to challenge her punishment beliefs; for example, asking her what she would say to her sister, a friend, or her niece. She acknowledges that she would tell a loved one that their actions as a teenager did not make them bad and worthy of punishment now and is able to come up with alternative appraisals (it must have been a terrifying experience to go through; acknowledging that she wasn't really given a choice but presented with a termination as the only option). However, despite identifying these alternative appraisals, Jessie may continue to feel that she deserves to be punished despite interventions targeted at challenging some of her punishment beliefs (responsibility pie chart around the termination; continua to explore her view of others who have had a termination; Socratic questioning that confirmed her beliefs in a benign God).

This suggests that Jessie has an intellectual understanding of theory B, but struggles to truly believe this at an emotional level. We can understand this in terms of Jessie making links at a propositional level, suggesting that she is able to come up with a plausible alternative that reflects her capacity to have a 'logical'/intellectual understanding ('*knowing* in her head' that she is not being punished). However, this has done little to challenge Jessie's punishment beliefs at an emotional/implicational level ('*feeling* in her heart' that she is not being punished). Despite being able to *understand* that her actions at the age of 14 years did not mean she deserves to be punished as an adult, she continues to *feel* that she deserves to be punished. Some work aimed at helping her to bridge this 'head–heart lag' may be indicated to undermine a strong *felt sense* of shame. Gilbert and Irons (2005) make sense of the difficulty a person may encounter in believing the alternative perspectives that (s)he has generated as difficulty in feeling safe enough to believe alternative appraisals.

Devoting some time in therapy to imagery rescripting can be time well spent in helping Jessie not only to generate alternative conclusions but to do so in a way that bridges this 'head–heart' lag, so she is able to not only 'know'/understand this is a more balanced perspective but also for this to resonate at an emotional level. This kind of work can help Jessie to make important shifts that enable her to let go of long-held beliefs that are pivotal in the maintenance of her OCD, making it easier for her to let go of existing obsessional behaviour and act according to her revised theory B.

4.4.7 Imagery rescripting to target shame-based memories

Imagery rescripting offers a powerful means of updating meanings that were formed at the time of key events that led to the formation of feelings of shame and associated beliefs. Arntz and Weertman (1999) offer a detailed description of their method, which is a three-phased approach that encourages the person to experience the situation from three different perspectives: their younger self experiencing events as they were actually experienced at the time (phase 1); the perspective of an older, wiser adult offering the child what was needed but absent at the time (phase 2); and from the perspective of their younger self receiving what they needed at the time (phase 3). An illustration of how imagery rescripting could be used with Jessie is outlined.

- Phase 1: ask Jessie to relive her memory of circumstances around the termination, particularly aspects that contributed to feelings of shame and deserving to be punished from the perspective of her 14-year-old self. Encourage her to do so in the first person, present tense, describing events as a 14-year-old. Begin by asking Jessie to close her eyes and to bring to mind an image of her 14-year-old self. Asking Jessie to describe what she can see around her, aspects of the room that she is in and tuning into other sensory aspects (what she can hear, smell, feel) can help her to connect with her 14-year-old self. In this first stage, it is important to help Jessie connect with the feelings of shame to identify where they have come from ('What is happening?' 'How are you feeling?' 'What are you thinking?'). Ask Jessie what she needs right now to help her with these feelings (e.g. 'What do you need from your mum and dad/God?').

- Phase 2: the second stage of this exercise requires viewing the same scene again, observing her 14-year-old self from the perspective of an older, wiser, non-judgemental, non-condemning other. This could be her current adult self or, if this is difficult for Jessie, ask her to identify someone that has these qualities and to view the scene from their perspective. Again, keeping the dialogue in the first person (the identified adult—whether older Jessie or someone else) and in the present tense, ask the adult to look into younger Jessie's eyes during the exercise to help him or her to empathize with this child. Ask what (s)he can see is happening, how (s)he feels towards 14-year-old Jessie, what (s)he can see that Jessie needs in this moment, and how (s)he would like to respond to her. This can lead to the identification of important messages (e.g. 'It is not your fault that you are in this situation, I still love you') and responses (e.g. being held and comforted, allowing younger Jessie to talk about her feelings, asking her what she would like to happen) that were not provided at the time and that would have been pivotal in protecting Jessie from developing feelings of shame and related self-condemning beliefs. Encourage the adult to respond to younger Jessie, providing what she needs and keeping in mind any needs that were identified by the child in stage 1.

◆ Phase 3: in the final stage, ask Jessie to adopt the perspective of her 14-year-old self again, this time experiencing the events in accordance with the rescripted version of this experience as identified in stage 2. Ensure that Jessie experiences these events in the first person present tense as a 14-year-old. Jessie is encouraged to *experience receiving* what she needed at the time, hearing the messages, and receiving the responses that were identified as important by the child in stage 1 and the adult in stage 2. Ask Jessie what is happening, how she now feels, and what she thinks about herself and the situation.

◆ Homework: audiorecording the imagery rescripting exercise is important so that Jessie can listen back to this several times before the next therapy session. Asking Jessie to re-rate her punishment beliefs and strength of feelings of shame after each listening will help to track the impact of the exercise.

Imagery rescripting can offer a powerful means of addressing feelings that are rooted in past experiences that continue to have strong emotional resonance. Engaging in such an exercise can enable Jessie to build an emotional bridge to the alternative appraisals that logically made sense to her but that she had previously struggled to accept. Doing so can help her to engage in the process of experimenting with living according to theory B owing to an erosion of the strong sense of shame she previously felt. There is a much stronger chance that Jessie will be able to continue with the usual treatment approach and can now be referred back to theory B and set behavioural experiments as homework tasks, in keeping with the typical approach to treatment (see Chapter 3).

4.4.8 **When shame and self-attacking present obstacles in therapy**

The imagery rescripting intervention described in Section 4.4.7 is likely to work if the person is able to access a non-judgemental and caring stance towards their younger self during the exercise, whether this is from the perspective of their older, wiser adult self or another person with these qualities. However, for some individuals, this may prove difficult. For example, Jessie may have got stuck in self-condemnation and may struggle to bring to mind anyone that would not judge or condemn her either. Jessie may always have felt this way about herself since the termination and may condemn herself for most things, not only the termination. The 'three-systems' (threat, drive, and soothing) model in CFT (Gilbert, 2010) offers a means of helping Jessie to make sense of why this may be the case. Jessie reported emotional memories of parents who were sometimes critical and withheld affection; while there were no memories of maltreatment, there was an absence of feelings of warmth and safeness in her early life, which contributed to a lack of feelings of soothing and safeness now. She had also internalized the critical messages from her parents and developed a tendency for self-criticism as a way of relating to herself from a young age, prior to the termination. This may help to make sense of why she struggled to engage in the imagery rescripting as she struggled to access a non-judgemental and caring stance towards herself, even from the perspective of another.

4.4.9 **Making sense of feelings of shame and their role in self-criticism**

Gilbert and Irons (2005) describe self-criticism as 'a form of self-to-self relationship where one part of self finds fault with, accuses, condemns or even hates the self' (page 265). Jessie's parents' reaction to her pregnancy was experienced as disapproving and rejecting by Jessie, and promoted a sense of reflected shame, which refers to the shame that one can cause others and the shame that others can bring to oneself (Gilbert, 2002). In Jessie's case, her failure to live up to her parents' expectations by being sexually active at 14 years of age and becoming pregnant was a violation of the values with which she had been raised. Bringing this shame on her parents evoked feelings of shame in herself (her perception of how she was now seen in their eyes) and guilt (feelings of remorse for having been the cause of distress and shame to her parents). Jessie's parents communicated their shame implicitly in their reluctance to discuss the pregnancy, their unilateral decision for Jessie to have a termination, and the implied message that her pregnancy and termination be kept secret. With respect to power, Jessie was in a subordinate position to her parents and was motivated to appease her parents by submitting to their wishes for fear of their rejection (withdrawal of their love and approval).

Jessie's experience of internal shame for 'destroying my baby' predisposed her to a self-critical pattern of relating to herself, which in turn primed her to be self-condemning for this 'transgression' in her adult life. Thus Jessie developed a vulnerability to self-blame, which was activated when she struggled to get pregnant 20 years later, leading her to blame herself rather than to make external attributions as other women may when struggling to conceive. Despite becoming pregnant, Jessie's self-condemning view of herself as undeserving of being a mum made it difficult to 'feel safe' with the idea that she would get to be a mother after all, triggering her obsessional fears of something happening to take her baby away. Her shame and self-condemnation for the termination in her teens led to her fear that God would punish her by taking her baby away, triggering intrusions about the many ways this could happen.

Jessie was motivated to appease God by engaging in strategies intended to reduce God's anger towards her, to avoid punishment or abandonment by God, and to invoke sympathy and forgiveness from God. These strategies were manifested in her obsessional rituals of praying to God for forgiveness for the termination. Social rank theory, as mentioned in Section 4.4.3, can help us to make sense of Jessie's praying as a 'safety strategy'. The issue of power is important in this context, as Jessie is in a relatively powerless relationship with God, who is perceived as all-powerful. Therefore, feeling that she has angered God is likely to elicit a much stronger appeasing response than would be elicited by others perceived as having less power over her. This can help us to make sense of her prayer rituals as damage limitation strategies aimed at making reparation for the termination and avoiding rejection; indeed, it may feel threatening for Jessie to behave in a non-submissive way, as this could lead to punishment by God if she is perceived to be without remorse.

In working with self-criticism, it is important to help the person gain insight into their 'inner critic' and to identify the functions of their inner critic (see Gilbert and Irons (2005) for illustrations of how to engage in this process). Engaging in chair work with Jessie revealed that her critic was motivated to ensure that Jessie had 'learned from her mistake' as a teenager. Her inner critic felt it was necessary to suffer and to show this suffering (initially to her parents, then later to God) to prove that her suffering was punishment in itself and that she had, in effect, 'paid for her mistake'. Jessie's critic argued that she was protecting Jessie from further rejection (in the form of withdrawal of love) by her parents and later, punishment by God (taking away Jessie's opportunity to be a mother). Jessie's self-criticism functioned as an act of redemption.

Chair work can help a person to gain insight into the impact of his or her self-criticism by offering a powerful emotional experience of what experiencing self-criticism is like. Moving between the role of the 'experiencing self' (i.e. being on the receiving end of self-criticism) and the 'critic' (the part of the self that is critical) can help the person to gain insight into the impact of self-criticism on himself or herself; for example, the powerlessness (s)he may feel and, crucially, the person's critic's rationale for maintaining this stance, which can reveal the function of the critic. Although the critic may be experienced as quite a powerful and dominant force, this exercise can also reveal a vulnerable part of the self that is relying on criticism to protect the self in some way. Engaging in chair work can support a dialogue that enables us to give voice to the vulnerability behind the angry/dominant critic and also to allow the experiencing self an opportunity to appeal to their critic by highlighting how the [self-]criticism is not helping, despite the critic's best intentions. One of Jessie's fears was that letting go of her inner critic was equivalent to letting herself off the hook and that, if she forgave herself, she may anger God even further, risking greater wrath and ultimately the punishment of having her baby taken away by God. This can help us to understand why it feels so risky for Jessie to give up her self-criticism.

Engaging in this process can help the person to recognize that it is understandable why (s)he has relied on his or her critic for such a long time, while supporting the person to recognize his or her self-condemnation as an understandable attempt to protect himself or herself that has led to unintended consequences. For example, ensuring that she never let herself 'off the hook' maintained Jessie's self-blame and feelings of shame. It is important for the therapist to be mindful of how (s)he reflects on these safety strategies and their unintended consequences, to avoid inadvertently activating further shame about Jessie's understandable yet misguided attempts to protect herself. This paves the way for Socratic dialogue to help the person explore how helpful his or her inner critic really is and to consider what kind of inner guide would be more helpful. Eliciting the qualities the person would like in such a guide can lay the foundations for compassionate mind training. Jessie identified that she needed a guide that was understanding and non-judgemental. This led to a discussion of 'compassion' and the qualities and attributes that may be associated with a 'compassionate other'.

4.4.10 Compassion-focused therapy/compassionate mind training

The definition of compassion in CFT is two-pronged: (1) having a sensitivity to the suffering of self and others; (2) with a deep commitment to try to relieve that suffering. Gilbert (2010) identifies key attributes of a compassionate mind: a motivation to care for wellbeing of self/others; sensitivity to own/others' distress; sympathy, which relates to being moved and emotionally in tune with own/others' feelings; distress tolerance, which refers to the capacity to tolerate rather than avoid distressing experiences; empathy, which enables us to understand our own/others' feelings; and non-judgement, with respect to developing an accepting rather than a condemning stance towards self/others. Related to these attributes are qualities that are also considered key in relating to oneself or others with compassion. These qualities include: wisdom, gained from life experience, to understand that we all find ourselves here, with experiences that we did not choose and a 'tricky (threat-focussed) brain' that influences how we feel and respond in difficult situations; strength, which involves having courage in the face of adversity to face our difficulties despite the urge to avoid them; warmth, which stimulates feelings of soothing, connectedness, and safeness; and a non-judgemental stance towards self/others, where the primary motivation is to understand and help.

Given that Jessie's self-criticism is keeping her stuck, this may indicate an intervention focussed on helping her to develop a compassionate mentality as an alternative way of relating to herself. Helping Jessie to develop her capacity for self-compassion would lay the foundations for her to undermine the well rehearsed pattern of self-criticism that has developed since her teens. This is likely to be more lengthy work, but is integral in supporting Jessie to overcome her OCD; supporting Jessie to adopt a compassionate (rather than self-critical) way of relating to herself is key to undermining the shame and self-attacking that are central in maintaining her OCD. It is important to discuss your rationale for engaging in this work, with both the individual with OCD and supervisor, and to receive appropriate supervision.

The aim of 'compassionate mind training' is to stimulate and strengthen alternative 'pathways' for relating to self (and others) in relation to three flows of compassion (other-to-self, self-to-other, and self-to-self), so that compassionate mind training develops the person's capacity to receive compassion from others, to offer compassion to others, and to cultivate self-compassion. Engaging in this process can essentially tone down self-condemning patterns, while stimulating self-caring patterns of relating to oneself (Gilbert and Irons, 2005).

- Jessie may benefit from practising some compassionate imagery exercises, aimed at developing her capacity for the three flows of compassion. For the highly critical person, this is likely to be a slower process, requiring careful pacing. See the work of Gilbert and colleagues (Gilbert, 2010; Gilbert and

Irons, 2005) for a fuller account of CFT. There are also some excellent self-help resources that Jessie could use to engage in this work independently or to support compassion-focussed work undertaken in therapy (Welford, 2012). An important aspect of this work is the use of imagery to develop a sense of an ideal compassionate other (other-to-self flow), which is essentially a fantasy figure that represents someone with whom the person can feel completely safe and unconditionally accepted (Lee, 2005). A key aspect of this work is to invoke key qualities of a compassionate other; for example, a commitment to care for her and motivation to free Jessie from her suffering, the strength to support Jessie in facing her difficulties despite her fears and distress, and the wisdom to understand how Jessie has come to find herself with the difficulties with which she is struggling. This is part of the process in our ultimate aim of supporting Jessie to develop her 'compassionate self' (self-to-self flow).

◆ Jessie can be encouraged to practise this imagery, initially when not distressed. Over time, she can be encouraged to bring her ideal compassionate other or compassionate self to mind at times of distress. When sufficiently developed, the ideal compassionate other and compassionate self can be drawn upon to offer a non-condemning response to oneself. This can help with various aspects of the intervention; for example, the ideal compassionate other can be drawn upon during imagery rescripting to offer Jessie the compassionate response she needed in childhood and to allow herself to experience receiving this during the imagery rescripting exercise. Similarly, Jessie can be encouraged to draw on her compassionate self to support her to engage in behavioural experiments; for example, disengaging from her prayer rituals.

◆ Jessie could be encouraged to write a 'compassionate letter' to herself. The focus of the letter could be to write to her 14-year-old self or her current self about her experience of having a termination, focussing on how it felt at the time and making sense of why this contributed to her current difficulties in relation to feelings of shame and the belief that she deserved to be punished. Encouraging Jessie to practise her compassionate imagery before writing this letter will support her to adopt a compassionate mindset (a sense of acceptance, wisdom, and non-judgemental understanding) while writing the letter. Jessie could also be encouraged to give herself advice on how to respond to her obsessional doubts. A compassionate letter can provide a nice alternative to a more traditional 'therapy blueprint' as it offers a new perspective that resonates at an emotional (versus purely intellectual) level.

4.4.11 **Compassionate letter writing**

An example of a compassionate letter that Jessie may have written to herself follows.

Dear Jessie

I'm so sorry that you have been having such a tough time. You've felt tormented these last few years struggling to get pregnant. The cycles of IVF have taken their toll and there were times when you felt this was never going to happen ... and then it did ... you became pregnant! What should have been a joyful time became a nightmare. You were convinced that something was going to happen to ruin things for you—that your baby would be taken away in some way. Other people just didn't understand—they assumed that you were anxious about things going wrong because it had been an uphill struggle to get pregnant with the IVF. They had no idea. But I understand why you became so terrified that your baby would be taken away.

It all started with the pregnancy when you were 14. It was hushed up and dealt with so quickly that nobody but mum and dad knew about it to this day—not even your best friend. You felt so ashamed. Mum and dad could barely look at you. They arranged a termination without even discussing it with you—you felt like you had made such a mistake and brought shame on them. You were so desperate to talk to someone, but you felt too ashamed to tell anyone, not even Sally. Even though you're still best friends with Sally, she has no idea about that pregnancy and what you went through. Mum and dad have never talked about it with you—it's been like a shameful family secret that's been buried.

I feel so sad for how alone you felt back then and how you have carried this with you all these years. The shame you felt has stopped you from ever telling anyone about the termination. You spent years terrified that God was angry with you and often worried that God would punish you by stopping you from having a baby. No wonder then, when you struggled to get pregnant, it felt like God was punishing you for destroying your first baby. You became convinced that he would never allow you to become a mother—that this was his punishment for the termination.

When you became pregnant, you were so relieved and felt that maybe God had punished you enough by making it so difficult to get pregnant but that he wasn't so angry that he would deny you becoming a mum. For a brief moment you felt that God had forgiven you and you prayed to thank him for this second chance and to tell him how you would be the best mum you could be to prove that you were worth his forgiveness. That's when the OCD kicked in. You were bombarded with thoughts of how your baby would come to harm in some way. Even though the therapist told you how common this was in OCD, it didn't feel like OCD. This felt different. It felt like God was having the last laugh—tormenting you by allowing you to get pregnant after such a long struggle, only to be waiting in the wings to snatch your baby away when you least expected. It felt like you were waiting for the inevitable and that it would all be your own fault.

Jessie—I want you to know that it's understandable that you're petrified. These experiences shaped your threat system. Feeling judged by mum and dad primed you to fear that everyone else, including God, would condemn you if they knew about the termination. Never talking to anyone about this made it feel more and more like a 'dirty secret' that needed to be hidden. It made sense then that when you became pregnant these fears came back to haunt you. I want you to know that you were just a child back then and that I want you to stop beating yourself up about the termination. Of course, mum and dad were shocked and even disappointed about your pregnancy at 14, but they wouldn't want you to be in such torment now. Perhaps they felt that never talking about it was the best thing for you. This was a mistake on their part and I wonder what they would think if they knew how tormented you've been.

I want you to know that these thoughts of your baby coming to harm are not a sign of what is going to happen, but they are OCD thoughts, primed by your threat system that has made you so sensitive to being judged and punished. We all have a tricky brain that can make us oversensitive to threats. That's why you have been bombarded by these thoughts that have convinced you that the ultimate punishment is around the corner. Praying to God for forgiveness keeps you locked in this state of threat. I understand that you feel you need to convince him of how sorry you are, but I want to help you understand that there is no punishment waiting for you and that you can continue to pray to God like you used to, but that you don't need to use prayer as a means of apologizing to prove how sorry you are.

I'm so sorry that you have been having such a tough time and I want you to know that I am here for you no matter what. I wish I could have been there for you back then so that you didn't feel so alone. I know that all you needed was someone to give you a big hug and tell you that everything was going to be okay, to tell you that God wasn't angry with you but understands how hard it was for you. It's not your fault that you couldn't keep your baby. You were only a child yourself and you weren't given a choice. If you had been able to understand this back then, you could have been spared years of anguish.

I know this feeling of being alone has returned over the last few years while you've been struggling to get pregnant. Going through the IVF and the rollercoaster of hope and disappointment has been so gruelling. In your darkest hours it felt like God was punishing you for destroying your first baby. I want you to know that it wasn't your fault that you struggled to get pregnant, that God wasn't angry with you and isn't punishing you. I want to remind you that the intrusive thoughts about your baby coming to harm is part of your OCD—it's not a sign that God is going to take your baby away. It's understandable that, after the struggle you've been through, it's hard to feel safe about being pregnant and to believe that you will get to be a mum after all. Lots of mums worry about things going wrong and it's natural, especially when it means so much to you.

I want you to feel safe enough to enjoy your pregnancy and to see it as a blessing. God doesn't want to punish you. He loves you and your baby and he wants you to enjoy this pregnancy without fear. He wants you to enjoy your baby when he or she arrives and to be able to do things without being restricted by the fear of something harming your baby.

When you're struggling, I want you to know that none of these things are your fault. You have suffered so much already and I want you to treat yourself kindly. You now have the wisdom that it was impossible to have as a 14-year-old, the wisdom that can help you to understand how you came to get caught up in feeling ashamed about the termination and feeling guilty towards your first baby. Draw on your wisdom to let go of feeling ashamed. Draw on your strength to guide you when you get a pang of shame or fear, so that you don't get caught in the cycles of doubt and praying for forgiveness. If you're struggling or feeling alone, remember to bring your compassionate self to mind—I will be there for you and guide you. I can give you the courage to talk about the pregnancy and termination with Sally or mum, if you would like to. Not talking about it when that is what you really needed added to the unnecessary feelings of shame. You may not feel the need to talk about it with either of them, but if you would like to, I'll be there with you.

With love and hugs, your compassionate self xxx

After writing her compassionate letter, Jessie talks to her mother about her memories of the termination and how she felt at the time. The de-shaming process in therapy reduces Jessie's urge to hide/deny this part of herself and gives her the courage to have the conversation with her mother that she has always craved.

4.4.11.1 A note on compassionate letter-writing

Emphasize the importance of handwriting the letter as this is more conducive to thoughts and feelings flowing unencumbered by the multitasking required when using a keyboard to type. People who are used to word processing and rarely write by hand may be reluctant, but encourage them to try this. Also encourage the person to approach the task as a 'first draft' that does not need to be 'right' or 'perfect'. It is fine to scribble out and insert words and to rewrite the version with which (s)he is happy.

Set this as a homework task and review the letter at the following session. Encourage the person first to spend a few minutes bringing his or her compassionate image to mind. This helps to engage the person in a compassionate mindset, which will be more responsive to accepting the contents of the compassionate letter. Once (s)he confirms (s)he has a strong sense of his or her compassionate image, ask the person to read the compassionate letter aloud to himself or herself in the session. This will give you an opportunity not only to review the content and tone of the letter (be on the lookout for a critical tone or an absence of warmth) but also to see how (s)he relates to the content of the letter. Notice how the person reads back the letter, paying particular attention to voice tone and looking out for shifts in affect. Emotional resonance will be indicated by noticeable shifts in affect while reading. If there is an absence of emotional resonance, it is important to explore this together. This may be related to the content of the letter and it may take the person a few attempts at redrafting their letter to arrive at content that 'hits the spot'. Alternatively, an absence of emotional resonance could be related to the way the person is engaging with the letter (e.g. not connecting with the meaning while reading). If the person reads the letter in a hurried way or in an emotionally detached way (rather like a newsreader), prompt him or her to pause, to slow the pace at which (s)he is reading, and to connect truly with the *meaning* of the words. The person may need more time to engage in compassionate imagery practice in the session before reading out the letter. It may be worth exploring whether (s)he is avoiding the emotions evoked by the letter. From experience, the level of emotion raised by reading the letter aloud can take the person by surprise, and (s)he may feel reluctant to continue if (s)he feels overwhelmed by the strength of emotion or may feel too exposed to experience such emotion in the therapist's presence. Providing a safe therapeutic environment and acknowledging these obstacles can help the person to overcome these difficulties.

While it can be tempting to ask the person to write a compassionate letter as an intervention in its own right aimed at addressing shame and self-criticism, this is likely to be of limited benefit without having engaged in the necessary groundwork to develop the person's capacity for self-compassion. After all, a compassionate letter can only be written once we have this capacity, being faced with the task of writing such a letter will understandably be daunting and difficult for the person who continues to feel ashamed or continues to relate to himself or herself in a critical way. Therefore it is important to engage the person in appropriate compassionate mind training before engaging him or her in compassionate letter writing. Indeed, when used as an intervention on its own in a piecemeal way, without being grounded in work aimed at cultivating greater self-compassion, the process could be experienced as ineffective and demoralizing.

4.4.12 Integrating a compassion-focussed approach with CBT for OCD

Taking time to engage Jessie in cultivating a compassionate mindset helped her to feel safe enough to believe the alternative appraisals she had previously generated in relation to her termination (see updated theory B, in Table 4.5), enabling her to shift away from the self-condemning attitude that maintained feelings of shame. Through this process Jessie was able to reappraise the circumstances around her termination to develop a compassionate reappraisal of the situation that undermined the self-condemning stance she had held for so long. This process of being able to let go of feelings of shame was instrumental in being able to give herself permission to practise the alternative (theory B) responses to her obsessional doubts that she had previously struggled to apply.

This section addresses the blocks in CBT for OCD that can be created by shame and self-criticism and how you may approach these difficulties when they play an important role in maintaining the person's obsessional difficulties. Your approach will vary depending on the nature and degree of these difficulties. Sometimes this may require more emphasis on particular aspects of a CBT approach; for example, normalizing and psychoeducation. At other times, you may identify a need to focus on a specific intervention to target difficulties with shame and self-criticism; rather than considering this a suspension or diversion in your work on the OCD, this may indeed be central to working on the person's obsessional problem. Interventions using imagery, whether this is to help the person to arrive at a more balanced, less self-condemning, appraisal of a past event or whether this is to help the person develop skills in adopting a more compassionate stance towards himself or herself in general, offer a useful therapy tool at times when we may otherwise feel stuck. In all cases it is important to remember not to 'throw the baby out with the bath water'. As always, your treatment should be formulation-driven and there needs to be a clear rationale for any intervention. Taking your case to supervision regularly will be essential in supporting this work.

For some individuals, it may be necessary to address directly feelings of shame that may be underpinning their obsessional problem. This may be particularly important when working with an individual who has had several courses of treatment that were considered good quality and in keeping with an evidence-based approach. Such a person may come to feel hopeless about their prospects of overcoming their difficulties, which could easily perpetuate beliefs about being beyond help. It is always worth offering the individual a further course of treatment, irrespective of the number of previous treatments; each new course of treatment offers the promise of a new therapist identifying a different focus for intervention that may be key to undermining the person's obsessional difficulties.

4.5 **Flexibility in applying CBT for OCD**

This section covers an emerging literature on various modes of delivery of CBT for OCD.

4.5.1 **Intensive delivery of CBT**

Traditionally, CBT has been delivered in approximately 1-hour long weekly sessions for reasons of general historical precedent and convenience (e.g. Beck, 1995).

However, there has been increasing recognition that this 'one size fits all' approach to treatment delivery may mean that additional difficulties in access-ing treatment are caused for certain groups of people; for example, those in full time work, those living remotely from the treatment centre, or those with small children. In addition, faster delivery of treatment is likely to be helpful where there are impending deadlines, such as a tribunal at work or pregnancy. Time-intensive CBT has been found to be effective in other anxiety disorders (social phobia, PTSD, panic; Deacon and Abramowitz, 2006; Ehlers *et al.*, 2014; Mortberg *et al.*, 2007).

Early behavioural therapy was delivered on a more intensive basis (e.g. Thornicroft *et al.*, 1991). In keeping with this precedent, more intensive for-mats have been examined to find out if comparable outcomes can be achieved in a shorter time with more intensive delivery. Equivalence of outcome has been found between intensive daily delivery and twice-weekly (Abramowitz *et al.*, 2003) or weekly sessions (Storch *et al.*, 2008). However, at follow-up, there was increased relapse for those in the intensive treatment group. In the UK, comparable results were found between weekly and intensively delivered treat-ment (consisting of 12 therapy hours in a 2-week period) using the techniques described in this book (Oldfield *et al.*, 2011). Intensive CBT in this format has also been used to good effect with postnatal women with OCD (Challacombe and Salkovskis, 2011). A comparison of a 2-week intensive programme against a 12-week programme in a residential setting found similar outcomes at dis-charge for the intensive option (Veale *et al.*, 2015a).

Although clinical results are promising, there have not as yet been any randomized trials comparing intensive treatment with other formats, not least because of the numbers needed for such studies.

A qualitative study examining the experience of treatment found intensively delivered CBT to be acceptable to participants, and was perceived as having the benefit of quickly getting momentum going (Bevan *et al.*, 2010). It is likely that, for some people, the weekly format is preferable as they feel it gives them time to reflect and put things into practice. For others prone to procrastination, avoidance, or rumination this can be more problematic. The choice of format is likely to be a decision based on a number of practical and perceived considerations. A particular issue for intensive delivery may be having ongoing support over a longer period of time in the form of follow-up sessions.

Home-based delivery of CBT has been shown to be as effective as office-based (Rowa *et al.*, 2007). These findings suggest that traditional delivery of therapy could be tailored to meet the needs of particular groups without loss of effectiveness.

A suggested format for intensive treatment:

Day 1: Two hours

> Formulation, theory A/B, goals
>
> Homework to include listening to recording of session

Day 2: Three hours

> Choosing to change; behavioural experiments, including modelling by therapist
>
> Homework to include self-directed behavioural experiments

Day 3: Two hours

> Further behavioural experiments; trouble-shooting avoidance or reluctance
>
> Homework to include more anti-OCD behavioural experiments and a focus on medium-term goals.

Two to four days later:

Day 4: Two hours

> Review of progress; therapy blueprint
>
> The remaining sessions could either be taken as another long session to consolidate gains or as more spaced out sessions to help with staying on track.

4.5.2 **Internet-guided CBT for OCD**

Given the difficulties for some clients in accessing CBT owing to geographical or OCD related limitations, increasing attention has turned to other ways to maximize the delivery of CBT approaches. Although many self-help books exist, there have not yet been any trials of bibliotherapy; research indicates that some therapist support is needed for effectiveness (Mataix-Cols and Marks, 2006). Reading self-help material alongside therapy is likely to be of help, and therapists commonly recommend specific reading as part of homework.

The advent of the internet has meant that CBT sessions can be delivered online. Webcam/video contact can allow for the exchange of visual information such as charts and diagrams, as well as real-time in-session behavioural experiments (Goetter et al., 2013). There is an increasing body of evidence that internet-guided CBT achieves comparable results to face-to-face CBT (Dettore et al., 2015; Mahoney et al., 2014; Pozza et al., 2014).

Computerized CBT has the potential to widen access to the principles of CBT for OCD, although it is not yet as effective as face-to-face therapy (Tumur et al., 2007).

4.5.3 **Group CBT for OCD**

The Improving Access to Psychological Therapies (IAPT) programme in the UK has enabled many more people to access psychological treatment than in previous years. As greater emphasis is placed on parity of esteem for mental health (Department of Health, 2014), services are placed under greater pressure to demonstrate ease of access and reduced waiting times. One of the ways in which some services have responded to this challenge is to offer group treatments. At the time of writing, NICE (National Institute for Health and Clinical Excellence, CG31, 2005) guidelines recommend group CBT, which includes ERP as a low-intensity treatment for those with mild symptoms of OCD.

This section will not address the more general considerations in running a group, as these are covered comprehensively elsewhere (e.g. Bieling et al., 2006; Morrison, 2001; Ryder, 2010). The focus will be to consider how to optimize a group CBT programme for OCD that goes beyond a focus on ERP, but also integrates aspects of the approach described in Chapter 3, to deliver a truly cognitive-behavioural approach.

With specific reference to group CBT for OCD, the benefits offered by group rather than individual therapy include:

Normalizing is supported through cultivating a sense of common humanity among group members—'I'm not alone', 'we are all in this together'

Scope for vicarious learning by group members through identifying with others' experiences

Group members can provide moral support for engaging in difficult tasks

Can use the group's creativity in planning behavioural experiments for one another

The drawbacks of group treatment compared to individual treatment may include limited scope to tailor the treatment to individuals.

To minimize this we suggest replacing one of the group sessions (session 4) with a series of brief individual sessions. For example, a 2-hour group session run by two facilitators could accommodate 8 × ½-hour sessions. This enables the therapist to review the person's understanding of the model as applied to himself or herself by reviewing the person's vicious flower and theory A/B, supporting them to develop this further if necessary.

The group dynamic may inhibit the person's progress. It is important to notice changes in affect among individual participants, particularly in relation to interactions with other group members, so that you can respond appropriately to minimize any disengagement by group members.

4.5.3.1 Suggested group CBT programme for OCD

Key features to include in group CBT for OCD:

Socializing participants to a cognitive model of OCD by developing a 'vicious flower' for selected group members. (The selection is based on identifying those who are happy to undergo this process during a group session and doing so for a range of difficulties that reflect most group members' experiences, while ensuring that individuals with an unusual presentation are also offered this opportunity to illustrate that the model still applies)

For each of the examples, identifying the key meanings maintaining the person's OCD (theory A) and developing an alternative perspective (theory B)

Having scope to check out each individual's vicious flower and theory A/ theory B individually, so that no individual participant gets left behind

Present the rationale for treatment: putting theory B to the test

In-session practice of planning, engaging in, and reviewing behavioural experiments

Encouraging group members to identify relevant experiments for one another and to support each other within the group.

Learning objectives for a CBT group programme:

Intrusive thoughts/images/urges/impulses are a normal human experience

Having the intrusive experience is *not* the problem

Trying to stop having intrusions is an impossible and unnecessary goal

Shift in perspective: being able to shrug the intrusions off as insignificant is the desired response to intrusions

Compulsions/SSBs are an understandable response to intrusions given the meaning attached to these experiences

Understanding OCD as a problem of anxiety/worry rather than of danger

Compulsions maintain anxiety in the long run and keep the OCD going

Role of behavioural experiments that test predictions about bad things happening to overcoming OCD.

4.5.3.2 Suggested session plan

Each session will have an agenda and follow a similar structure to a typical CBT session:

Agenda

Review homework (except session 1)

Recap of main points from previous session.

Main topic for this session (refer to Table 4.6):

Summarize key learning points

Plan homework (includes obsessive-compulsive inventory (OCI) and mood measures each session).

Table 4.6 Group programme: session by session

Session	Main topic
1	Introductions
	Group rules
	What is OCD? Psychoeducation and normalizing around intrusions
	Socialize to basic CBT model (appraisal is key in emotional and behavioural response)
	Considering the costs of OCD and how to start reclaiming your life Recommend self-help book: *Break Free from OCD*
	Homework: goals (three timeframes, i.e. short, medium, long)

(continued)

Table 4.6 Continued

Session	Main topic
2	Introduce vicious flower using case vignettes
	Review examples from the group (willing participants)
	Different types of maintenance factors (rituals, reassurance-seeking, selective attention, avoidance)
	Homework: draw out own examples of vicious flower
3	Develop theory A/theory B for each example from previous week (or new examples if other participants are willing to share)
	Introduce rationale for therapy: testing out theory B
	In-session thought suppression experiment (polar bear, pink elephant) to illustrate paradoxical effects of thought suppression
	Homework: develop own theory A/theory B sheet
4	The group is replaced by a brief individual session (30 minutes) for each participant, in which they get to meet with one of the group facilitators to review their own vicious flowers and theory A/theory B—this is an important opportunity to identify anyone who is struggling and to support them with this process before the next group session
5	Psychoeducation: three anxiety curves
	Introduce in-session experiments that include ERP
	Socialize participants in process of planning behavioural experiments, ensuring that each participant has planned one experiment
	Homework: planned behavioural experiment
6	Introduce metaphors: OCD as a bully; coach A/coach B (compassionate versus critical coach)
	Homework: defying the bully (more behavioural experiments) and practising self-encouragement (versus bullying self)
7	Midpoint: review therapy goals
	In-session ERP-based experiments
	Planning behavioural experiments for each other
	Troubleshooting obstacles
	Advice for friends and families
	Homework: experiments that were set in session and planning own experiments
8	Introduce three choices (OCD, non-OCD, and anti-OCD)
	Identify anti-OCD experiments for each group member
	Homework: planned anti-OCD experiments
9	Reclaiming your life
	Homework: identify additional goals related to reclaiming your life

Table 4.6 Continued

Session	Main topic
10	Becoming your own therapist: introduce therapy blueprint
	Homework: begin drafting therapy blueprint
11	Review session:
	Review progress with therapy goals
	Review therapy blueprints and continue working on them
	Develop a 'group blueprint' together that can complement the individual therapy blueprints
	Homework: identify post-therapy goals; complete therapy blueprint
12	End of therapy progress review
	Planning for the future
	Any items from previous session the group wish to recap
	Go round group with each member identifying advice for each other
	Goodbyes
	Information re further support (contact details for support groups and charities, e.g. OCD-UK, OCD-Action, Maternal OCD)
Follow-up (1 month after final session)	Review progress, identifying any setback experiences
	Encourage group members to identify solutions/guidance for one another
	Identify anyone who may be struggling and may benefit from an individual follow-up/referral for further individual CBT for OCD or other comorbid problem

Recommending a self-help book that can be read alongside the group session (e.g. *Break Free from OCD*; Challacombe *et al.*, 2011) will help to support the learning that takes place in the group.

4.6 Involving family and friends in CBT for OCD

4.6.1 What is the impact on family members

OCD can affect the lives of family members; Magliano *et al.* (1996) found moderate to severe levels of burden in family members, which were similar and in most domains greater than in relatives of people with severe depression (major depressive disorder; MDD). Both groups endorsed feeling they had 'given up on living life as they wanted' (58% OCD versus 57% MDD), having 'health problems as a result of the situation' (59% OCD versus 57% MDD) and 'being at the relative's beck and call' (62% OCD versus 46% MDD). Both groups perceived a significant burden on social relationships, with 74% (versus 61% MDD) feeling that social relationships were compromised, with 59% (versus

48% MDD) saying this was entirely caused by their relative's problem. Relatives of people with OCD differed from those related to people with depression in their own feelings of depression (84% recording such feelings, against 61% in the depression group) and 'nervous tension' (75% in the OCD group versus 50% in the depression group). Taking a clinical threshold, higher rates of MDD but not other disorders were also found in family members of people with OCD compared with non-clinical controls (Cicek *et al.*, 2013).

Sadly the damage caused by a prolonged period of OCD may not be fully reversible and can continue to reverberate, such as the impact from divorce or separation (Goodwin *et al.*, 2002; Subramaniam *et al.*, 2012) or consequences of the decision not to have children because of OCD when biologically able (Neziroglu *et al.*, 1992). Therapy may involve people coming to terms with these losses and ideally will help to reinforce further the motivation not to lose further time and resources on OCD and truly live OCD-free.

4.6.2 **Family 'accommodation' of symptoms**

Because of the nature of the problem, the person with OCD may demand that family members change their behaviour as a result of the person's own fears, to mimic the compulsions and safety behaviours in which they are themselves engrossed. Family accommodation (the term given to the concept of adapting behaviour to the symptoms of the person with OCD) is commonplace in family members, and the degree to which it takes place has been linked to poor family functioning (Albert *et al.*, 2007; Calvocoressi *et al.*, 1995). It seems to be very prevalent: one study found that 96.9% of families accommodated symptoms, with 59% saying it was a daily occurrence (Stewart *et al.*, 2008). The provision of reassurance, participation in rituals, and assisting the person with OCD in avoidance are the most frequent practices (occurring on a daily basis in 47%, 35%, and 43% of family members, respectively) (Albert *et al.*, 2010). Contamination/cleaning is the symptom dimension most associated with family accommodation in these studies.

As well as the impact on others, accommodation of symptoms by family members has been found to predict poorer CBT treatment response in adults and children (Boeding *et al.*, 2013; Ferrao *et al.*, 2006; Waters and Barrett, 2000). Accommodation can have the effect of transferring responsibility for the behaviour and preventing disconfirmation of the obsessional beliefs (Salkovskis, 1991).

Some family members may simultaneously be fulfilling a supportive role in accommodating symptoms, trying to 'help' the person where his or her OCD makes something intolerable, or at best time-consuming. It may be a way of avoiding conflict or managing their own distress at seeing their loved one caught in OCD. An intriguing study found that partner accommodation of obsessional behaviour was associated with less relationship satisfaction in partners but not in people with OCD. However, partner accommodation was also associated with increased perceptions of criticism by the partner regarding the person's OCD (Boeding *et al.*, 2013). In many cases trying to get other people to follow obsessional rules will cause conflict and may cause hostility on both sides. Unfortunately, negative emotional responses from others have been linked to severity of symptoms and also predict worse outcome in therapy (Renshaw *et al.*, 2003; Van Noppen and Steketee, 2009).

4.6.3 Addressing family and relationship issues

The relationship between family accommodation and treatment outcome suggests that it is an important and potentially fruitful target for interventions that could increase treatment effectiveness. In practical terms it can be a very useful exercise to ask people with OCD to consider not only costs to themselves but also costs to others, including partners and children. Although this can sometimes be painful and difficult, it can also help generate goals that have the benefit of helping both the person with OCD and those around them. Questions might include:

> Do you ask others to follow your obsessional rules or perform compulsions?
>
> Do you get irritable with others when they interrupt you during compulsions?
>
> Do you ask others the same questions repeatedly (reassurance)?
>
> Are you often late or change arrangements because of obsessions or compulsions? How does this affect others?
>
> Do you avoid particular activities, places, or people due to compulsions? How does this affect others?
>
> Do you delegate tasks because OCD makes them too difficult for you, or you feel you can't trust yourself?
>
> Do you prevent others from doing things because you feel they can't be trusted to do it properly?
>
> Are others worried about you because of your anxiety?

These questions may be asked at the point of assessment, when discussing theory A/B and the costs of the problem, and/or when the person is starting to test things out and challenge the OCD. It can be useful to engage with the wider impact on others if the person is struggling with changing his or her obsessional behaviour.

Jessie was avoiding thinking about how much the problem was affecting Gus.

THERAPIST: Jessie, can you tell me a bit about how your OCD affects Gus?

JESSIE: Affects him? Well, I suppose we have got so used to it, it's just how things are. I don't think he minds too much as I'm the one that's really bothered by it … but now I think about it, I do get him to do a lot of the housework for me because of my fears. He probably thinks I'm just lazy! I do get very upset if he forgets to take his shoes off and change his clothes right away when he gets home. I know he'd rather not but he does it. Hmm, now I really think about it, we haven't talked about much apart from OCD lately. It's a bit tough to think how it's dragged him down too.

THERAPIST: Do you think it might be important to think about all the costs of this problem on you and Gus?

JESSIE: Yes, OCD has really taken a lot from me, hasn't it?

4.6.4 Working with family and friends

Family and friends (termed partners here for ease of reference) may have strong opinions on how the person should change. Meaningful and lasting change can only come from the person with OCD. However, given that the involvement of partners in OCD can limit treatment gains and the involvement in treatment can enhance them, partner views and accommodation of rituals is an important area to consider. Partners can be involved at any point, and some researchers are developing 'couples' protocols' for CBT (Abramowitz *et al.*, 2013). The following are areas for consideration:

Has the person with OCD discussed what is going on with the person/people with whom (s)he lives? If not, what are the reasons for this? On occasion, people can give other explanations for their behaviour which are plausible but can cause problems in their own right. For example, a woman who could not touch bins made a series of excuses why she had not cleaned up, which led her partner to conclude that she was lazy. In another case, a mother who performed many of her rituals behind a locked bathroom door eventually told her children, who expressed relief as they strongly believed that this behaviour was due to the fact that she had a drug problem! Furthermore, as discussed in Section 4.4, shame can be a huge maintaining factor in OCD as the person can be left alone with thoughts and symptoms with no reality checks.

Does the partner agree with the person's description of the problem? Often people manage to disguise their obsessions and compulsions very well from others. Sometimes, they are less good than they think at doing this, but find it very difficult to acknowledge the true extent of the problem, even to loved ones. People can feel very guilty about the impact of their behaviour on others, even if in the moment they find it hard to act otherwise. It is important to remind them that, before therapy, they had little choice but to act to prevent harm, etc. as they had no 'theory B'.

In some rare and unfortunate instances, the person with OCD is not insightful about the impact of his or her problem on others. In these cases it will be necessary clearly to make the person aware of the risks of his or her behaviour and the implications of continuing to act in an obsessional way. This may include the fact that the OCD is having a negative effect on relationships but may also include safeguarding issues, such as cases where extensive volumes of cleaning products are used on a child's skin, or the person is prevented from having contact with other children. See Section 2.7, Assessing risk, for a fuller consideration of these points.

When involving partners in treatment, part of the initial intervention may be to facilitate a useful discussion that helps a sharing of perspectives. This may involve the therapist or person with OCD explaining the theory A meaning of obsessional behaviour to a partner, and giving the partner a chance to talk about the impact of the behaviour on him or her. Ideally at this point, the person will have a good understanding of theory B and the types of things that need to change. Explaining this to a partner can be a useful way of reinforcing their own understanding and joining forces to think of ways in which they can do things differently. It can help the partner or friend feel involved in supporting his or her loved one.

Lydia brought her husband Mike into a joint session.

THERAPIST: OK, Lydia, we have been talking a lot about your OCD. I thought it might be helpful if you could explain some of our work to Mike, so that we can think together about how you can move on from OCD and the best ways he can support you.

LYDIA: Yes, that's a good idea. I've been doing all my checking and asking you for reassurance as I've been so terrified that something bad will happen if I don't. I get stuck in the moment, focussing on how bad it would be if I caused the flat to burn down. I've felt that I couldn't live with it. What I've learned is that I'm too focussed on danger because I'm so worried. All the things I've been doing to keep safe keep me worried … and part of that is all the things I make you do, including giving me reassurance.

MIKE: OK, that makes sense now. I wish I could help you more but you never believe me when I tell you I've checked something. It drives me mad.

LYDIA: Now I realize that asking you is part of me making the problem worse.

MIKE: So do you think you can trust me more?

LYDIA: I know I have to!

A blanket ban on families and partners giving reassurance is sometimes difficult in practice and it is useful to keep the onus on the person with OCD to stop *asking* for reassurance.

As well as stopping counterproductive and limiting obsessional behaviours, putting positive things in their place is a key part of fighting an obsessional problem. These can include finding more positive ways for a partner to help a person with OCD, e.g. substituting reassurance with encouragement. In more global ways, people can capitalize on the fight against OCD by increasing the range of activities that OCD has prevented them doing—going out for a meal, booking a family holiday. These might also serve as specific behavioural experiments. Having longer term strategies and things outside OCD can be very helpful in getting the person (back) on track. Working out a plan together can facilitate discussion and understanding of the problem and how to tackle it.

Lydia and Mike's fighting OCD plan:

Mike will: try not to reassure and will remind you of theory B if you're stressed

Mike will: remind you of how great it was before OCD got really bad—and how it can be again

Lydia will: try not to ask for reassurance but will ask for cuddles. Will also ask for a cuddle if I forget and do ask for reassurance

Lydia will: definitely not check Mike's checking

Lydia will: come back from work on time. Just leave at 6—tomorrow is another day!

Lydia will: book that holiday we have been talking about for years (and actually get to the airport this time—sorry, Mike)

Both: remember that we are doing our best to fight OCD!

Jessie and Gus worked together on a behavioural experiment, as shown in Table 4.7.

It is helpful for all parties to make time to do enjoyable things, both together and apart, and remember themselves apart from OCD.

If the relationship is very conflictual at the point of therapy, joint sessions may be limited in what they can achieve. In these cases, joint work might be deferred or relationship goals added to the person's medium or longer term goal list. It is likely to be easier to deal with relationship difficulties if they have addressed the OCD that is limiting their life together.

4.7 Continuing to develop as a therapist

This book should act as a detailed guide to how to use CBT with people with all forms of OCD. We will now consider how you may continue to develop your competence and confidence in working with obsessional problems beyond reading and applying the skills learned from this book.

Table 4.7 Behavioural experiment record for challenging contamination concerns and reassurance-seeking

Complete before		Complete after		
Planned experiment	**Specific predictions and how much I believe them**	**What happened? Did the predictions come true?**	**Conclusions? What do you make of this?**	**Does it fit best with theory A or B?**
Cook chicken dish for Gus	I will need reassurance: 70%	I did wash hands before and after preparing the food (down from 20%)	Surprisingly I can manage to reduce reassurance and washing	B—I don't feel as convinced as before. Gus had two helpings as I couldn't eat much and he was still okay. Next time I'll have more
	I will get salmonella poisoning	I got strong urges to ask for reassurance throughout. I cracked at one point and asked—he reminded me it was theory B and it was best to go with it	Cooking chicken was not fatal	
	I will be hospitalized and the baby will die: 100%		I need to do more	
	Gus will be ill: 80%	Felt very anxious		
		We didn't get ill But I found it hard to eat much		

4.7.1 Competencies

Roth and Pilling's (2007) competence framework offers a useful point of reference for reflecting on your skills as a CBT therapist. The competence is organized into five domains:

1. Generic competences, relevant to all psychological therapies.
2. Basic CBT competences.
3. Specific core CBT techniques employed in most forms of CBT.
4. Problem-specific competences.
5. Metacompetences.

The competence framework for CBT has provided a vital anchor for both training novice therapists and for experienced clinicians continuing to develop their skills. The existing OCD competences are based on an ERP model and include 'assessment and treatment planning', 'a capacity to engage the client with the intervention', and 'relapse prevention', which are entirely consistent with Chapters 2 and 3 of this book. Roth and Pilling's (2007) competences go on to detail 'in vivo exposure', 'imaginal exposure', and 'ritual prevention'. We suggest the competencies shown in Box 4.2 for a cognitive behavioural approach.

Box 4.2 'CBT competences' for OCD

◆ A capacity to engage the client with the intervention

◆ An ability to use metaphor to illustrate the nature of OCD

◆ An ability to work with the client to identify the pros and cons of change and staying the same

◆ Establishing a framework and rationale for the components of the intervention

◆ An ability to help the client to understand that intrusive thoughts are normal and common, and that they only become problematic when negatively appraised (normalizing)

◆ An ability collaboratively to develop a maintenance formulation that shows the relationship between intrusions, the appraisal of these intrusions, anxiety, SSBs (compulsions/rituals), avoidance, and attentional processes

◆ An ability collaboratively to develop a credible, alternative, less-threatening belief (theory A/theory B) and to consider the implications of the two competing belief systems

◆ An ability to generate goals aimed at reclaiming life that do not accommodate OCD.

Methods of change: evidence gathering and discovery

◆ An ability collaboratively to develop behavioural experiments that effectively test the client's beliefs about threat and/or build up evidence for the alternative, less-threatening, belief

◆ An ability to execute behavioural experiments, including therapist modelling where appropriate, home visits, field visits

◆ An ability to work with the client to encourage behavioural experiments when alone and in a variety of settings

◆ An ability to challenge beliefs about responsibility, the over-importance of thoughts, perfectionism, and other beliefs using Socratic method, responsibility pie charts, continua, and other techniques

◆ An ability to identify obstacles to change and how to overcome these

◆ An ability to manage complications that may arise, such as subtle SSBs or avoidance.

4.7.2 **Moving from competent adherence to metacompetent adherence**

Throughout this volume we have sought not just to explain theory and demonstrate techniques, but to engender an understanding of the principles behind effective CBT for OCD, and how these must be skilfully applied with each individual with OCD—thus developing metacompetence. Roth and Pilling (2007) developed the metacompetences as a superordinate competences that 'focus on the ability to implement models in a manner that is flexible and tailored to the needs of the individual client' (page 9). The metacompetences represent the fluent translation between the empirically grounded clinical intervention and the specific nature of the concerns of the person with whom you are working— using clinical skill, judgement, and wisdom to adapt the evidence-based techniques to the idiosyncratic needs of the person.

Whittington and Grey (2014), in a chapter on mastering metacompetence, note that, often, metacompetence will lead to a clinician tightly following the usual evidence-based methods rather than following less well tested methods. They define metacompetent adherence as 'making therapy decisions based on evidence that clearly supports the practice and on a sound theroretical rationale where the evidence is less clear' (page 4). A generic metacompetence is the capacity to use clinical judgement when implementing treatment models—this does not mean 'throwing the baby out with the bath water' and abandoning evidence-based treatment. When working with someone with a chronic, baffling, and complicated form of OCD, it is tempting to think that a 'straightforward' CBT approach will not work—we suggest that this is exactly the time to stick to the core elements of treatment.

Roth and Pilling's (2007) metacompetences are listed in Table 4.8, with examples from CBT for OCD as described in previous chapters.

Roth and Pilling (2007), in *The Competences Required to Deliver Effective Cognitive and Behavioural Therapy for People with Depression and with Anxiety Disorders*, suggest that skilful implementation of clinical work rests on an ability to implement 'procedural rules'—using clinical judgment to decide when, how, and whether to carry out a particular action or set of actions to make an intervention or a procedure responsive to the needs of each individual. Whittington and Grey (2014) has devised a 'training target tool' for novice and experienced therapists that includes these procedural rules. We suggest that this is a useful device for developing competence and metacompetence in delivering CBT for OCD. An example is shown in Table 4.9.

In terms of competencies for the treatment described here, we recommend the use of the Revised Cognitive Therapy Scale (CTS-R OC; Forrester *et al.*, in preparation; Appendix 4), which took as its starting point the CTS-R developed

Table 4.8 Roth and Pilling's metacompetences for OCD with examples from a formulation-driven CBT approach

Metacompetences	
Generic metacompetences	**Examples from a formulation driven CBT approach**
Capacity to use clinical judgement when implementing treatment models	e.g. Comorbidity—comorbidity need not be complex. Collaborative formulation will reveal a route through multiple problems
Capacity to adapt interventions in response to client feedback	e.g. If a client is already very insightful, less need for weighing up pros and cons of change; accelerate to behavioural experiments
	e.g. If the onset is very recent—'theory B'/ living without OCD is recallable, less need for building up the competing theories
Capacity to use and respond to humour	There is ample opportunity for humour when working with a person with OCD, e.g. putting one's hands down the toilet is often accompanied with broad grins
CBT-specific metacompetences	**Examples from a formulation-driven CBT approach**
Capacity to implement CBT in a manner consonant with its underlying philosophy	e.g. Overcoming OCD is a collaborative journey that starts with a shared understanding, normalizing, and working together to find ways to overcome the problem
Capacity to formulate and apply CBT models to the individual client	The vicious flower model is endlessly adaptable and can accommodate infinite variations of OCD
Capacity to select and apply the most appropriate behavioural and CBT method	Once the formulation is established, this is the guide through treatment
Capacity to structure sessions and maintain appropriate pacing	e.g. Generally CBT for OCD is delivered as a short-term intervention with active work on the problem from the start
Capacity to manage obstacles to CBT therapy	e.g. Myriad ways that OCD can sneak in and undermine everyone's best efforts; being tuned into new and/or subtle SSBs, including mental rituals/arguments/avoidance

Table 4.9 Training target tool for developing competence and metacompetence in CBT for OCD

Method	Specific activity to support my learning	Specific questions for this activity/ targets for your learning from each activity	Procedural rules identified (from the activities undertaken)
Specific supervised case work: What specific types of cases can you seek out/take on to support your learning?	Take on people with contamination OCD under supervision of Alison, an expert in this field	How collaboratively to formulate when the person has multiple contamination concerns and other forms of OCD	Use different examples in vicious flower formulations to identify the same underlying threat appraisals
Observed practice: How can you be formally observed and receive feedback, e.g. live, audio, video, CTS-R	Ensure Alison listens to part/whole of my recordings	Am I actually getting to the meaning/ appraisal attached to the thoughts?	Ensure the person with OCD understands the importance of the appraisal of the thoughts Persist with a 'downward arrow' approach to identifying the meaning
Observation of practice: How can you observe an expert at work in this area live, or by audio or video, e.g. your supervisor or an expert on commercially available video	Watch a video of Alison's sessions working on contamination concerns	How does Alison generalize learning from one contamination concern, e.g. touching shoes, to another, e.g. touching door handles?	Use Socratic method to facilitate the person with OCD to learn that his or her underlying belief about contamination is the same in all the different physical settings
Self-practice/ self-reflection: What specific SPSR activities might support your learning in this area, e.g applying methods to your own life?	Explore my own reluctance to 'contaminate' myself	What do I believe is going to happen to me if I touch the sole of my shoe and then eat something?	Acknowledge my own disgust/anxiety with the person with OCD and use to strengthen the therapeutic relationship

Table 4.9 Continued

Method	Specific activity to support my learning	Specific questions for this activity/ targets for your learning from each activity	Procedural rules identified (from the activities undertaken)
Training events: What events are available that you could attend that can add to your learning in this area?	Attend a masterclass on OCD by an expert in the field	How do I address the most difficult/ last remaining contamination fears?	Use metaphor, e.g. reinfected wound to highlight the importance of addressing all the concerns
Reading: What books or journal articles are particularly relevant?	Fear of contamination (Rachman, 2006) Treatment of mental contamination (Rachman et al., 2015)	What is the relationship between physical and mental contamination?	Ask questions about an internal feeling of contamination
Other: Any other learning activities that are relevant	Reading web fora run by people with OCD about their experiences of treatment	What do people with OCD value in their experience of CBT?	Actively collaborative with the person with OCD; be honest about my level of experience

by James *et al.* (2001), modified by Elizabeth Forrester and colleagues. Note that, unlike the base CTS-R, not all components can occur in every session so, for some of the more specific treatment strategies, 'not applicable' can be registered. In such instances, these items are pro-rated to obtain a total score if required. There is a comprehensive manual for the rater.

4.8 Supervision and supervising

4.8.1 Making effective use of your own supervision

The following key elements are needed for effective supervision.

4.8.1.1 Preparation for supervision

Preparation for supervision begins with formulating a supervision question related to the person you wish to discuss. Your supervisor may encourage you to do some formal preparation using a supervision record. Formulating a question will not only help you to focus your supervision, but the process of preparation promotes reflection that can facilitate 'internal supervision' that may help you to answer your supervision question.

4.8.1.2 The formulation as a point of reference

Have your formulation with you in supervision and refer to this when introducing your client, describing your intervention to date, and the question you are bringing to supervision.

4.8.1.3 Audio recording/video recording

Seeking your client's consent to record the sessions can support you in your own development as a therapist. Reviewing taped sessions allows opportunities to reflect on progress with a specific client, identifying what is working well and areas that you may benefit from taking to supervision. The process of reviewing a recorded session enables you to notice things that occurred during the session that you may have missed at the time. It also offers an opportunity to reflect on how you may approach a particular scenario differently next time and to reflect on your own practice, including whether any of your own beliefs are interfering in progress. Identify particular sections of the session for 'live supervision', in which you can play excerpts of the therapy session in supervision to give your supervisor a sense of the issue you are bringing to supervision.

4.8.1.4 Seek formal feedback using therapist rating tools

While this is common practice during CBT training, many therapists will not continue to seek such feedback post-qualification. Asking your supervisor to review a recorded session using the CTS-R (Blackburn *et al.*, 2001) can identify areas of strength and areas for further development. The Cognitive Behaviour Therapy Rating Scale for OCD (CTS-OC; Forrester *et al.*, in preparation) was developed as an adaptation of the CTS-R that highlights the skills essential in working with OCD—see Appendix 4.

4.8.1.5 Seek consultative supervision when necessary

If your supervisor is not familiar with OCD or does not have much experience in this area, you may benefit from some consultative supervision with a clinician who has more experience in working with OCD.

4.8.1.6 Joint work

Seek opportunities to engage in joint work with therapists that are more experienced in working with OCD. This offers a powerful means of developing your skills through observing a co-therapist, who can model how (s)he approaches different aspects of therapy and provides scope to be observed (and to receive feedback outside the session).

4.8.2 **Developing as a clinical supervisor**

As we develop as therapists it is common to take on a supervisory role. A skilled therapist does not necessarily make a skilled supervisor, so it is important to develop your skills by seeking supervision training and reading relevant literature. Pilling and Roth's (2008) guidelines on generic supervision competencies and specific CBT supervision competencies can support you in your role as a supervisor. Their framework can support you to identify any skills deficits and consider how you can support your supervisee to address these.

You may be supervising therapists in a service where there may be pressure to offer group supervision. While there are some benefits of group supervision (for example, vicarious learning), it is important that all clinicians have some individual supervision that enables supervisor and supervisee to focus on the individual learning needs of that therapist.

4.8.2.1 Feedback on your supervision/supervision of supervision

Just as we have supervision to support our therapeutic work, it is important to seek supervision of your supervision. This could be with your clinical supervisor or through a supervisors' group. Audio or video taping your supervision sessions will enable you to review your supervision and to seek feedback from your supervisor on excerpts or a whole session. You may seek feedback using supervisor rating scales (e.g. OCTC's Supervisor Competency Scale; OCTC, 2009). You may also use your own professional supervision to support your development as a therapist and a supervisor. This provides a forum for highlighting areas for development and negotiating how this can be supported; for example, through training or access to opportunities such as secondments.

4.8.2.2 Structuring supervision

As a supervisor, you will have an important teaching role in which you will support your supervisees to develop their skills. Structuring your supervision session as you would a CBT therapy session can help to 'model the model':

> Identify goals at the start of your supervisory relationship and review these goals regularly
>
> Agree an agenda
>
> Follow up actions agreed at previous supervision and seek a brief update on clients discussed at last supervision session
>
> Use Socratic questioning rather than didactic teaching
>
> Offer feedback that is specific and makes reference to examples
>
> Agree 'homework' and review this at the next supervision session

Elicit key learning points at the end of each supervision session and seek feedback on what was helpful and what was less helpful.

'Live' supervision provides a valuable means of offering feedback, as does joint work with your supervisee in an area that (s)he has identified for development. Modelling and role play within your supervision to demonstrate how an issue may be approached offer a useful means of addressing the 'how to' questions that can arise in supervision. You can also support your supervisee to develop their knowledge and skills outside of the supervision session by signposting him or her to relevant literature and opportunities for further skill development. Throughout this book we have provided examples of typical supervision questions and suggestions on how to address them.

4.9 **Conclusion: OCD is an unnecessary problem ...**

In this book we have presented 'state of the art' information for formulation-driven CBT. The loosening up of the key responsibility and threat beliefs that either implicitly or explicitly motivate the pervasive compulsive behaviour is always the crucial component of successful psychological treatment, be that CBT as described here or ERP as applied currently and historically.

People trapped in the hell of suffering and endless and pointless toil, which is what OCD becomes over time, have to decide to resist and to begin to fight back. To do so requires, at the very least, some inkling that their fears are not justified, that they do not need to do the things that they feel compelled to do. They need to take a risk, to make a leap of faith, and to think the unthinkable and do the impossible. For that to happen requires an extraordinary degree of trust in their therapist (or perhaps their self-help book). They have to be able at least to consider it possible that their fears are not justified, that the solution has indeed become the problem, and that confronting their fears without responding has a possibility of not only working in the short term but also of helping them regain the life that they have lost. Put in the terminology of this book, they have to begin to consider the possibility that 'theory B' could be true, even if not phrased in that way. As therapists, we have absolutely no right to say 'Trust me', but we can and should say 'Don't trust me without question; work with me'. A sense of mutual respect and willingness to be flexible is required of both therapist and the individual with OCD.

In summary, for treatment of OCD to be effective, there are several components, all of which are necessary, none of which are sufficient alone. First is forming a good therapeutic relationship; second is the person being empowered to consider that there might be an alternative, less negative, explanation of what is happening to them; third, that (s)he is able to draw on past experience to evaluate this alternative view better; and, finally, for the person to find ways to test it out actively, and in doing so benefit from this new experience in the context of the more flexible thinking that (s)he has begun to apply to his or her OCD.

Where things do not work in treatment (of any kind), this is usually because the therapist has failed to understand the person's experience and offer the right solutions in the right way. There are no hopeless cases, but there are, we fear, ineffective therapists, as well as those therapists who simply do not help as much as they should through lack of understanding and effort. It is clear that in many cases of 'treatment failure', what has previously been offered to those suffering from OCD has not only been substandard but at times pitiful (Stobie et al., 2007). Any worthwhile therapist will first and foremost consider and try to deal with his or her contribution to failing treatment rather than seek to blame the person with whom they are working. By the same token, when treatment goes well, it is crucial that both therapist and the individual with OCD realize and acknowledge that this is due to how the person has used the therapy offered. As therapists, we do not change or 'treat' people; we help them to identify the changes needed and then to try such changes out as part of self-treatment. To even try this requires an initial shift in attitudes and beliefs about OCD, which is then consolidated through the interplay of formulation, discussion, and the acquisition of new experience, usually in the form of behavioural experiments, including but not confined to exposure.

There is another big issue, almost the elephant in the room. We know that there is a gap between people developing OCD to the point of meeting diagnostic criteria. On average, OCD is developed around the age of 20, and diagnosed at 28 (e.g. Stobie et al., 2007). Treatment follows on some years or even decades later, and, as has already been said, can be inadequate, contributing more to a sense of hopelessness than to recovery. Consider both the time involved and the timing: in the period between being 20 and entering one's 30s, key life choices are made, education is gained, jobs are taken, relationships forged. For those with OCD this represents the most colossal loss. It could reasonably be described as 'collateral damage' or 'the human cost of OCD'. Working with severe and chronic OCD the authors have been struck by the fact that much of the work done in helping those with OCD has to focus on helping the person deal with this damage, with the loss sometimes being harder to deal with than the OCD itself. Part of treatment for some involves working with the real sense of grief linked to the lost opportunities in the years or decades over which patients have fought their OCD and it has gradually consumed their lives. That is not to devalue the way that most people with OCD manage to keep going, and the huge bravery required to manage on a daily basis despite their problems. But this should be unnecessary. OCD itself, as already indicated, is entirely and always treatable, but what is offered mostly is too little too late. Why is this?

Firstly, there are the ever-present issues of stigma, shame, and misunderstanding. OCD is widely misunderstood as a 'trivial problem' ('I'm a bit OCD, because I like things to be tidy'). Conversely, some services massively and horribly overreact to OCD, for example in parents, up to and including inappropriately taking children into care (Challacombe and Wroe, 2013). It is not surprising, then, that people are slow in seeking help for OCD. Robinson *et al.* (2016) have carried out an in-depth analysis of the barriers and enablers in seeking help in OCD. For most people with OCD the issues that finally lead to them seeking help and treatment are a sense of crisis, things falling apart, and desperation. This is by turns both sad and a scandal. Also notable is that one of the strongest enablers found was the notion that, when they did seek help, the professionals would be kind and understanding. This idea gave people the courage to seek help, but this expectation was by no means universal. It should be.

So what conclusions can be drawn? We consider that future efforts towards improving the understanding and treatment of OCD should focus on the broad theme of prevention. Prevention can be considered as primary, secondary, and tertiary. The development of such an agenda would, in our view, render chronic OCD a thing of the past; it should reduce the incidence of the problem and result in people who do develop it receiving appropriate help in a timely way.

4.9.1 Prevention in OCD

Primary prevention usually involves population or community interventions delivered in a public health or general education type of context. The aim of primary prevention is to seek to lower the incidence of problems in the general population, to reduce the likelihood that everyone, regardless of risk, has a decreased vulnerability. For OCD, there is a strong case for including an understanding of the psychological mechanisms involved in OCD into information/education packages. This might include education in the prevalence of worry and intrusive thoughts and how safety-seeking/neutralizing, thought suppression, and avoidance are counterproductive. Given the data on delay in seeking help, interventions that normalize and destigmatize in general are likely to be helpful, such as making available the stories of people with personal experience of OCD and its successful treatment. An evaluation of such prevention strategies is long overdue. The role of 'third sector' (specialist anxiety disorder and OCD charities) is likely to be important and may provide a useful focus for empirical work. School-based programmes are also likely to be effective, and mass media, broadcast, and the internet should be part of such efforts.

Secondary prevention involves identifying those at relatively high risk of developing OCD and related problems, but who have not yet developed the problem. Some effort has gone into conceptualizing the role of psychological factors in the origins of OCD (Salkovskis *et al.*, 1999) based on cognitive-behavioural theory and research. As described in Section 1.8, the main candidates are conditional beliefs, particularly concerning responsibility and the closely related concept of importance of thoughts. This in turn can be linked to beliefs absorbed in early years and critical incidents that have sensitized the person both to responsibility beliefs and the tendency to deploy particular safety-seeking strategies. Further work on how to deploy secondary prevention is required, but the main focus of research so far has been on triggering events.

An obvious example is recent work on maternal OCD; childbirth typically is associated with an increase in perceived responsibility and concern about harm (Fairbrother and Abramowitz, 2007). There is considerable evidence that, for some, childbirth can act as a trigger for first episode and worsening in pre-existing OCD (Neziroglu *et al.*, 1992; Russell *et al.*, 2013). In a recent prospective study we found that detectable cognitive variables can identify those at risk as well as those having a history of OCD (Challacombe, 2014), which may offer chances for early intervention and prevention (Timpano *et al.*, 2011). Note also that fathers also appear to be vulnerable to perinatal OCD (Abramowitz *et al.*, 2001).

Other examples of such trigger points need to be investigated, such as young people leaving home for the first time or promotion to a more responsible job. It may be important to consider the extent to which particular vulnerabilities 'mesh' with events, a line of research likely to result in better focussed prevention strategies.

Given that there is some evidence of familial transmission, there may be opportunities in this area as well. Note, however, that the evidence suggests that the children of women with severe OCD do not show any obvious tendency towards OCD themselves (Challacombe and Salkovskis, 2009). However, treatment of mothers with OCD should be prioritized, as there is some evidence of more subtle impacts on maternal bonding and enjoyment of parenting (Challacombe *et al.*, 2016), which appears not to be substantially diminished by treatment (Challacombe *et al.*, 2017).

Tertiary prevention is of course the primary focus of the book; this is about what happens after the problem has developed, and how it can be stopped from progressing. This involves treatment interventions in ways that mitigate the extent of damage done by OCD. The pressing imperative, beyond treating those who have sought help and ensuring that treatment is appropriate, is for early recognition, detection, and presentation. Again, the issue of stigma is central to this, to diminish the fears that so many sufferers experience as a barrier to seeking help (Robinson *et al.*, 2016).

Ensuring that people receive appropriate evidence-based treatment as early as possible is also a priority. Although the use of stepped care, in which lower intensity interventions are offered for less severe/chronic OCD may be indicated, there is potential for harm if they are not effective, leaving the individual with OCD with the impression that treatment has failed. This is not well understood and requires proper investigation. Using low intensity treatment as a kind of filter or stage that has to be passed through before more targeted and higher intensity treatment is offered is inappropriate.

Another key component in tertiary prevention/treatment is the training, skills, and attitudes of those to whom people with OCD turn for help. Robinson found that the expectation of being received kindly if the person went to the GP to discuss OCD was a particularly important enabler. Adherence to evidence-based Clinical Guidelines, such as those produced by NICE (2005), and a willingness to share evidence with people with OCD are important characteristics. Routine outcome monitoring is, in our view, a necessary aspect of treatment, allowing both patient and therapist to identify the extent of change and respond to patterns of non-response or partial response. As described in Section 4.5.1, all therapists, however skilled and experienced, should be able to reflect and should in addition receive supervision, preferably on a 'live' basis.

A better and more comprehensive understanding of OCD in these terms would mean that fewer people would develop the problem and those who did would receive rapid, effective, and kindly offered and delivered treatment. This means that OCD would, more than 50 years after effective psychological treatments were developed and trialled, become an unnecessary problem that no one need suffer for more than a short time.

Recommended reading

Bieling, P., McCabe, R. & Antony, M. (2006). *Cognitive Behavioural Therapy in Groups.* New York: Guildford Press.

Challacombe, F., Bream Oldfield, V. & Salkovskis, P. (2011). *Break Free from OCD.* London: Vermilion.

Egan, S. J., Wade, T. D., Shafran, R., & Antony, M. M. (2014). *Cognitive-behavioral Treatment of Perfectionism.* New York, NY: Guilford Press.

Gilbert, P. (2010). *Compassion Focused Therapy.* London: Routledge.

Morrison, N. (2001). Group cognitive therapy: treatment choice or sub-optimal option? *Behavioural and Cognitive Psychotherapy, 29*, 311–32.

Pilling, S. & Roth, A. (2008). *A Competence Framework for the Supervision of Psychological Therapies.* Available at: http://www.ucl.ac.uk/clinical-psychology/CORE/CBT_Framework.htm (accessed 25 March 2015).

Roth, A. & Pilling, S. (2007). *The Competences Required to Deliver Effective Cognitive and Behavioural Therapy for People with Depression and with Anxiety Disorders.* Available at: http://www.ucl.ac.uk/clinical-psychology/CORE/CBT_Competences/CBT_Competence_List.pdf (accessed 25 March 2015).

Ryder, J. (2010). CBT in groups. In M. Mueller, H. Kennerley, F. McManus, & D. Westbrook (Eds.), *Oxford Guide to Surviving as a CBT Therapist* (p.157–73). Oxford: Oxford University Press.

Whittington, A. & Grey, N. (Eds.) (2014). *How to Become a More Effective CBT Therapist.* Chichester: Wiley Blackwell.

References

Abramowitz, J., Moore, K., Carmin, C., Wiegartz, P., & Purdon, C. (2001). Acute onset of obsessive-compulsive disorder in males following childbirth. *Psychosomatics: Journal of Consultation Liaison Psychiatry, 42*(5), 429–31.

Abramowitz, J. S., Baucom, D. H., Wheaton, M. G., *et al.* (2013). Enhancing exposure and response prevention for OCD: A couple-based approach. *Behavior Modification, 37*(2), 189–210. doi: http://dx.doi.org/10.1177/0145445512444596

Abramowitz, J. S., Foa, E. B., & Franklin, M. E. (2003). Exposure and ritual prevention for obsessive-compulsive disorder: Effects of intensive versus twice-weekly sessions. *Journal of Consulting and Clinical Psychology, 71*(2), 394–8.

Albert, U., Bogetto, F., Maina, G., Saracco, P., Brunatto, C., & Mataix-Cols, D. (2010). Family accommodation in obsessive-compulsive disorder: Relation to symptom dimensions, clinical and family characteristics. *Psychiatry Research, 179*(2), 204–11. doi: http://dx.doi.org/10.1016/j.psychres.2009.06.008

Albert, U., Maina, G., Forner, F., & Bogetto, F. (2004). DSM-IV obsessive-compulsive personality disorder: Prevalence in patients with anxiety disorders and in healthy comparison subjects. *Comprehensive Psychiatry, 45*(5), 325–32. doi: http://dx.doi.org/10.1016/j.comppsych.2004.06.005

Albert, U., Salvi, V., Saracco, P., Bogetto, F., & Maina, G. (2007). Health-related quality of life among first-degree relatives of patients with obsessive-compulsive disorder in Italy. *Psychiatric Services, 58*(7), 970–6. doi: http://dx.doi.org/10.1176/appi.ps.58.7.970

American Psychiatric Association. (2013). *Diagnostic and Statistical Manual of Mental Disorders* (5th ed.). Washington, DC: American Psychiatric Association.

Ansell, E. B., Pinto, A., Crosby, R. D., *et al.* (2010). The prevalence and structure of obsessive-compulsive personality disorder in Hispanic psychiatric outpatients. *Journal of Behavior Therapy and Experimental Psychiatry, 41*(3), 275–81. doi: http://dx.doi.org/10.1016/j.jbtep.2010.02.005

Arntz, A. & Weertman, A. (1999). Treatment of childhood memories: theory and practice. *Behaviour Research and Therapy, 37*, 715–40.

Beck, A. T. (1995). Cognitive therapy: Past, present, and future. In *Cognitive and Constructive Psychotherapies: Theory, research, and practice* (pp. 29–40). New York, NY: Springer Publishing Co.

Bevan, A., Oldfield, V. B., & Salkovskis, P. M. (2010). A qualitative study of the acceptability of an intensive format for the delivery of cognitive-behavioural therapy for obsessive-compulsive disorder. *British Journal of Clinical Psychology, 49*(2), 173–91. doi: http://dx.doi.org/10.1348/014466509X447055

Bieling, P., McCabe, R. & Antony, M. (2006). *Cognitive Behavioural Therapy in Groups.* New York: Guildford Press.

Blackburn, I.-M., James, I. A., Milne, D. L., *et al.* (2001). The revised cognitive therapy scale (CTS-R): Psychometric properties. *Behavioural and Cognitive Psychotherapy, 29*(4), 431–46. doi: http://dx.doi.org/10.1017/S1352465801004040

Boeding, S. E., Paprocki, C. M., Baucom, D. H., *et al.* (2013). Let me check that for you: Symptom accommodation in romantic partners of adults with obsessive-compulsive disorder. *Behaviour Research and Therapy, 51*(6), 316–22. doi: http://dx.doi.org/10.1016/j.brat.2013.03.002

Calvocoressi, L., Lewis, B., Harris, M., *et al.* (1995). Family accommodation in obsessive-compulsive disorder. *American Journal of Psychiatry, 152*(3), 441–3.

Challacombe, F., & Salkovskis, P. (2009). A preliminary investigation of the impact of maternal obsessive-compulsive disorder and panic disorder on parenting and children. *Journal of Anxiety Disorders, 23*(7), 848–57. doi: http://dx.doi.org/10.1016/j.janxdis.2009.04.002

Challacombe F. L. (2014). *OCD in the Postnatal Period: An investigation into the impact on mothers, parenting and infants.* Unpublished PhD thesis. King's College, London.

Challacombe, F. L., & Salkovskis, P. M. (2011). Intensive cognitive-behavioural treatment for women with postnatal obsessive-compulsive disorder: A consecutive case series. *Behaviour Research and Therapy, 49*(6–7), 422–6. doi: http://dx.doi.org/10.1016/j.brat.2011.03.006

Challacombe, F. L., & Wroe, A. L. (2013). A hidden problem: Consequences of the misdiagnosis of perinatal obsessive-compulsive disorder. *British Journal of General Practice, 63*(610), 275–6. doi:http://dx.doi.org/10.3399/bjgp13X667376

Challacombe, F., Bream Oldfield, V. & Salkovskis, P. (2011). *Break Free from OCD.* London: Vermilion.

Challacombe, F. L., Salkovskis, P. M., Woolgar, M., Wilkinson, E. L., Read, J., & Acheson, R. (2016). Parenting and mother–infant interactions in the context of maternal postpartum obsessive-compulsive disorder: Effects of obsessional symptoms and mood. *Infant Behavior and Development, 44*, 11–20. doi: http://dx.doi.org/10.1016/j.infbeh.2016.04.003

Challacombe, F. L., Salkovskis, P. M., Woolgar, M., Wilkinson, E. L., Read, J., & Acheson, R. (2017). A pilot RCT for postpartum OCD: effects on maternal symptoms, mother infant interactions and attachment. *Psychological Medicine*, epub ahead of print.

Challacombe, F. L., et al. (2017). A pilot randomized controlled trial of time-intensive cognitive–behaviour therapy for postpartum obsessive–compulsive disorder: effects on maternal symptoms, mother–infant interactions and attachment. *Psychological Medicine*, 1–11.

Cicek, E., Cicek, I. E., Kayhan, F., Uguz, F., & Kaya, N. (2013). Quality of life, family burden and associated factors in relatives with obsessive-compulsive disorder. *General Hospital Psychiatry, 35*(3), 253–8. doi: http://dx.doi.org/10.1016/j.genhosppsych.2013.01.004

Coles, M. E., Pinto, A., Mancebo, M. C., Rasmussen, S. A., & Eisen, J. L. (2008). OCD with comorbid OCPD: A subtype of OCD? *Journal of Psychiatric Research, 42*(4), 289–96. doi: http://dx.doi.org/10.1016/j.jpsychires.2006.12.009

de Silva, P., & Marks, M. (1999). The role of traumatic experiences in the genesis of obsessive-compulsive disorder. *Behaviour Research and Therapy, 37*(10), 941–51. doi: http://dx.doi.org/10.1016/S0005-7967%2898%2900185-5

Deacon, B., & Abramowitz, J. (2006). A pilot study of two-day cognitive-behavioral therapy for panic disorder. [Evaluation Studies.] *Behaviour Research and Therapy, 44*(6), 807–17. doi: 10.1016/j.brat.2005.05.008

Department of Health. (2014). *Achieving Better Access to Mental Health Services by 2020.* Available at: https://www.gov.uk/government/uploads/system/uploads/attachment_data/file/361648/mental-health-access.pdf.

Dettore, D., Pozza, A., & Andersson, G. (2015). Efficacy of technology-delivered cognitive behavioural therapy for OCD versus control conditions, and in comparison with therapist-administered CBT: Meta-analysis of randomized controlled trials. *Cognitive Behaviour Therapy, 44*(3), 190–211. doi: http://dx.doi.org/10.1080/16506073.2015.1005660

Egan, S. J., Wade, T. D., & Shafran, R. (2011). Perfectionism as a transdiagnostic process: A clinical review. *Clinical Psychology Review, 31*(2), 203–12. doi: http://dx.doi.org/10.1016/j.cpr.2010.04.009

Egan, S. J., Wade, T. D., Shafran, R., & Antony, M. M. (2014). *Cognitive-behavioral Treatment of Perfectionism.* New York, NY: Guilford Press.

Ehlers, A., & Clark, D. M. (2000). A cognitive model of posttraumatic stress disorder. *Behaviour Research and Therapy, 38*(4), 319–45. doi: http://dx.doi.org/10.1016/S0005-7967%2899%2900123-0

Ehlers, A., Hackmann, A., Grey, N., *et al.* (2014). A randomized controlled trial of 7-day intensive and standard weekly cognitive therapy for PTSD and emotion-focused supportive therapy. *The American Journal of Psychiatry, 171*(3), 294–304. doi: http://dx.doi.org/10.1176/appi.ajp.2013.13040552

Fairbrother, N., & Abramowitz, J. S. (2007). New parenthood as a risk factor for the development of obsessional problems. *Behaviour Research and Therapy, 45*(9), 2155–63. doi: http://dx.doi.org/10.1016/j.brat.2006.09.019

Ferrao, Y. A., Shavitt, R. G., Bedin, N. R., *et al.* (2006). Clinical features associated with refractory obsessive-compulsive disorder. *Journal of Affective Disorders, 94*(1–3), 199–209.

Fineberg, N. A., Reghunandanan, S., Kolli, S., & Atmaca, M. (2014). Obsessive-compulsive (anankastic) personality disorder: toward the ICD-11 classification. *Revista Brasiliera de Psiquiatria, 1*, 40–50.

Foa, E. B., Cashman, L., Jaycox, L., & Perry, K. (1997). The validation of a self-report measure of posttraumatic stress disorder: The Posttraumatic Diagnostic Scale. *Psychological Assessment, 9*(4), 445–51. doi: http://dx.doi.org/10.1037/1040-3590.9.4.445

Foa, E. B., Ehlers, A., Clark, D. M., Tolin, D. F., & Orsillo, S. M. (1999). The Posttraumatic Cognitions Inventory (PTCI): Development and validation. *Psychological Assessment*, *11*(3), 303–14. doi: http://dx.doi.org/10.1037/1040-3590.11.3.303

Forrester, E., Bream, V., & Salkovskis, P. (in preparation). Assessing quality in the treatment of obsessive-compulsive disorder: development of the Obsessive-Compulsive Disorder Cognitive Therapy Scale (OCD-CTS).

Frost, R. O., Steketee, G., Tolin, D. F., Sinopoli, N., & Ruby, D. (2015). Motives for acquiring and saving in hoarding disorder, OCD, and community controls. *Journal of Obsessive Compulsive and Related Disorders*, *4*, 54–9. doi: http://dx.doi.org/10.1016/j.jocrd.2014.12.006

Gershuny, B. S., Baer, L., Parker, H., Gentes, E. L., Infield, A. L., & Jenike, M. A. (2008). Trauma and posttraumatic stress disorder in treatment-resistant obsessive-compulsive disorder. *Depression and Anxiety*, *25*(1), 69–71. doi: http://dx.doi.org/10.1002/da.20284

Gershuny, B. S., Baer, L., Radomsky, A. S., Wilson, K. A., & Jenike, M. A. (2003). Connections among symptoms of obsessive-compulsive disorder and posttraumatic stress disorder: A case series. *Behaviour Research and Therapy*, *41*(9), 1029–41. doi: http://dx.doi.org/10.1016/S0005-7967%2802%2900178-X

Goetter, E. M., Herbert, J. D., Forman, E. M., *et al.* (2013). Delivering exposure and ritual prevention for obsessive-compulsive disorder via videoconference: Clinical considerations and recommendations. *Journal of Obsessive-Compulsive and Related Disorders*, *2*(2), 137–45. doi: http://dx.doi.org/10.1016/j.jocrd.2013.01.003

Gilbert, P. (2002). Body shame: a biopsychosocial conceptualisation and overview, with treatment implications. In P. Gilbert and J. N. V. Miles (Eds.), *Body Shame: Conceptualisation, assessment and intervention* (pp. 3–54). London: Routledge.

Gilbert, P. (2010). *Compassion Focused Therapy*. London: Routledge.

Gilbert, P. & Irons, C. (2005). Focused therapies and compassionate mind training for shame and self-attacking. In P. Gilbert (Ed.), *Compassion: Conceptualisations, research and use in psychotherapy* (pp. 263–325). London: Routledge.

Gilbert, P. & McGuire, M. T. (1998). Shame, status, and social roles: psychobiology and evolution. In P. Gilbert and B. Andrews (Eds.), *Shame: Interpersonal behavior, psychopathology, and culture* (pp. 99–125). Oxford: Oxford University Press.

Goodwin, R., Koenen, K. C., Hellman, F., Guardino, M., & Struening, E. (2002). Helpseeking and access to mental health treatment for obsessive-compulsive disorder. *Acta Psychiatrica Scandinavica*, *106*(2), 143–9. doi: http://dx.doi.org/10.1034/j.1600-0447.2002.01221.x

Gordon, O. M., Salkovskis, P. M., & Bream, V. (2016). The impact of obsessive compulsive personality disorder on cognitive behaviour therapy for obsessive compulsive disorder. *Behavioural and Cognitive Psychotherapy*, *44*(4), 444–59.

Gordon, O. M., Salkovskis, P. M., Oldfield, V. B., & Carter, N. (2013a). The association between obsessive compulsive disorder and obsessive compulsive personality disorder: Prevalence and clinical presentation. *British Journal of Clinical Psychology*, *52*(3), 300–15. doi: http://dx.doi.org/10.1111/bjc.12016

Gordon, O. M., Salkovskis, P. M., & Oldfield, V. B. (2013b). Beliefs and experiences in hoarding. *Journal of Anxiety Disorders*, *27*(3), 328–39.

Grabe, H. J., Ruhrmann, S., Spitzer, C., *et al.* (2008). Obsessive-compulsive disorder and posttraumatic stress disorder. *Psychopathology, 41*(2), 129–34. doi: http://dx.doi.org/ 10.1159/000112029

Grey, N. (2009). A casebook of cognitive therapy for traumatic stress reactions. In *A Casebook of Cognitive Therapy for Traumatic Stress Reactions* (pp. xvi, 310). New York, NY: Routledge/Taylor & Francis Group.

Grey, N., Young, K., & Holmes, E. (2002). Cognitive restructuring within reliving: A treatment for peritraumatic emotional "hotspots" in posttraumatic stress disorder. *Behavioural and Cognitive Psychotherapy, 30*(1), 37–56. doi: http://dx.doi.org/ 10.1017/S1352465802001054

Huppert, J. D., Moser, J. S., Gershuny, B. S., *et al.* (2005). The relationship between obsessive-compulsive and posttraumatic stress symptoms in clinical and non-clinical samples. *Journal of Anxiety Disorders, 19*(1), 127–36. doi: http://dx.doi.org/10.1016/ j.janxdis.2004.01.001

James, I. A., Blackburn, I. M. & Reichelt, R.A. (2001). *Manual of the Revised Cognitive Therapy Scale.*

Kim, S., Thibodeau, R., & Jorgensen, R. S. (2011). Shame, guilt, and depressive symptoms: A meta-analytic review. *Psychological Bulletin, 137*(1), 68–96.

Lee, D. (2005). The perfect nurturer: a model to develop a compassionate mind within the context of cognitive therapy. In P. Gilbert (Ed.), *Compassion: Conceptualisations, research and use in psychotherapy* (pp. 326–51). London: Routledge.

Macdonald, J. (1998). Disclosing shame. In P. Gilbert and B. Andrews (Eds.), *Shame: Interpersonal behavior, psychopathology, and culture* (pp. 141–57). Oxford: Oxford University Press.

Magliano, L., Tosini, P., Guarneri, M., *et al.* (1996). Burden on the families of patients with obsessive-compulsive disorder: A pilot study. *European Psychiatry, 11*(4), 192–7.

Mahoney, A. E., Mackenzie, A., Williams, A. D., Smith, J., & Andrews, G. (2014). Internet cognitive behavioural treatment for obsessive compulsive disorder: A randomised controlled trial. *Behaviour Research and Therapy, 63*, 99–106. doi: http://dx.doi.org/ 10.1016/j.brat.2014.09.012

Mancebo, M. C., Eisen, J. L., Grant, J. E., & Rasmussen, S. A. (2005). Obsessive compulsive personality disorder and obsessive compulsive disorder: Clinical characteristics, diagnostic difficulties, and treatment. *Annals of Clinical Psychiatry, 17*(4), 197–204. doi: http://dx.doi.org/10.1080/10401230500295305

Mataix-Cols, D., & Marks, I. M. (2006). Self-help for obsessive-compulsive disorder: How much therapist contact is necessary? *Clinical Neuropsychiatry: Journal of Treatment Evaluation, 3*(6), 404–9.

Mataix-Cols, D., Frost, R. O., Pertusa, A., *et al.* (2010). Hoarding disorder: A new diagnosis for DSM-V? *Depression and Anxiety, 27*(6), 556–72. doi: http://dx.doi.org/10.1002/da.20693

Millar, J., Salkovskis, P., & Brown, C. (2016). Mental contamination in the "Dirty Kiss": Imaginal betrayal or bodily fluids? *Journal of Obsessive-Compulsive and Related Disorders, 8*(1), 70–4.

Morrison, N. (2001). Group cognitive therapy: treatment choice or sub-optimal option? *Behavioural and Cognitive Psychotherapy, 29*, 311–32.

Mortberg, E., Clark, D., Sundin, O., & Wistedt, A. (2007). Intensive group cognitive treatment and individual cognitive therapy vs. treatment as usual in social phobia: A randomized controlled trial. *Acta Psychiatrica Scandinavica, 115*(2), 142–54. doi: http://dx.doi.org/10.1111/j.1600-0447.2006.00839.x

Nacasch, N., Fostick, L., & Zohar, J. (2011). High prevalence of obsessive-compulsive disorder among posttraumatic stress disorder patients. *European Neuropsychopharmacology, 21*(12), 876–9. doi: http://dx.doi.org/10.1016/j.euroneuro.2011.03.007

National Institute for Health and Clinical Excellence. (2005). NICE Clinical Guideline 31: Core interventions in the treatment of obsessive-compulsive disorder and body dysmorphic disorder. Available at: http://www.nice.org.uk/guidance/cg31

Neziroglu, F., Anemone, R., & Yaryura-Tobias, J. A. (1992). Onset of obsessive-compulsive disorder in pregnancy. *American Journal of Psychiatry, 149*(7), 947–50.

OCTC (2009). Supervisor competency scale. In M. Mueller, H. Kennerley, F. McManus, & D. Westbrook (2010). *The Oxford Guide to Surviving as a CBT Therapist.* Oxford: Oxford University Press.

Oldfield, V. B., Salkovskis, P. M., & Taylor, T. (2011). Time-intensive cognitive behaviour therapy for obsessive-compulsive disorder: A case series and matched comparison group. *British Journal of Clinical Psychology, 50*(1), 7–18. doi: http://dx.doi.org/10.1348/014466510X490073

Pertusa, A., Frost, R. O., & Mataix-Cols, D. (2010). When hoarding is a symptom of OCD: A case series and implications for DSM-V. *Behaviour Research and Therapy, 48*(10), 1012–20. doi: http://dx.doi.org/10.1016/j.brat.2010.07.003

Pertusa, A., Fullana, M. A., Singh, S., Alonso, P., Menchon, J. M., & Mataix-Cols, D. (2008). Compulsive hoarding: OCD symptom, distinct clinical syndrome, or both? *The American Journal of Psychiatry, 165*(10), 1289–98. doi: http://dx.doi.org/10.1176/appi.ajp.2008.07111730

Pilling, S. & Roth, A. (2007) *Psychological Interventions with People with Personality Disorder.* Available at: https://www.ucl.ac.uk/pals/research/cehp/research-groups/core/pdfs/Personality_Disorders/Personality_background_document.pdf (accessed 3 July 2016).

Pilling, S. & Roth, A. (2008). *A Competence Framework for the Supervision of Psychological Therapies.* Available at: http://www.ucl.ac.uk/clinical-psychology/CORE/CBT_Framework.htm (accessed 25 March 2015).

Pozza, A., Andersson, G., Antonelli, P., & Dettore, D. (2014). Computer-delivered cognitive-behavioural treatments for obsessive compulsive disorder: Preliminary meta-analysis of randomized and non-randomized effectiveness trials. *The Cognitive Behaviour Therapist, 7.* doi: http://dx.doi.org/10.1017/S1754470X1400021X

Rachman, S. (1994). Pollution of the mind. *Behaviour Research and Therapy, 32*(3), 311–14. doi: http://dx.doi.org/10.1016/0005-7967%2894%2990127-9

Rachman, S. J. (2006). *The fear of contamination: Assessment and treatment.* Oxford: Oxford University Press.

Rachman, S., Coughtrey, A., Shafran, R., & Radomsky, A. (2015). *Oxford Guide to the Treatment of Mental Contamination.* New York, NY: Oxford University Press.

Rachman, S., Elliott, C. M., Shafran, R., & Radomsky, A. S. (2009). Separating hoarding from OCD. *Behaviour Research and Therapy, 47*(6), 520–2. doi: http://dx.doi.org/10.1016/j.brat.2009.02.014

Radomsky, A. S., & Elliott, C. M. (2009). Analyses of mental contamination: Part II, individual differences. *Behaviour Research and Therapy, 47*(12), 1004–11. doi: http://dx.doi.org/10.1016/j.brat.2009.08.004

Radomsky, A. S., Rachman, S., Shafran, R., Coughtrey, A. E., & Barber, K. C. (2014). The nature and assessment of mental contamination: A psychometric analysis. *Journal of Obsessive-Compulsive and Related Disorders, 3*(2), 181–7. doi: http://dx.doi.org/10.1016/j.jocrd.2013.08.003

Renshaw, K. D., Chambless, D. L., & Steketee, G. (2003). Perceived criticism predicts severity of anxiety symptoms after behavioral treatment in patients with obsessive-compulsive disorder and panic disorder with agoraphobia. *Journal of Clinical Psychology, 59*(4), 411–21. doi: http://dx.doi.org/10.1002/jclp.10048

Robinson, K. J., Rose, D., Salkovskis, P. M. (2016). Seeking help for obsessive compulsive disorder (OVCD): A qualitative study of the enablers and barriers conducted by a researcher with personal experience of OCD. *Psychology and Psychotherapy: Theory Research and Practice* 2017, doi 10.1111/papt.12090

Roth, A. D. & Pilling, S. (2007). *The Competences Required to Deliver Effective Cognitive and Behavioural Therapy for People with Depression and with Anxiety Disorders.* London: Department of Health.

Rowa, K., Antony, M. M., Summerfeldt, L. J., Purdon, C., Young, L., & Swinson, R. P. (2007). Office-based vs. home-based behavioral treatment for obsessive-compulsive disorder: A preliminary study. *Behaviour Research and Therapy, 45*(8), 1883–92. doi: http://dx.doi.org/10.1016/j.brat.2007.02.009

Russell, E. J., Fawcett, J. M., & Mazmanian, D. (2013). Risk of obsessive-compulsive disorder in pregnant and postpartum women: A meta-analysis. *Journal of Clinical Psychiatry, 74*(4), 377–85.

Ryder, J. (2010). CBT in groups. In M. Mueller, H. Kennerley, F. McManus, & D. Westbrook (Eds.), *Oxford Guide to Surviving as a CBT Therapist* (pp. 157–73). Oxford: Oxford University Press.

Salkovskis, P., Shafran, R., Rachman, S., & Freeston, M. H. (1999). Multiple pathways to inflated responsibility beliefs in obsessional problems: Possible origins and implications for therapy and research. *Behaviour Research and Therapy, 37*(11), 1055–72.

Salkovskis, P. M. (1991). The importance of behaviour in the maintenance of anxiety and panic: A cognitive account. *Behavioural Psychotherapy, 19*(1), 6–19.

Seaman, C., Oldfield, V. B., Gordon, O., Forrester, E., & Salkovskis, P. M. (2010). The impact of symptomatic hoarding in OCD and its treatment. *Behavioural and Cognitive Psychotherapy, 38*(2), 157–71. doi: http://dx.doi.org/10.1017/S1352465809990695

Shafran, R., Cooper, Z., & Fairburn, C. G. (2002). Clinical perfectionism: A cognitive-behavioural analysis. *Behaviour Research and Therapy, 40*(7), 773–91. doi: http://dx.doi.org/10.1016/S0005-7967%2801%2900059-6

Shafran, R., Egan S. & Wade T. (2010). *Overcoming Perfectionism.* London, Constable & Robinson Ltd.

Steketee, G., & Frost, R. (2013). *Treatment for Hoarding Disorder.* Treatments that work series: Oxford, Oxford University Press.

Stewart, S., Beresin, C., Haddad, S., Stack, D. E., Fama, J., & Jenike, M. (2008). Predictors of family accommodation in obsessive-compulsive disorder. *Annals of Clinical Psychiatry, 20*(2), 65–70.

Stobie, B., Taylor, T., Quigley, A., Ewing, S., & Salkovskis, P. M. (2007). Contents may vary: A pilot study of treatment histories of OCD patients. *Behavioural and Cognitive Psychotherapy, 35*(3), 273–82. doi:http://dx.doi.org/10.1017/S135246580700358X

Storch, E. A., Merlo, L. J., Lehmkuhl, H., *et al.* (2008). Cognitive-behavioral therapy for obsessive-compulsive disorder: A non-randomized comparison of intensive and weekly approaches. *Journal of Anxiety Disorders, 22*(7), 1146–58. doi: http://dx.doi.org/10.1016/j.janxdis.2007.12.001

Subramaniam, M., Abdin, E., Vaingankar, J. A., & Chong, S. A. (2012). Obsessive-compulsive disorder: Prevalence, correlates, help-seeking and quality of life in a multiracial Asian population. *Social Psychiatry and Psychiatric Epidemiology, 47*(12), 2035–43. doi: http://dx.doi.org/10.1007/s00127-012-0507-8

Tangney, J. P. & Dearing, R. L. (2002). *Shame and Guilt*. New York: Guilford Press.

Thordarson, D. S., Radomsky, A. S., Rachman, S., Shafran, R., Sawchuk, C. N., & Hakstian, A. (2004). The Vancouver Obsessional Compulsive Inventory (VOCI). *Behaviour Research and Therapy, 42*(11), 1289–314. doi: http://dx.doi.org/10.1016/j.brat.2003.08.007

Thornicroft, G., Colson, L., & Marks, I. M. (1991). An in-patient behavioural psychotherapy unit: Description and audit. *The British Journal of Psychiatry, 158*, 362–7. doi: http://dx.doi.org/10.1192/bjp.158.3.362

Timpano, K. R., Abramowitz, J. S., Mahaffey, B. L., Mitchell, M. A., & Schmidt, N. B. (2011). Efficacy of a prevention program for postpartum obsessive-compulsive symptoms. *Journal of Psychiatric Research, 45*(11), 1511–17. doi: http://dx.doi.org/10.1016/j.jpsychires.2011.06.015

Torgersen, S., Kringlen, E., & Cramer, V. (2001). The prevalence of personality disorders in a community sample. *Archives of General Psychiatry, 58*(6), 590–6. doi: http://dx.doi.org/10.1001/archpsyc.58.6.590

Tumur, I., Kaltenthaler, E., Ferriter, M., Beverley, C., & Parry, G. (2007). Computerised cognitive behaviour therapy for obsessive-compulsive disorder: A systematic review. *Psychotherapy and Psychosomatics, 76*(4), 196–202. doi: http://dx.doi.org/10.1159/000112646

Van Noppen, B., & Steketee, G. (2009). Testing a conceptual model of patient and family predictors of obsessive compulsive disorder (OCD) symptoms. *Behaviour Research and Therapy, 47*(1), 18–25. doi: http://dx.doi.org/10.1016/j.brat.2008.10.005

Veale, D., Naismith, I., Miles, S., *et al.* (2015). Outcome of intensive cognitive behaviour therapy in a residential setting for people with severe obsessive compulsive disorder: A large open case series. *Behavioural and Cognitive Psychotherapy, 44*, 331–46.

Veale, D., Page, N., Woodward, E., & Salkovskis, P. (2015). Imagery rescripting for obsessive compulsive disorder: A single case experimental design in 12 cases. *Journal of Behavior Therapy and Experimental Psychiatry, 49*, 230–6.

Waters, T. L., & Barrett, P. M. (2000). The role of the family in childhood obsessive-compulsive disorder. *Clinical Child and Family Psychology Review, 3*(3), 173–84. doi: http://dx.doi.org/10.1023/A:1009551325629

Weingarden, H., & Renshaw, K. D. (2015). Shame in the obsessive compulsive related disorders: A conceptual review. *Journal of Affective Disorders, 171*, 74–84.

Weiss, D. S., & Marmar, C. R. (1997). The Impact of Event Scale-Revised. In: Wilson, J. P., & Keane, T. M. (eds.) *Assessing Psychological Trauma and PTSD* (pp. 399–411). New York, NY: Guilford Press.

Welford, M. (2012). *The Compassionate Mind Approach to Building Self-confidence.* London: Robinson.

Whittington, A., & Grey, N. (2014). How to become a more effective CBT therapist: Mastering metacompetence in clinical practice. In: Whittington, A., & Grey, N. (eds.) *How to Become a More Effective CBT Therapist: Mastering metacompetence in clinical practice,* (pp. xviii, 318). Wiley-Blackwell, Chichester.

CBT for OCD appendices

Appendix 1

Blank theory A/B sheet

Which is the best description of the problem I have? Which problem do I need to solve?	
Theory A Belief rating:	Theory B Belief rating:
What is the evidence? Why do I believe this?	
What are the implications? What do I need to do if this is true?	
What does this say about me as a person?	
What will my life be like if I carry on acting this way?	

Blank behavioural experiment form

COMPLETE BEFORE		COMPLETE AFTER		
Planned experiment	Specific predictions and how much I believe them	What happened? Did the predictions come true?	Conclusions? What do you make of this?	Does it fit best with theory A or B?

Blank blueprint

Development and understanding of the problem

♦ What sort of background factors made me more likely to develop OCD?

♦ How did the problem develop (what was going on in my life)?

♦ What were the intrusive thoughts/images/urges/doubts and what did I think they meant when they were bothering me?

♦ What were the underlying ideas about myself, responsibility or how the world works that kept the problem going?

♦ Once the problem took hold, what was it that I was doing, thinking, and paying attention to that kept the problem going? (Draw a vicious flower if you can.)

Change

♦ *Intrusive thoughts*: what do I know now about intrusive thoughts? Who gets them and when do they feel important?

♦ What did they mean to me at the start of treatment?

♦ *Beliefs about the world/others/myself*: how did I challenge these and what did I learn? (Describe the most useful behavioural experiments and metaphors, and any other ways you identified or challenged the processes.)

♦ What are more helpful versions of these ideas?

Costs of OCD and benefits of changing

◆ What can I do now that the OCD was stopping me from doing?

◆ What can I continue to do to reclaim my life from OCD and beyond?

◆ What is the best thing about me standing up to OCD?

Future planning

◆ What sort of situations might I find difficult in the future and why? What would I do?

• Possible difficult situations:

• What OCD might say:

• What I need to remember and do:

Obsessive Compulsive Inventory (OCI)

The following statements refer to experiences which many people have in their everyday lives. Under the column labelled FREQUENCY, please CIRCLE the number next to each statement that best describes how **FREQUENTLY YOU HAVE HAD THE EXPERIENCE IN THE PAST MONTH**. The numbers in this column refer to the following labels:

0 = Never   1 = Almost never   2 = Sometimes   3 = Often   4 = Almost always

Then, in the column labelled DISTRESS, please **CIRCLE** the number that best describes **HOW MUCH** that experience has **DISTRESSED** or **BOTHERED YOU DURING THE PAST MONTH**. The numbers in this column refer to the following labels:

0 = Not at all   1 = A little   2 = Moderately   3 = A lot   4 = Extremely

FREQUENCY	DISTRESS

1. **Unpleasant thoughts come into my mind against my will and I cannot get rid of them**

   0   1   2   3   4   0   1   2   3   4

2. **I think contact with bodily secretions (perspiration, saliva, blood, urine, etc.) may contaminate my clothes or somehow harm me**

   0   1   2   3   4   0   1   2   3   4

3. **I ask people to repeat things to me several times, even though I understood them the first time**

   0   1   2   3   4   0   1   2   3   4

4. **I wash and clean obsessively**

   0   1   2   3   4   0   1   2   3   4

5. I have to review mentally past events, conversations and actions to make sure that I didn't do something wrong

    0   1   2   3   4   0   1   2   3   4

6. I have saved up so many things that they get in the way

    0   1   2   3   4   0   1   2   3   4

7. I check things more often than necessary

    0   1   2   3   4   0   1   2   3   4

8. I avoid using public toilets because I am afraid of disease or contamination

    0   1   2   3   4   0   1   2   3   4

9. I repeatedly check doors, windows, drawers, etc.

    0   1   2   3   4   0   1   2   3   4

10. I repeatedly check gas and water taps and light switches after turning them off

    0   1   2   3   4   0   1   2   3   4

11. I collect things I don't need

    0   1   2   3   4   0   1   2   3   4

12. I have thoughts of having hurt someone without knowing it

    0   1   2   3   4   0   1   2   3   4

13. I have thoughts that I might want to harm myself or others

    0   1   2   3   4   0   1   2   3   4

14. I get upset if objects are not arranged properly

    0   1   2   3   4   0   1   2   3   4

15. I feel obliged to follow a particular order in dressing, undressing and washing myself

    0   1   2   3   4   0   1   2   3   4

16. I feel compelled to count while I am doing things

    0   1   2   3   4   0   1   2   3   4

17. I am afraid of impulsively doing embarrassing or harmful things

    0   1   2   3   4   0   1   2   3   4

18. I need to pray to cancel bad thoughts or feelings

    0   1   2   3   4   0   1   2   3   4

19. I keep on checking forms or other things I have written

    0   1   2   3   4   0   1   2   3   4

20. I get upset at the sight of knives, scissors and other sharp objects in case I lose control with them

    0   1   2   3   4   0   1   2   3   4

21. I am excessively concerned about cleanliness

    0   1   2   3   4   0   1   2   3   4

22. I find it difficult to touch an object when I know it has been touched by strangers or certain people

    0   1   2   3   4   0   1   2   3   4

23. I need things to be arranged in a particular order

    0   1   2   3   4   0   1   2   3   4

24. I get behind in my work because I repeat things over and over again

    0   1   2   3   4   0   1   2   3   4

25. I feel I have to repeat certain numbers

    0   1   2   3   4   0   1   2   3   4

26. After doing something carefully, I still have the impression I have not finished it

    0   1   2   3   4   0   1   2   3   4

27. I find it difficult to touch garbage or dirty things

    0   1   2   3   4   0   1   2   3   4

28. I find it difficult to control my own thoughts

    0   1   2   3   4   0   1   2   3   4

29. I have to do things over and over again until it feels right

    0   1   2   3   4   0   1   2   3   4

30. I am upset by unpleasant thoughts that come into my mind against my will

    0   1   2   3   4   0   1   2   3   4

31. Before going to sleep I have to do certain things in a certain way

    0   1   2   3   4   0   1   2   3   4

32. I go back to places to make sure that I have not harmed anyone

    0   1   2   3   4   0   1   2   3   4

33. I frequently get nasty thoughts and have difficulty in getting rid of them

    0   1   2   3   4   0   1   2   3   4

34. I avoid throwing things away because I am afraid I might need them later

    0   1   2   3   4   0   1   2   3   4

35. I get upset if others change the way I have arranged my things

    0   1   2   3   4   0   1   2   3   4

36. I feel that I must repeat certain words or phrases in my mind in order to wipe out bad thoughts, feelings or actions

    0   1   2   3   4   0   1   2   3   4

37. After I have done things, I have persistent doubts about whether I really did them

    0   1   2   3   4   0   1   2   3   4

38. I sometimes have to wash or clean myself simply because I feel contaminated

    0   1   2   3   4   0   1   2   3   4

39. I feel that there are good and bad numbers

    0   1   2   3   4   0   1   2   3   4

40. I repeatedly check anything which might cause a fire

    0   1   2   3   4   0   1   2   3   4

41. Even when I do something very carefully I feel that it is not quite right

    0   1   2   3   4   0   1   2   3   4

42. I wash my hands more often or longer than necessary

    0   1   2   3   4   0   1   2   3   4

OCI © Wellcome Trust Obsessive Compulsive Disorder Group (Oxford) 2000.

Responsibility Assumptions Scale (RAS)

This questionnaire lists different attitudes or beliefs which people sometimes hold. Read each statement carefully and decide how much you agree or disagree with it.

For each of the attitudes, show your answer by putting a circle round the words which BEST DESCRIBE HOW YOU THINK. Be sure to choose only one answer for each attitude. Because people are different, there is no right answer or wrong answer to these statements.

To decide whether a given attitude is typical of your way of looking at things, simply keep in mind what you are like MOST OF THE TIME.

1. **I often feel responsible for things which go wrong.**

   TOTALLY AGREE   AGREE   NEUTRAL   DISAGREE   DISAGREE   TOTALLY
   AGREE   VERY   SLIGHTLY   SLIGHTLY   VERY   DISAGREE
      MUCH   MUCH

2. **If I don't act when I can foresee danger, then I am to blame for any consequences if it happens.**

   TOTALLY AGREE   AGREE   NEUTRAL   DISAGREE   DISAGREE   TOTALLY
   AGREE   VERY   SLIGHTLY   SLIGHTLY   VERY   DISAGREE
      MUCH   MUCH

3. **I am too sensitive to feeling responsible for things going wrong.**

   TOTALLY AGREE   AGREE   NEUTRAL   DISAGREE   DISAGREE   TOTALLY
   AGREE   VERY   SLIGHTLY   SLIGHTLY   VERY   DISAGREE
      MUCH   MUCH

4. **If I think bad things, this is as bad as *doing* bad things.**

   TOTALLY AGREE   AGREE   NEUTRAL   DISAGREE   DISAGREE   TOTALLY
   AGREE   VERY   SLIGHTLY   SLIGHTLY   VERY   DISAGREE
      MUCH   MUCH

5. **I worry a great deal about the effects of things which I do or don't do.**

TOTALLY AGREE   AGREE   NEUTRAL   DISAGREE   DISAGREE   TOTALLY
AGREE   VERY SLIGHTLY   SLIGHTLY   VERY   DISAGREE
         MUCH   MUCH

6. **To me, not acting to prevent disaster is as bad as making disaster happen.**

TOTALLY AGREE   AGREE   NEUTRAL   DISAGREE   DISAGREE   TOTALLY
AGREE   VERY SLIGHTLY   SLIGHTLY   VERY   DISAGREE
         MUCH   MUCH

7. **If I know that harm is possible, I should always try to prevent it, however unlikely it seems.**

TOTALLY AGREE   AGREE   NEUTRAL   DISAGREE   DISAGREE   TOTALLY
AGREE   VERY SLIGHTLY   SLIGHTLY   VERY   DISAGREE
         MUCH   MUCH

8. **I must always think through the consequences of even the smallest actions.**

TOTALLY AGREE   AGREE   NEUTRAL   DISAGREE   DISAGREE   TOTALLY
AGREE   VERY SLIGHTLY   SLIGHTLY   VERY   DISAGREE
         MUCH   MUCH

9. **I often take responsibility for things which other people don't think are my fault.**

TOTALLY AGREE   AGREE   NEUTRAL   DISAGREE   DISAGREE   TOTALLY
AGREE   VERY SLIGHTLY   SLIGHTLY   VERY   DISAGREE
         MUCH   MUCH

10. **Everything I do can cause serious problems.**

TOTALLY AGREE   AGREE   NEUTRAL   DISAGREE   DISAGREE   TOTALLY
AGREE   VERY SLIGHTLY   SLIGHTLY   VERY   DISAGREE
         MUCH   MUCH

11. **I am often close to causing harm.**

TOTALLY AGREE   AGREE   NEUTRAL   DISAGREE   DISAGREE   TOTALLY
AGREE   VERY SLIGHTLY   SLIGHTLY   VERY   DISAGREE
         MUCH   MUCH

12. **I must protect others from harm.**

TOTALLY AGREE   AGREE   NEUTRAL   DISAGREE   DISAGREE   TOTALLY
AGREE   VERY SLIGHTLY   SLIGHTLY   VERY   DISAGREE
         MUCH   MUCH

13. **I should never cause even the slightest harm to others.**

TOTALLY AGREE   AGREE   NEUTRAL   DISAGREE   DISAGREE   TOTALLY
AGREE   VERY SLIGHTLY   SLIGHTLY   VERY   DISAGREE
         MUCH   MUCH

14. I will be condemned for my actions.

TOTALLY AGREE   AGREE   NEUTRAL   DISAGREE   DISAGREE   TOTALLY
AGREE   VERY   SLIGHTLY   SLIGHTLY   VERY   DISAGREE
         MUCH   MUCH

15. If I can have even a slight influence on things going wrong, then I must act to prevent it.

TOTALLY AGREE   AGREE   NEUTRAL   DISAGREE   DISAGREE   TOTALLY
AGREE   VERY   SLIGHTLY   SLIGHTLY   VERY   DISAGREE
         MUCH   MUCH

16. To me, not acting where disaster is a slight possibility is as bad as making that disaster happen.

TOTALLY AGREE   AGREE   NEUTRAL   DISAGREE   DISAGREE   TOTALLY
AGREE   VERY   SLIGHTLY   SLIGHTLY   VERY   DISAGREE
         MUCH   MUCH

17. For me, even slight carelessness is inexcusable when it might affect other people.

TOTALLY AGREE   AGREE   NEUTRAL   DISAGREE   DISAGREE   TOTALLY
AGREE   VERY   SLIGHTLY   SLIGHTLY   VERY   DISAGREE
         MUCH   MUCH

18. In all kinds of daily situations, my inactivity can cause as much harm as deliberate bad intentions.

TOTALLY AGREE   AGREE   NEUTRAL   DISAGREE   DISAGREE   TOTALLY
AGREE   VERY   SLIGHTLY   SLIGHTLY   VERY   DISAGREE
         MUCH   MUCH

19. Even if harm is a very unlikely possibility, I should always try to prevent it at any cost.

TOTALLY AGREE   AGREE   NEUTRAL   DISAGREE   DISAGREE   TOTALLY
AGREE   VERY   SLIGHTLY   SLIGHTLY   VERY   DISAGREE
         MUCH   MUCH

20. Once I think it is possible that I have caused harm, I can't forgive myself.

TOTALLY AGREE   AGREE   NEUTRAL   DISAGREE   DISAGREE   TOTALLY
AGREE   VERY   SLIGHTLY   SLIGHTLY   VERY   DISAGREE
         MUCH   MUCH

21. Many of my past actions have been intended to prevent harm to others.

TOTALLY AGREE   AGREE   NEUTRAL   DISAGREE   DISAGREE   TOTALLY
AGREE   VERY   SLIGHTLY   SLIGHTLY   VERY   DISAGREE
         MUCH   MUCH

22. I have to make sure other people are protected from all of the consequences of things I do.

TOTALLY AGREE	AGREE VERY MUCH	AGREE SLIGHTLY	NEUTRAL	DISAGREE SLIGHTLY	DISAGREE VERY MUCH	TOTALLY DISAGREE

23. Other people should not rely on my judgement.

TOTALLY AGREE	AGREE VERY MUCH	AGREE SLIGHTLY	NEUTRAL	DISAGREE SLIGHTLY	DISAGREE VERY MUCH	TOTALLY DISAGREE

24. If I cannot be *certain* I am blameless, I feel that I am to blame.

TOTALLY AGREE	AGREE VERY MUCH	AGREE SLIGHTLY	NEUTRAL	DISAGREE SLIGHTLY	DISAGREE VERY MUCH	TOTALLY DISAGREE

25. If I take sufficient care then I can prevent any harmful accidents.

TOTALLY AGREE	AGREE VERY MUCH	AGREE SLIGHTLY	NEUTRAL	DISAGREE SLIGHTLY	DISAGREE VERY MUCH	TOTALLY DISAGREE

26. I often think that bad things will happen if I am not careful enough.

TOTALLY AGREE	AGREE VERY MUCH	AGREE SLIGHTLY	NEUTRAL	DISAGREE SLIGHTLY	DISAGREE VERY MUCH	TOTALLY DISAGREE

Responsibility Interpretations Questionnaire (RIQ)

Name.. Date........................   *RIQ*

We are interested in your reaction to intrusive thoughts that you have had in the *last 2 weeks*.

Intrusive thoughts are thoughts that suddenly enter your mind, may interrupt what you are thinking or doing and tend to recur on separate occasions. They may occur in the form of words, mental image, or an impulse (a sudden urge to carry out some action). We are interested in those intrusive thoughts that are unacceptable. Research has shown that most people experience or have experienced such thoughts which they find unacceptable in some way, at some time in their lives to a greater or lesser degree, so there is nothing unusual about this.

Some examples of unpleasant intrusions are:

> *Repeated image of attacking someone*
>
> *Suddenly thinking that your hands are dirty and you may cause contamination*
>
> *Suddenly thinking you might not have turned off the gas, or that you left a door unlocked*
>
> *Repeated senseless images of harm coming to someone you love*
>
> *Repeated urge to attack or harm somebody (even though you would never do this)*

These are just a few examples of intrusions to give you some idea of what we are looking at; people vary tremendously in the type of thoughts that they have.

<u>IMPORTANT</u>

Think of INTRUSIONS OF THE TYPE DESCRIBED ABOVE that you have had in the last 2 weeks, and answer the following questions with these intrusions in mind. The questions do *NOT* relate to all thoughts but specifically to your negative intrusions.

Please write down intrusions that you have had in the last 2 weeks:

1.

2.

3

4.

5.

Beliefs

Over the last two weeks. When you were bothered by these worrying intrusive thoughts, how much did you **believe** each of these ideas to be true? Rate the belief you had of these ideas *when you had the intrusions*, using the following scale; mark the point on the line that most accurately applies to your belief at the time of the intrusion.

B1

| I did not believe this idea at all | | | | | | | | I was completely convinced this idea was true |

If I don't resist these thoughts it means I am being irresponsible

0   10   20   30   40   50   60   70   80   90   100

I could be responsible for serious harm

0   10   20   30   40   50   60   70   80   90   100

I can not take the risk of this thought coming true

0   10   20   30   40   50   60   70   80   90   100

If I don't act now then something terrible will happen and it will be my fault

0   10   20   30   40   50   60   70   80   90   100

I need to be certain something awful won't happen

0   10   20   30   40   50   60   70   80   90   100

I should not be thinking this kind of thing

0   10   20   30   40   50   60   70   80   90   100

It would be irresponsible to ignore these thoughts

0   10   20   30   40   50   60   70   80   90   100

I'll feel awful unless I do something about this thought

| 0 | 10 | 20 | 30 | 40 | 50 | 60 | 70 | 80 | 90 | 100 |

Because I've thought of bad things happening then I must act to prevent them

| 0 | 10 | 20 | 30 | 40 | 50 | 60 | 70 | 80 | 90 | 100 |

Since I've had this thought I must want it to happen

| 0 | 10 | 20 | 30 | 40 | 50 | 60 | 70 | 80 | 90 | 100 |

Now I've thought of bad things which could go wrong I have a responsibility to make sure I don't let them happen

| 0 | 10 | 20 | 30 | 40 | 50 | 60 | 70 | 80 | 90 | 100 |

Thinking this could make it happen

| 0 | 10 | 20 | 30 | 40 | 50 | 60 | 70 | 80 | 90 | 100 |

I must regain control of these thoughts

| 0 | 10 | 20 | 30 | 40 | 50 | 60 | 70 | 80 | 90 | 100 |

This could be an omen

| 0 | 10 | 20 | 30 | 40 | 50 | 60 | 70 | 80 | 90 | 100 |

It's wrong to ignore these thoughts

| 0 | 10 | 20 | 30 | 40 | 50 | 60 | 70 | 80 | 90 | 100 |

Because these thoughts come from my mind, I must want to have them

| 0 | 10 | 20 | 30 | 40 | 50 | 60 | 70 | 80 | 90 | 100 |

Manual for the CTS-OC

(Reprinted with kind permission of
Dr Elizabeth Forrester)

About the rating scale

This is a scale for assessing therapists' skill in cognitive therapy for OCD. Whilst a widely used Cognitive Therapy Scale (CTS; Young and Beck, 1980; 1988) has been available for some time, and a more recent variant developed (Cognitive Therapy Scale—Revised [CTS-R]; James *et al.*, 2001), both provide a measure of generic cognitive therapy skills. The development of the Cognitive Behaviour Therapy for Obsessive-Compulsive Disorder: Cognitive Therapy Scale (CTS-OC) is derived from the premise that some disorders require very specific strategies and interventions, and although one might be a skilled cognitive therapist in general terms, it is not always the case that one is skilled at CBT for a particular disorder. Whilst it can be treated as a 'stand alone' scale, it is intended to be a supplementary scale to the CTS-R (James *et al.*, 2001).

Because of the detail and clarity of the CTS-R (James *et al.*, 2001), an earlier version of this scale was adapted to utilize a similar format and range of criteria. It has been divided into three parts:

1. *General therapeutic skills*: some cognitive therapy skills provide the core to a good intervention, and in general apply across the spectrum of disorders.

2. *Conceptualization, strategy, and technique*: whilst some of the items included in this section may still be considered to apply across all disorders, there are a number of strategies and techniques that have particular salience in the treatment of OCD.

3. *Observations regarding the therapeutic intervention*: this section considers the complexity of the person (e.g. interpersonal style, multiple difficulties),

which may make it difficult for the therapist to adhere to the general treatment protocol. As a research team, it is also of importance to assess whether the way in which the therapy was delivered fits sufficiently closely with treatment trial protocol as we strive for consistency amongst trial therapists.

Use of the rating scale

The seven-point scales utilized for this measure extend from 0, where the therapist did not adhere to that aspect of therapy (non-adherence), to 6, where there is not only 'adherence' to the protocol, but the therapist demonstrates a very high level of skill. Thus the checklist assesses both adherence to therapy method and skill of the therapist. To aid with the rating of each item on the scale, an outline of the key features for each item is provided at the top of each section. A description of the various rating criteria is given in the right hand margin.

The examples are intended as useful guidelines only. They are not meant to be used as prescriptive rating criteria, but as illustrative anchor points and guides. The assessor should be familiar with the protocol for CBT for OCD, and have sufficient clinical expertise to be able to identify particular skills and strategies, and to recognize acceptable variations in the basic approach and be proficient to score them accordingly. However, the manual and the checklist provide sufficient detail for the novice therapist to be able to use it in his or her practice, and identify strengths and weaknesses of the therapy sessions in a meaningful way. That is, the checklist scale provides a description of appropriate CBT skills at different levels of expertise. It should enable the practitioner to identify aspects in need of improvement, with appropriate suggestions for doing so, as well as providing feedback on aspects that are examples of good practice.

Example of the rating layout

Key features: this is an operationalized description of the item (see examples within the scale).

Circle the rating pertaining to the level to which you think the therapist has fulfilled the core function. The descriptive features on the right are designed to guide your decision. If the therapist does not quite meet all criteria for a level, it is acceptable to circle two levels (the resulting rating will be the average, e.g. level 3 and 4 = 3.5).

The following is intended as an overall guide:

Competence level		Examples
	0	Absence of feature, or highly inappropriate performance
Incompetent	1	Inappropriate performance, with major problems evident
Novice	2	Evidence of competence, but numerous problems and lack of consistency
Advanced beginner	3	Competent, but some problems and/or inconsistencies
Competent	4	Good features, but minor problems and/or inconsistencies
Proficient	5	Very good features, minimal problems and/or inconsistencies
Expert	6	Excellent performance, or even very good in the face of patient difficulties

It should be noted that the items shown in Sections 17 and 18 of this Appendix are not scored in this way (see below for a detailed explanation).

Rating distribution

It should be noted that the rating profile for this scale should approximate to a normal distribution (i.e. midpoint 3), with relatively few therapists rating at the extremes. Raters should refer to page 3 of the *Manual of the Revised Cognitive Therapy Scale (CTS-R)* for a full explanation of the scoring system. The CTS-R has a maximum score on the scale of 72 (i.e. 12 items × maximum 6 points per item), and the Newcastle Cognitive Therapy Centre sets a minimum 'competency' standard of 36, which would be an average of 3 marks per item. The OCD-CTS has a total of 18 items, 16 of which are scored on a 6-point scale, with item 17 (client complexity) scored on a 4-point scale, and item 18 (consistency with trial protocol) rated simply as Yes/Subthreshold/No. This final item would not be included in a total score as it was included for the purpose of setting a minimum standard for therapy skills whilst training therapists to conform to treatment protocol for a randomized control trial, and does not necessarily provide a measure of skill in cognitive therapy for the treatment of OCD (for example, a highly skilled therapist may successfully and appropriately use schema change techniques with the person they are working with but would be deemed as not adhering to trial protocol as the remit prescribes adherence to specific strategies).

Because the OCD-CTS contains more items, any overall score is not directly comparable with the CTS-R. Ratings on the OCD-CTS are not in fact intended to give an overall score, but can be used on the accompanying summary sheet to give a general profile. This is thought to be more helpful in identifying aspects where sufficient levels of skill are evident, and where attention should be paid to refining emerging competencies. Educational research has shown that this is a wise move (e.g. Black and Wiliam, 1998): when students are provided with a mark or grade, they pay more attention to this than to any qualitative feedback, even when such feedback is fulsome in its praise of a particular piece of work.

References

Black, P., & Wiliam, D. (1998). Assessment and classroom learning. *Assessment in Education*, 5, 1–74.

Blackburn, I., James, I. A., Milne, D. L., *et al.* (2001). The Revised Cognitive Therapy Scale (CTS-R): Psychometric properties. *Behavioural & Cognitive Psychotherapy*, 29, 431–446.

James, I., Blackburn, I., & Reichelt, F. K. (2001). *Manual of the Revised Cognitive Therapy Scale (CTS-R)*. Unpublished manuscript.

Young, J., & Beck, A. T. (1980). *Cognitive Therapy Rating Scale: Rating manual*. Unpublished manuscript, University of Pennysylvania, Philadelphia, PA.

Young, J, & Beck, A. T. (1988). *Cognitive Therapy Scale*. Unpublished Manuscript, University of Pennysylvania, PA.

Obsessive-compulsive disorder: checklist of therapist skill

The contents of this section are as follows:

Part 1: General therapeutic skills

1. Rationale

2. Agenda setting

3. Dealing with questions

4. Reassurance-seeking

5. Clarity of communication

6. Pacing and efficient use of time

7. Interpersonal effectiveness

Part 2: Conceptualization, strategy, and technique

8. Reviewing previously set homework

9. Use of feedback and summaries

10. Guided discovery

11. Conceptual integration and focus on OCD-related cognitions

12. Normalizing the client's experience

13. Application of appropriate strategies for cognitive change and modifying compulsions

14. Therapeutic focus

15. Integration of exposure into a cognitive framework

16. Homework setting

Part 3: Observations regarding the therapeutic intervention

17. Client complexity

18. Consistency with trial protocol

Part 1: General therapeutic skills

Introduction

This section enables the assessor to reflect on the general therapeutic skills evident in the treatment session. Some of these skills are not specific to CBT for OCD, but are more general skills in either the practice of CBT or therapy from a different theoretical orientation. For example, interpersonal effectiveness, clarity of communication, pacing and effective use of time, and dealing with questions are quite broad skills, of which any therapist would reasonably be expected to demonstrate a basic command.

Rating of this section may not necessarily be done in strict order; indeed, it may be appropriate for the assessor to return to the questions once the entire therapy session has been reviewed as some items rely on an overall impression (e.g. interpersonal effectiveness) or can only be adequately assessed at the end of the session (e.g. pacing and efficient use of time).

1 Rationale

The way in which a rationale is presented can vary according to the stage in therapy. Initially, the therapist would be expected to explain the treatment rationale clearly and thoroughly (i.e. provide an overview of the theoretical model).

Rationale is not necessarily explicit. As treatment progresses, it is likely (and hopeful) that the client will have taken on board the theoretical model. In that case, the rationale may become *implicit*, i.e. it is evident from the content of the dialogue and the kinds of behavioural experiments and homework activities that there is a firm theoretical underpinning to the session which is clearly shared by both client and therapist.

Examples of level 1 rationale might be that the therapist proposes that an exposure-based experiment is carried out 'to prove that the things you worry about don't happen'.

Examples of level 5/6 rationale: the therapist uses Socratic questioning to check the client's understanding, e.g. when devising an appropriate behavioural experiment or homework exercise. Examples would include, 'In what way do you think it would be helpful to do ...' or 'Why do you think it would be better to do [something extreme like deliberately "contaminate" bottles for recycling] when it's not what most people would do?'

Key features: *the format of therapy is clearly explained. Procedures closely follow an explicit theoretical model which is made clear by the therapist and understood by the client.*

0   No rationale given for any procedures used, and no attempt to establish client's understanding of procedures used

1   Rationale attempted, but is wrong, misleading, or poorly delivered. No attempt to establish client's understanding

2   Appropriate rationale is provided, but major difficulties evident (e.g. vague, confusing, or incomplete, poorly delivered). Some attempt to check client's understanding, but explicit feedback not sought and misunderstandings not clearly identified or addressed

3   Appropriate rationale is provided, some difficulties present (e.g. unclear at times, problems in content or style of delivery). Some attempts to check client's understanding and obtain feedback, misunderstandings not fully addressed

4   Appropriate rationale provided, generally clear, well delivered, client's understanding is established, feedback sought, and difficulties or misunderstandings addressed. Minor difficulties evident (e.g. unclear at times, explanations not always complete).

5   Highly appropriate rationale, given clearly and well delivered, client's understanding is checked, feedback sought, and misunderstandings addressed. Minimal problems

6   Excellent rationale given clearly, client's understanding checked, feedback sought, and misunderstandings addressed collaboratively or appropriate

rationale delivered clearly and well, understanding and feedback sought in the face of difficulties.

2 Agenda setting

Introduction

'The agenda ensures that the most important issues are addressed in an efficient manner. Therapist and patient must establish these issues jointly. The agenda should review items from the previous session(s), in particular the homework assignment, and include one or two items for the session. Once set, it should be appropriately adhered to. However, if changes are necessary, because of a new issue arising, the deviation from the agenda should be made explicit.'

(James *et al.*, 2001, page 4)

Agenda setting may be formal or informal. An example of a 'formal' approach to agenda setting may be where the therapist explicitly says, for example, 'Let's begin by setting an agenda for today's session', and then goes on to do so with the assistance of the client. A more informal approach (and equally acceptable) may be when the therapist forestalls the client's eagerness to launch into what is pressing for him or her (perhaps (s)he is too eager to give feedback on homework, or launch into reasons why (s)he's had a bad week, for example), and attempts to contain this by drawing up an agreed outline for the session with the client. The therapist may have to deftly field any topics the client introduces that are not appropriate or helpful to cover in the session (e.g. the client may wish to talk about a recent argument at work which is unrelated to the OCD problem). Without unilaterally vetoing the client, the therapist is likely (in such a scenario) to ask how the client feels that their 'agenda' fits with the overall focus of therapy. Without addressing it directly, the therapist may help reach an acceptable compromise by suggesting that it might be appropriate and timely to look at the way in which emotional upsets (such as that arising from the argument) contribute to the experience of OCD. In this way, both specific current concerns of the client and the overall rationale and goals for therapy are reflected in the agenda.

As with the section on 'Rationale', clients who are more familiar with the format of therapy may automatically 'adhere' to an implied agenda, where the therapist has no need to itemize feedback on developments formally between sessions or even setting of homework. The client would in that case have the expectation that this is the way in which the session will progress—(s)he will automatically give feedback at the beginning of the session, and may even specify what (s)he thinks needs to be covered in the session (with minimal prompting from the therapist, who may simply ask: 'So, what would it be useful to cover today?' and allow the client to take responsibility—a longer term goal in CBT for OCD—for setting an appropriate agenda).

It is also important that any agenda is not too elaborate or lengthy. There should not be so many agenda items that it is unrealistic to expect to cover everything adequately. Where the client has multiple needs, a highly skilled therapist would help the client to identify what would be most fitting to cover in this session, and perhaps either to reserve other topics for a future date or to leave time at the end of the session to review whether or not lower priority issues may have been adequately tackled through targeting key matters arising. In a similar vein, some clients will highlight numerous unrelated matters that they consider of equal importance. It is crucial that the therapist avoids a 'fly-swatting' approach by tackling each issue individually. This can be a particular issue with obsessional clients, who may have a tendency to view not dissimilar problems/occurrences as matters requiring individual attention. In terms of aiding the development of an overall shared understanding of OCD problems it is essential that the therapist does not conclude with this, but encourages the client to consider these seemingly disparate issues under one 'umbrella'. For example, when the client says, 'I know that if I let the thoughts about being contaminated with toxoplasmosis just come and go naturally without trying to fix them at all, or trying to push them out of my head, but it's different when I get images of stabbing my dogs …'

Key features: *to make optimal use of time available in the therapy session, discrete, appropriate, and realistic topics need to be identified for the session. The agenda should be set in a collaborative way, reflecting both specific current issues that the client may have and the overall rationale and goals for therapy.*

0   No agenda set, or highly inappropriate

1   Inappropriate agenda set (e.g. lack of focus, unrealistic, no account of client's presentation, homework not reviewed)

2   An attempt at an agenda made, but major difficulties evident (e.g. unilaterally set). Poor adherence

3   Appropriate agenda, which was set well, but some difficulties evident (e.g. poor collaboration). Some adherence

4   Therapist worked with the client to set a mutually satisfactory agenda that included specific problems in understanding or overcoming OCD. Minor difficulties evident (e.g. no prioritization), but appropriate features covered (e.g. review of homework). Moderate adherence

5   Appropriate agenda set with discrete and prioritized targets, reviewed at the end. Agenda adhered to. Minimal problems

6 Excellent agenda set, which was highly appropriate for available time and stage in therapy, or highly effective agenda set in the face of difficulties.

3 Dealing with questions

Introduction

The therapist should be able to deal appropriately with questions that the client may raise during the sessions whilst being able to maintain appropriate control over the agenda to avoid unscheduled deviations and to prevent using up too much time in the session on non-agenda matters. Some questions are, of course, entirely appropriate. For example, the client may be seeking clarification or feedback on a particular matter. In such cases, dealing with questions is unlikely to pose much of a problem for the therapist: the questions will be dealt with swiftly and deftly as part of an overall uninterrupted therapeutic dialogue. It will be neither time-consuming nor lead to a gross deviation.

However, in OCD, clients' questions can be a particular feature of the presentation of their obsessional difficulties. Constant reassurance-seeking, for example, can mean that the client is continually seeking for the therapist to put their mind at ease about whether, say, (s)he had become contaminated by a bottle of detergent (s)he had spotted on his or her way in to the office. In other cases, questions are driven by a need 'to be sure': 'to be sure' (s)he's understood what therapy entails, 'to be sure' (s)he knows when today's session started or would finish, 'to be sure' the therapist had understood the point (s)he was trying to make. Such a constant barrage of questions undeniably eats into therapy time, can obstruct any agenda that may have been set, lead to unprofitable deviations, and sabotage any attempts to target the obsessional problem in any helpful and meaningful way.

It can be difficult for the therapist to maintain an appropriate level of control with such clients, but this is crucial to being able to conduct satisfactory therapy. There are various methods of dealing with frequent questions. These range from simply answering the question to the adoption of a more collaborative means where the client is encouraged to decide whether the question is a 'genuine' one (i.e. (s)he does not know the answer, and it is relevant to the present discourse) or an 'obsessional' one (i.e. (s)he may have already asked the question, and is trying to make himself or herself feel less anxious or more certain, it does not relate to what is being discussed in the present). With frequent 'such issues', the therapist may propose that questions are kept until the end of the session when time will be made available to address any that have not been adequately dealt with as part of the content of the therapy session (if this is a problem that has previously been encountered with the client, 'question time' should be included on the agenda at the outset).

Key features: *an important aspect of good therapy is to be able to deal with any questions from the client and objections or problems that the client may have with any aspect of the therapy or therapeutic relationship. The therapist should elicit any problems or objections and deal with them sensitively and directly, also obtaining feedback on this in the session. This is similar to, but distinct from, eliciting feedback on the therapy session as a whole.*

0   Therapist fails to acknowledge questions, dismisses them, or makes no attempt to answer them

1   Therapist shows no understanding of questions, and responds inappropriately, inadequately, or too briefly

2   Therapist responds to client's questions, but major difficulties evident (e.g. some misunderstanding, answers may be unclear, client does not understand answer)

3   Therapist is sensitive to questions, generally understands them, and has some success in answering appropriately and clearly; some difficulties evident (e.g. some answers may be incomplete or overly detailed, fails to check client's understanding of/response to the answer)

4   Therapist is sensitive to questions, answers them clearly and appropriately, generally seeks feedback from client. Minimal problems

5   Therapist is sensitive to, and understands questions, answers them appropriately, and seeks feedback from client

6   Therapist is sensitive to, and understands questions, answers them appropriately, and seeks feedback from client. Makes links between questions and conceptualization or broader picture.

4 Reassurance-seeking

Introduction

Reassurance-seeking is frequently encountered in the treatment of OCD. This is particularly prevalent during early sessions (when the client is not familiar with the theoretical understanding of his or her problem), but may persist (or re-emerge) later on—perhaps because (s)he has not fully understood the rationale for treatment and that seeking reassurance is a means of 'neutralizing' obsessional worries.

A full explanation of reassurance-seeking can be found in the introduction to Section 3 on Dealing with Questions.

Key features: *the counterproductive nature of reassurance-seeking is an issue that is well established in the cognitive approach to the treatment of OCD. Therapists*

must be mindful that reassurance can be sought in many subtle ways and when this occurs should be identified and dealt with appropriately in the session.

0   Therapist ignores or shows no understanding of direct or indirect requests for reassurance

1   Therapist responds to requests by providing reassurance when it is inappropriate to do so, or has difficulty in recognizing reassurance-seeking

2   Therapist is generally sensitive to requests for reassurance, and attempts to deal with them appropriately, but some difficulties evident (e.g. gets hooked into a debate regarding the focus of the OCD concern, misses more subtle methods of reassurance-seeking, overly didactic, or vague in their response)

3   Therapist is sensitive to requests for reassurance, tries to deal with them collaboratively, and generally responds effectively. Minor difficulties (e.g. inconsistent, may miss indirect requests)

4   Therapist recognizes direct and indirect requests for reassurance, and responds effectively, enabling client to become more aware of the effect of reassurance-seeking in maintaining the problem

5   Consistent and competent recognition of and response to direct and indirect requests for reassurance, or very good work done in the face of difficulties

6   Excellent recognition of and response to all forms of reassurance-seeking. Facilitates the client to recognize this behaviour and to identify when this is happening without prompting by therapist.

5 Clarity of communication

Introduction

Good therapy demands clarity of communication. This means that the language that the therapist uses should be clear and at a level appropriate to the client's ability. Jargon should be avoided, although it is entirely appropriate to introduce the client to appropriate terminology not in everyday usage with which to talk about his or her problems. For example, 'neutralizing' is not a term commonly understood, but is a useful term for the kinds of things the client does to reduce their anxiety in OCD-relevant situations. However, if the client already has their own term for what (s)he does (e.g. 'fixing' thoughts), it is often better if the therapist continues to use this term rather than introducing what may be considered unnecessary jargon.

In more general terms, therapists should strive to employ vocabulary that the client can easily understand and not use words that the client is unlikely to understand. As a rule of thumb, plain English should be the norm and the therapist should not try to 'impress' by showing off his or her knowledge of difficult or obscure language. However, the therapist also needs to guard against appearing 'patronizing' to clients, who may feel that their intelligence is being insulted if too simple language is used, or the therapist constantly explains things in detail when there is no evidence that such an explanation is required. It is often sensible for the therapist generally to adopt a straight-forward language style that would need few alterations to meet the needs of individual clients.

Clarity of communication does not only apply to the kind of vocabulary used. The therapist should also demonstrate a sound grasp of the treatment approach and be able to present this in a clear, well ordered fashion. At the highest level, the therapist should be able to rephrase easily for the benefit of a client who may not have readily understood the point (s)he had been making rather than simply reiterating their original statement.

The use of analogies and metaphors is encouraged to help elucidate further. However, these should be appropriate to both the point being made and the experience of the client. For example, a metaphor using the concept of home insurance can be useful to illustrate how the cost of the client's rituals may far outweigh the perceived benefits, but may not be fitting for younger clients who are not home owners nor acquainted with the details of insurance policies. Similarly, metaphors about traffic lights can sometimes be lost on non-drivers.

Key features: *an essential aspect of good therapy is clarity of communication. This involves clear use of language at a level that is appropriate to the client's ability, avoiding jargon, and generally presenting information in a style that is clear and easily understood.*

0 Therapist was muddled in his or her presentation of information and over-used jargon, or used language that was highly inappropriate for the client's level of understanding

1 Therapist had difficulty presenting information in straightforward language. Overuse of jargon

2 Therapist generally presented information in a coherent fashion, but was overly technical or found it hard to simplify information to aid client's understanding

3 Therapist was generally clear in communications, but at times struggled to get appropriate points across. Did not use examples to illustrate, or used inappropriate examples

4 Therapist presented information in a clear way. Some minor problems evident (e.g. occasionally lapsed into jargon, used language that the client may struggle to comprehend)

5 Therapist presented information in a clear and well ordered fashion, using language and terminology appropriate to the client. Provided appropriate examples/metaphors. Minimal communication problems

6 Therapist had excellent communication skills, and used language and terminology appropriate to the client. Used many appropriate examples/metaphors, which were highly effective in illustrating specific points.

6 Pacing and efficient use of time
Introduction

'The therapist should make optimal use of the time in accordance with items set in the agenda. He/she must maintain sufficient control, limit discussion of peripheral issues, interrupt unproductive discussion, and pace the session appropriately. Nevertheless, the therapist should avoid rushing the crucial features of the session.'

'The session should be well time managed, such that it is neither too slow nor too quick. For example, the therapist may unwittingly belabour a point after the patient has already grasped the message, or may gather much more data than is necessary before formulating a strategy for change. In these cases, the sessions may seem painfully slow and inefficient. On the other hand, the therapist may switch from topic to topic too rapidly, thus not allowing the patient to integrate the new material sufficiently. The therapist may also intervene before having gathered enough data to conceptualise the problem. In summary, if the therapy is conducted too slowly or too quickly, it may impede therapeutic change and could de-motivate the patient.

The pacing of the material should always be accommodated to the patient's needs and speed of learning. For example, when there is evidence of difficulties (e.g. emotional or cognitive difficulties), more time and attention may need to be given. In such circumstances the agenda items may be shuffled or adapted accordingly. In some extreme circumstances (e.g. disclosure of suicidal thoughts), the structure and pacing of the session will need to change drastically in accordance with the needs of the situation.

The therapy should move through discrete phases. At the start, there should be a structured agenda. Then the agreed plan of the session should be handled efficiently during the main phase.

It is important that the therapist maintains an overview of the session to allow correct pacing throughout. This may involve the therapist politely interrupting peripheral discussion and directing the patient back to the agenda.

A well paced session should not need to exceed the time allocated for the period and should cover the items set in the agreed agenda. It will also allow sufficient time for the homework task to be set appropriately, and not be unduly rushed.'

(James et al. 2001)

Key features: *the session should be well 'time-managed' in relation to the agenda, and to allow smooth progression through start, middle, and concluding phases. Work must be paced to suit the client's needs (e.g. learning speed) and, whilst important issues need to be followed, unproductive digressions should be dealt with smoothly. The session should not go over time without good reason.*

0   Poor time management leads to either an aimless or overly rigid session or therapist made no attempt to manage manifestations of OCD, which enabled the client to dominate the session completely

1   The session is too slow or too fast for the current needs and capacity of the client

2   Reasonable pacing, but digression or repetitions from therapist and/or client lead to inefficient use of time, or therapist unable to manage appropriately the client's obsessional behaviour manifested during the session. Unbalanced allocation of time, or session over-ran without good reason

3   Good pacing evident some of the time with discrete start, middle, and concluding phases, but diffuse at times. Some problems evident (e.g. therapist had some difficulties managing obsessional behaviours, which interfered with efficient use of time)

4   Balanced allocation of time with discrete start, middle, and concluding phases. Minor problems evident (e.g. therapist occasionally lets session become dominated by obsessional behaviours)

5   Good time management skills evident, session runs smoothly. Therapist working effectively in controlling the flow within the session, and for the most part able to limit inappropriate or unproductive discussions. Minimal problems

6 Excellent time management, enabling the agenda to be covered in its entirety, or highly effective management evident in the face of difficulties. Therapist able to limit inappropriate or unproductive discussions, and helps the client to recognize them as a feature of obsessional difficulties.

7 Interpersonal effectiveness

Introduction

'The ability of the therapist to form a good relationship with the patient is deemed crucial to the therapy. Indeed, in order for the patient to be able to disclose difficult material, there must be both trust and confidence in the therapist. Rogers suggests that the non-specific factors of "empathy, genuineness, and warmth" are key features of effective therapy.'

'In order that the appropriate levels of [these] 3 features are conveyed, careful judgment is required from the therapist. Personal and contextual needs must be taken into account. For example, towards the end of therapy lower levels of warmth may be used, as compared to the beginning, in order to promote patient disengagement.

Empathy concerns the therapist's ability to make the patient aware that their difficulties are recognised and understood on both an emotional and cognitive level. The therapist needs to show that he/she shares the patient's feelings imaginatively. For example, the promotion of a shared value system between therapist and patient will help to enhance this aspect of the relationship. The therapist should avoid appearing distant, aloof or critical.'

'A good therapist should adopt a genuine and straight forward therapeutic style. A sincere and open style will promote a trusting, collaborative working relationship. The therapist should avoid appearing condescending or patronising.

It is also important for the therapist to convey warmth and concern through both his/her verbal and non-verbal behaviour. The therapist should avoid being critical, disapproving, impatient or cold. He/she should convey an attitude of acceptance of the person, but not of course with respect to the style of thinking.

It is important to highlight that appropriate use of humour can often help to establish and maintain a good therapeutic relationship.'

(James *et al.*, 2001)

Key features: *the client is put at ease by the therapist's verbal and non-verbal (e.g. listening skills) behaviour. The client should feel that the core conditions (e.g. warmth, genuineness, empathy, and understanding) are present. However, it is important to maintain professional boundaries.*

0 Therapist has poor interpersonal skills. His or her manner and interventions make the client disengage and become distrustful and/or hostile (e.g. the therapist seemed hostile, demeaning, or in some other way destructive towards the client)

1 Therapist had difficulty showing empathy, genuineness, and warmth or had difficulty conveying confidence and competence

2 Therapist's style (e.g. intellectualization) at times impedes his or her empathic understanding of the client's communications *or* therapist displayed little confidence

3 The therapist is able to understand explicit meanings of client's communications, resulting in some trust developing. Some evidence of inconsistencies sustaining the relationship

4 The therapist is able to understand both implicit and explicit meanings of client's communications, and demonstrates it in his or her manner. Minor problems evident (e.g. inconsistent). Displays a satisfactory degree of warmth, concern, confidence, genuineness, and professionalism

5 The therapist demonstrates very good personal effectiveness. Client appears confident that (s)he is being understood, which facilitates self-disclosure. Minimal problems

6 Excellent interpersonal effectiveness, or highly interpersonally effective in the face of difficulties. Therapist displays optimal levels of warmth, genuineness, professionalism, etc. appropriate for this particular client in this session.

Part 2: Conceptualization, strategy, and technique

8 Reviewing previously set homework

Introduction

Since homework is considered an essential part of therapy, it is crucial that its importance is reflected by a thorough review in the therapy session. Besides discovering how successful the client has been with tasks, the therapist also needs to obtain feedback about the client's experience of carrying out the homework, identify any difficulties there have been, and (perhaps most importantly) what the client has learned from the task. Information gained from reviewing the homework should ideally be incorporated into the agenda for that session, to build on the conceptualization in a concrete way (i.e. to test out hypotheses generated by the treatment model). An example of this might be that the client believed that he would be unable to sleep as his mind would be beset by ruminations about how dirty he was if he did not bathe in his usual (obsessional) manner before retiring. The homework task may have required him to go to bed without washing at all. After doing so, the client may report that, although he initially spent time worrying, he eventually fell asleep and slept soundly until morning.

Reviewing questionnaire measures is equally important. Clients often find completing them difficult—perhaps because of the way their OCD interferes with completing the task, or because they stir up feelings they are trying to suppress, or simply because they find them tedious due to the frequency with which they are requested to complete them. It is important that the therapist does not simply accept them and file them away without even a cursory glance. Whilst care should be taken not to allow the entire therapy session to be taken up by a review of measures, it is helpful to the therapeutic process briefly to assess changes that have been detected, particularly in levels of anxiety and depression, which should then be discussed in the light of recent experiences (perhaps adverse life events may account for an increase in depression scores, or a reduction of anxiety may be the result of avoiding situations that trigger OCD symptoms rather than habituation!). Questionnaires that focus on responsibility appraisal provide important information about strength of beliefs, and can help identify the reasons for resistance to changing behaviour. It is important to target these in treatment. Conversely, less eloquent clients may demonstrate significant decreases in compulsive behaviour but be unable to express what has facilitated their behavioural changes. By providing examples of OCD-relevant appraisals, the client is better able to recognize the beliefs under which they are operating.

To summarize, the role of homework assignments is to bring about a cognitive shift. Similarly, the use of questionnaires is to provide a measure of change. Thus the importance of reviewing these activities and incorporating them into the overall format of therapy is essential.

Key features: *homework is an essential part of therapy to test out ideas, develop new understanding, and try new experiences. To ascertain how successful the client has been with the tasks, and what they have learned, it is important to allocate time to review their activities.*

Homework should regularly involve self-directed exposure, which the client should be actively engaged in between sessions. To monitor changes (which can be minimized by clients once they have managed to achieve a particular exposure goal) it is important that these activities are monitored and measured. Similarly, questionnaire responses are clinically important as they can identify belief changes that have resulted from behavioural changes, or to highlight strongly held beliefs that may hinder improvements. Review of questionnaires and other measures/records reinforces the importance of 'homework'.

0   Therapist did not review previous homework, nor look at measures or exposure diary

1   Therapist took a cursory look at previous homework, measures, or diary, but did not comment or commented in an unhelpful manner

2   Therapist reviewed homework/measures/exposure diary, but commented on it in a cursory fashion. Did not attempt to elicit what the client had learned from the experience

3   Therapist reviewed homework/measures/exposure diary, noted any changes and made some attempt to use this information in the session. Some problems evident; for example, review not integrated into main body of agenda or failed to address some of the points identified in the session. Some problems and inconsistencies evident

4   Therapist reviewed previous homework/exposure/measures in detail and had some success in clarifying its outcome or what the client had learned from the task. Minor problems evident; for example, insufficient time allowed for discussion, inconsistent use of Socratic questioning to establish client's learning, but generally competent

5   Therapist skilfully reviewed previous homework/exposure/measures, identified problems, established the outcome of the homework/exposure assignment, and was generally able to work with the client to maximize what could be learned from the assignment. However, little or no attempt was made to integrate any new learning into everyday life. Only minimal problems evident

6   Therapist skilfully reviewed previous homework/exposure/measures, identified any problems, established the outcome of the assignment, worked with the client to maximize what could be learned from the assignment, and identified how any new learning could be integrated into daily life.

9 Use of feedback and summaries

Introduction

The therapist should both provide and elicit feedback throughout the session. The therapist's feedback should occur at regular intervals and is particularly important at the end of the session. The way in which the feedback is given can be brief and concise, perhaps just reflecting back to the client, or rephrasing what has been said in a succinct way. At other times (particularly when there has been a major cognitive shift) feedback should be more detailed, and ideally the client should also be encouraged to make the summary. Feedback helps to focus the client on the main therapeutic issues and assists in reducing vague or amorphous issues into manageable units. It also helps both client and therapist to determine whether they have a shared understanding of the problems and concerns.

Eliciting feedback ensures that the client understands the therapist's interventions, formulations, and lines of reasoning. It also allows the individual to express positive and negative reactions during therapy.

Major summaries should occur at the beginning and end of each session, to help reinforce and consolidate therapeutic material. It is important that the feedback is appropriate. For example, when providing feedback the therapist must choose the salient material presented to him or her, and then summarize these features in a way that both clarifies and highlights key issues. This form of summarizing and feeding back is the foundation for many forms of cognitive techniques (e.g. Socratic questioning). When eliciting feedback, the therapist should be aware that some clients (especially people suffering from depression) often indicate understanding simply out of compliance. Hence, it is important that the therapist explores the client's understanding and attitude towards the therapy carefully.

The manner in which the feedback is elicited and delivered is also important. For example, the therapist should be sensitive to negative and covert reactions expressed both verbally and non-verbally by the client, and should also ask for the client's thoughts when such clues are noticed. Whenever appropriate, the therapist should ask the client either for suggestions about how to proceed, or choose among alternative courses of action.

When giving feedback the therapist should deliver it in a manner that is constructive and helps to move the therapy forward. This will involve anticipation of how the information may be received (e.g. perceived as criticism).

Key features: *the client's and therapist's understanding of key issues should be helped through the use of two-way feedback. The main ways of doing this are through the use of a general summary and chunking important units of information (capsule summaries). The therapist should seek regular feedback from the client to help him or her understand the patient's situation and to ascertain the client's understanding of therapy and so facilitate the client's ability to gain new insights and make therapeutic shifts. It also keeps the client focussed.*

0   Therapist did not ask for feedback to determine the client's understanding at any point during the session, or feedback was highly inappropriate

1 Minimal appropriate feedback (verbal and/or written)

2 Appropriate feedback, but not given frequently enough by therapist, with insufficient attempts to elicit and give feedback (e.g. feedback too vague to provide opportunities for understanding and change)

3 Appropriate feedback given and elicited frequently, although some difficulties evident in terms of content or method of delivery

4 Appropriate feedback/summaries given and elicited during the session, facilitating moderate therapeutic gains. Session summarized at the end. Minor problems evident (e.g. inconsistent or didactic)

5 Highly appropriate feedback given and elicited regularly throughout the session (e.g. at beginning and end of session), facilitating shared understanding and enabling significant therapeutic gains. Time for therapist and client to reflect on sessions. Therapist encourages client to summarize at the end of session. Minimal problems

6 Excellent use of feedback throughout the session (e.g. at beginning and end), or highly effective feedback given and elicited in the face of difficulties. Time for therapist and client to reflect on session.

10 Guided discovery
Introduction

'Guided discovery is a form of presentation and questioning which assists the patient to gain new perspectives for himself/herself without the use of debate or lecturing. It is used throughout the sessions in order to help promote the patient to gain understanding. It is based on the principles of Socratic dialogue, whereby a questioning style is used to promote discovery, to explore concepts, synthesise ideas and develop hypotheses regarding the patient's problems and experiences.

It has been observed that patients are more likely to adopt new perspectives, if they have been able to come to such views and conclusions for themselves. Hence, rather than adopting a debating stance, the therapist should use a questioning style to engage the patient in a problem solving process.

Skilfully phrased questions, which are presented in a clear manner, can help to highlight either links or discrepancies in the patient's thinking. In order to accommodate the new information or learning, new insight is often achieved. Padesky (1993) emphasises that the aim of questioning is not to "change minds" through logic, but to engage the patient in a Socratic dialogue. Within this dialogue the patient can arrive at new perspectives and solutions for themselves.'

(James et al., 2001)

The therapist's questioning technique should reveal a constant flow of inquiry from concrete and specific ('Does your anxiety reduce every time you check the electricity is turned off?') to abstract ('How do you decide when to stop checking?' or 'What would be so bad about not checking?') and back again. Good questions are those asked in the spirit of inquiry, while less helpful ones are those which lead the client to a predetermined conclusion.

Whilst it is a sound basic principle of CBT to avoid leading the client to a predetermined conclusion, there are occasions when this would be appropriate when working with OCD. With their 'rational' (i.e. non-obsessional) minds, clients will generally concur that, for example, they overestimate threat in certain situations. However, when operating under obsessional principles they are unlikely to attend to any alternate views that conflict with, or undermine, their OCD beliefs. To identify the idiosyncrasies of the client's obsessional beliefs, it is often necessary to 'play the dumb therapist' to encourage the client to describe in sufficient details the often surprising links (s)he may make between his or her actions (or inactions) and a feared catastrophe. The therapist can honestly claim that this line of questioning is genuinely in the spirit of enquiry as it is crucial that the therapist should not make assumptions about the links without checking them out with the client.

The techniques may also permit the client to make both lateral and vertical linkages. The lateral links are those of day-to-day features of the client's life that produce and maintain his or her difficulties (i.e. the responsibility appraisals, neutralizing actions, moods, and physical sensations). The vertical links are the historical patterns and cycles, which manifestly relate to the client's current problems (i.e. childhood issues, parenting, relationship difficulties, work issues, etc.).

The questions posed should not be way beyond the patient's current level of understanding, as this is unlikely to promote effective change. Rather they should be phrased within, or just outside, the client's current understanding so that (s)he can make realistic attempts to answer them. The product of attempting to deal with such intelligently phrased question is likely to be new discoveries.

The therapist should appear both inquisitive and sensitive without coming across as patronizing.

(Drawing on James et al., 2001, with alterations to examples to fit an OCD
treatment rationale)

Key features: *the client should be helped to develop hypotheses regarding his or her current situation and to generate potential solutions for himself or herself through guided discovery. To facilitate this, the therapist should maintain an open and inquisitive style and use Socratic questioning to lead the client towards new ways of looking at things.*

0 No attempt at guided discovery (e.g. hectoring or lecturing). Therapist seemed to be 'cross-examining' the client, putting the client on the defensive, or forcing his or her view on the client

1 Therapist relied heavily on persuasion or 'lecturing', with little opportunity for discovery by the client. However, the therapist's style was sufficiently supportive that the client did not feel attacked or defensive

2 Minimal opportunity for discovery. Some use of questioning, but unhelpful in assisting the client to gain access to his or her thought or emotions or to make connections between themes

3 Some reflection evident. Therapist uses primarily a questioning style that is following a productive line of discovery

4 For the most part, the therapist helped the client see new perspectives through the skilled use of questioning (e.g. examining the evidence, considering alternatives) rather than through debate. Minor problems evident; for example, some inconsistency, occasionally lapses into a didactic approach

5 Effective reflection evident. Therapist uses skilful questioning style leading to reflection, discovery, and synthesis. Minimal problems

6 Therapist was adept at using guided discovery during the session to explore OCD-related problems, and help the client draw his or her own conclusions. Achieved a balance between skilful questioning and other modes of intervention. Evidence of a deeper understanding having been developed.

11 Conceptual integration and focus on OCD-related cognitions

Introduction

Conceptualization concerns the provision of an appropriate knowledge base that promotes understanding and facilitates therapeutic change. It encompasses both the cognitive therapy rationale and the cognitive formulation. Through the conceptualization the client will gain an understanding of the cognitive rationale of his or her disorder, its underlying and maintaining features, and relevant triggers. Importantly, the client should also gain an understanding of the relative efficacy of the neutralizing strategies and SSBs currently being used to deal with the problem.

The conceptualization process involves initially socializing the client to the therapeutic rationale and a less threatening explanation of his or her experience. For example, at the beginning of therapy the client may believe that his or her thoughts mean that (s)he is a child molester, a potential murderer, a blasphemer, and so on. Given such beliefs, it is not surprising that (s)he seeks to deal with the situation by fighting these thoughts and neutralizing any consequence of their occurrence in attempts to ensure that (s)he cannot be responsible for any harm or be otherwise blamed. It is therefore necessary that, in the early stages of treatment, the client is helped to see that there may be an alternative explanation of the difficulties (s)he is experiencing. The client is introduced to a idiosyncratically based cognitive model which offers a quite different and less threatening account of the problems. The therapist and client work together to draw a diagram summarizing the formulation agreed, using the specific beliefs and reactions discussed during the session (from Salkovskis *et al.*, 1998). An example of the general format of the conceptualization or formulation can also be found there).

Whilst the formulation (in diagrammatic form) should be devised early on in therapy (usually within the first three sessions), throughout treatment the two possible explanations for the client's problems are considered alongside each other, and the details of the formulation are used to guide and 'drive' the therapeutic process. It is often necessary to review the formulation from time to time to ascertain whether it can explain other OCD symptoms with which the client presents (i.e. whether the formulation is able to provide a more general model of OCD concerns).

Thus, the conceptualization should provide a thread to link all therapy sessions. As well as identifying maintaining features to the problem (the 'here and now') as a vicious circle (or more likely, a cluster of vicious circles), it should also incorporate broader influences upon the development of the problem (such as historical factors, underlying core beliefs, etc.). Following the formulation, the client must acquire the knowledge of what needs to be changed and the most appropriate change mechanisms (e.g. the importance of exposure to situations that trigger OCD concerns, the role of neutralizing in the maintenance of obsessional beliefs, etc.). The appropriately constructed formulation should be able to explain most of the features of the client's difficulties (historical and present) and, as a shared 'frame of reference' with the therapist, then leads on to choice of treatment techniques that help inform potential change mechanisms.

Conceptualization is one of the key processes of therapy through which change takes place. It provides the theoretical overview of the work. Its absence can lead to disjointed therapy, which might prevent major insight being gained by the patient. When it is not appropriately integrated within therapy, the work may lose its focus and only consist of a set of unrelated techniques.

It is of note when scoring this item that the conceptualization per se (i.e. the actual diagram) is not necessarily used in each session, but the focus of the intervention should reflect the model (both implicitly and explicitly) through the topics of discussion and change techniques used.

Key features: *a comprehensive conceptualization of the presenting problem is crucial to the effective treatment of OCD as it underpins the focus of the intervention. The therapist should help the client to gain an understanding of how his or her perceptions and interpretations, beliefs, attitudes, and rules relate to the current problems, the historical factors that may be responsible for their development, and current maintaining factors.*

0   The absence of an appropriate conceptualization

1   Lack of an appropriate OCD conceptualization which leads to aimless application of procedures

2   Evidence of a rudimentary conceptualization, but does not lead to a clear rationale for interventions. Therapist failed to elicit or discuss meanings attached to the occurrence of intrusive thoughts, images, or urges

3   Conceptualization partially developed with some integration with goals of therapy. Therapist discussed in general terms the role of meanings attached to the occurrence of OCD phenomena and/or the role of responsibility appraisals. However, the therapist failed to focus on the client's specific appraisals. Some difficulties evident, although sufficient foundation for a coherent intervention

4   Conceptualization is moderately developed and integrated within therapy. Therapist elicited and discussed idiosyncratic meanings attached to the client's OCD phenomena and was able to link these to the model

5   Well developed conceptualization. Therapist generally able to utilize it effectively in the session, and share it with the client in a useful way. Minor problems evident (e.g. some difficulties generalizing the model to explain other obsessional concerns)

6   Excellent development and integration evident. Therapist skilfully elicited and discussed relevant meanings and appraisals specific to OCD, established their role in the maintenance of the problem, and linked them to the cognitive model of OCD. Highly effective in the face of difficulties.

12 **Normalizing the client's experience**

Introduction

As an essential component of providing an alternative, less threatening explanation of the client's experience, it is important that the therapist emphasizes that obsessional thoughts are not an abnormal phenomenon per se. Many clients consider the obsessional thoughts to be so strange that they fear that they amount to insanity, or worry that the frequency of their occurrence means that they are in danger of losing control.

One of the major goals of therapy is to help the client to recognize that intrusive thoughts are likely to occur, but that the problem lies with the way in which (s)he interprets the occurrence and content of the thoughts that is in fact the problem.

The therapist should take every opportunity to provide normalizing information during therapy. In the early stages of treatment in particular it can be helpful to use examples to illustrate. 'Normalizing' can simply take the form of a Socratic question, such as: 'What kind of person would be most likely to be worried by thoughts about the devil?' It can also be helpful to illustrate the way that a non-clinical population often behaves is in a manner that is similar to that of those with OCD. An example of this is the way in which most people (including mental health professionals) are reluctant to write down 'I wish that ____ would die horribly in an accident', completing the blank with the name of a loved one (and those who do frequently score out what they have written, or tear up the paper).

Key features: *normalizing the client's experience of his or her problems is an essential aspect of reaching a shared understanding and facilitating change. It helps to reduce clients' anxiety about what is happening (e.g. that they are not 'going mad') and engenders a positive attitude towards overcoming their problems. Whilst it may be done as a discrete topic addressed in therapy, the accomplished therapist successfully interweaves normalizing as a thread that runs throughout therapy.*

0 Therapist makes no attempt to normalize the client's experience, or uses a biological/pathological explanation (e.g. brain 'hiccups')

1 Therapist makes some rudimentary attempts to normalize the client's experience, but uses highly inappropriate examples (e.g. leans towards a biological/pathological explanation). Major problems evident

2 Therapist exhibits some competence at normalizing, but numerous problems and lack of consistency (e.g. applied as a technique, weak examples, etc.)

3 Competent use of normalizing, uses some good examples, but applied as a technique

4 Good features. Some indication that normalizing is an emerging thread in therapy, but minor problems and inconsistencies (e.g. misses opportunities to normalize recent experiences described by the client)

5 Therapist uses normalizing skilfully, often using opportunities arising during the session to do so. Minimal problems

6 The therapist appropriately emphasizes the way in which obsessional concerns are an exaggeration of the client's normal concerns, reactions to ideas they find unacceptable, etc. and this is interwoven with therapy. Facilitates the patient to use a normalizing explanation.

13 Application of appropriate strategies for cognitive change and modifying compulsions
Introduction
Change methodologies are cognitive and behavioural strategies employed by the therapist that are consistent with the cognitive rationale and/or formulation and designed to promote therapeutic change. The potency of the techniques will depend upon whether they are applied at the appropriate stage in therapy and the degree to which they are implemented skilfully. It is important to note that during some sessions it may not be appropriate to use a wide range of methods; a rater should take this into account when scoring this item.

The therapist skilfully uses, and helps the client to use, appropriate cognitive and behavioural techniques in line with the formulation. The therapist helps the client to devise appropriate cognitive methods to evaluate the key cognitions associated with distressing emotions, leading to major new perspectives and shifts in emotions. The therapist also helps the client to apply behavioural techniques in line with the formulation. The therapist helps the client to identify potential difficulties and think through the cognitive rationales for performing the tasks. Whilst the methods provide useful ways for the client to test out beliefs practically and gain experience in dealing with high levels of emotion in the treatment of OCD, the fundamental mechanism of change would be for the client to establish (through a combination of discussion techniques and behavioural experiments) that the formulation does indeed provide an accurate maintenance model of the difficulties. The methods used allow the therapist to obtain feedback regarding the client's level of understanding of prospective practical assignments (i.e. by the client performing the task in-session). During earlier stages, the therapist is also likely to 'model' some tasks (e.g. touching the sole of their shoe before eating a sandwich).

Three features need to be considered:

1. The appropriateness and range of both cognitive methods (e.g. cognitive change diaries, continua, responsibility pie charts, evaluating alternatives, examining pros and cons, determining meanings, imagery restructuring, etc.) and behavioural methods (e.g. behavioural diaries, behavioural tests, role play, graded task assignments, response prevention, reinforcement of patient's work, modelling, etc.).

2. The skill in the application of these methods; however, skills such as feedback, interpersonal effectiveness, etc., should be rated separately under their appropriate items.

3. The suitability of the methods for the needs of the client (i.e. not too difficult or complex).

In deciding the appropriateness of a method it is important to determine whether the technique is a coherent strategy for change, following logically from the formulation.

Clinical judgement is required in assessing the degree of skill with which a particular methodology is applied. This feature goes beyond mere adherence (i.e. the preciseness with which a technique is applied). Indeed, the rater should be concerned with the manner of the application, i.e. the therapist must be articulate, comprehensible, sensitive, and systematic when discussing and implementing the technique. The therapist should also be creative and resourceful in his or her selection of methods. (S)he should be able to draw upon a wide range of suitable cognitive and behavioural methodologies.

It is important to remember that the same technique can have a different function depending on the stage of therapy. For example, a diary can act as an assessment tool early on in therapy, but later may serve as an effective way of promoting the re-evaluation of thought processes or changes in the amounts of rituals carried out in a day. The timing of the intervention is vital and must be suited to the needs of the client. For example, if a therapist challenges basic assumptions or core beliefs too early in therapy, before (s)he has a clear understanding of the client's view of the world, (s)he could feel misunderstood and alienated. Only after sufficient socialization should the therapist ask the client to start to reassess that level of cognition. The evaluation of automatic thoughts and responsibility appraisals starts earlier, first as part of the socialization into the cognitive mode, and then as a change method to improve on mood and improve on coping behaviour.

As with the application of cognitive techniques, the therapist must display skill in applying behavioural methodologies. The rationale for employing the tasks should be carefully explored, and clear learning goals established. It is important to remember that behavioural tasks play a key role with respect to reinforcement of new learning. For example, by engaging a client in a role-play, one can assess whether the theoretical information has been truly learned and integrated into his or her behavioural repertoire. The role-play will also allow the person to practise new skills. Behavioural tasks are also useful methodologies to employ prior to asking the client to use the activity in a homework task. Initially, the therapist would model the required behaviour and then observe the client. However, the client is encouraged to take increasing responsibility for the task (to avoid either deliberate or inadvertent reassurance). Eventually, the client is expected to assign their own behavioural tasks without discussion with the therapist (to assume complete responsibility for his or her actions). Again, it is important that behavioural methodologies are timely. For example, encouraging response prevention before the client has understood the formulation is likely to lead to failure, which may compromise further attempts at response prevention.

In addition, the therapist needs to elicit and develop practical plans with the client so that effective change takes place (e.g. the where, what, when, and how of an exposure programme). Indeed, part of the process of producing effective behavioural change is the development of plans that will help test out hypotheses and break unhelpful patterns of behaviour. In planning the task, relevant questions should be asked of the person's concepts, cognitions, affective and physiological states, and behavioural repertoire.

13 APPLICATION OF APPROPRIATE STRATEGIES FOR COGNITIVE CHANGE AND MODIFYING COMPULSIONS

Introduction

Change methods are cognitive and behavioural strategies employed by the therapist which are consistent with the cognitive rationale and/or formulation and designed to promote therapeutic change. The potency of the techniques may depend on whether they are applied at the appropriate stage in therapy, and the skill with which they are applied, although sometimes change with OCD patients is slower and the fruits of particular techniques may not be immediately apparent but contribute to more gradual change over time. The rater should bear this in mind when rating the item as it is the skill with which a technique is applied rather than how *effective* it appears to have been at the time (the rater may wish to consider whether the technique seems timely and logical, and is likely to facilitate a change in the way the client appraises his or her situation). It is important to note that, during some sessions, it may not be appropriate to use a wide range of methods; the rater should take this into account when scoring this item.

In deciding the appropriateness of a method it is important to determine whether the technique is a coherent strategy for change, following logically from the client's formulation and the content of the discussion. The indiscriminate use of a range of techniques is not considered a demonstration of advanced skill.

Key features: *a range of techniques can be used to promote cognitive change. These include identifying alternative explanations for OCD (e.g. is the problem contamination or worry about contamination?), reviewing evidence for misinterpretations, pie charts, probability step analysis, designing behavioural experiments, etc. Note: the focus is on the quality of the therapist's strategy, not on how effective the strategy was.*

0 Therapist fails to use or misuses techniques for cognitive change or modifying neutralizing behaviours

1 Therapist applies either insufficient or inappropriate methods, or attempts to challenge intrusive thoughts rather than their meaning. Limited skill or flexibility evident

2 Therapist selected appropriate techniques for cognitive change and/or modifying neutralizing behaviours. However, major difficulties evident (e.g. techniques did not seem promising for the client, therapist had limited repertoire of techniques and/or had difficulties moving between them)

3 Therapist applies a number of methods in competent ways, although some problems evident (e.g. interventions are incomplete)

4 Therapist applies a range of methods with skill and flexibility, enabling the client to develop new perspectives. Minor problems evident

5 Therapist systematically applies an appropriate range of methods in a creative, resourceful, and effective manner. Minimal problems

6 Excellent range and application, or successful application in the face of difficulties. Therapist followed a coherent, consistent therapeutic strategy, incorporating the most appropriate techniques for cognitive change and modifying neutralizing behaviours.

14 Therapeutic focus

Introduction

Therapeutic goals should be discussed and agreed at the outset of therapy. They should be discreet, readily achievable, and concrete objectives that the client and therapist have collaboratively agreed. Ideally, they should be divided into short-, medium-, and long-term aims.

The focus of the therapy should thus be directed towards achieving those goals, which should be consistent with the formulation. However, it is important that the therapist does not become so 'goal-driven' that the sessions become so task-orientated that there is insufficient flexibility to encompass important issues raised during the session. The therapist should be generally adept at picking up on other issues arising and making links with the presenting problem. This is particularly salient with the client who introduces a problem which (s)he views as 'different' to the presenting obsessional concern. An example of this may be the person who worries a lot about contamination and has extensive rituals to prevent accidental poisoning of his or her family, who then complains that 'another problem' has occurred that is quite different, and that they keep having intrusive thoughts about deliberately pushing people into a busy road. In such cases, it is important that the therapist does not become sidetracked by this but is able to help the client fit this new experience into his or her existing formulation to generalize understanding of the way in which obsessional problems work.

The interpersonal style of the client can mean that (s)he is not very focussed and has a tendency to try to talk about a range of subjects which bear no relevance to therapy (from discussing the weather and the queue at the bus stop to asking the therapist about his or her family, or seeking information about other problems that the therapist is not qualified to comment on such, as health or financial concerns). The therapist should be mindful of this tendency, and be able tactfully to bring the client back to the appropriate therapeutic focus (for which a firm agenda is extremely useful). However, the skilful therapist should be able to elicit whether the digression is likely to lead to information relevant to therapy and be able to guide the client towards the point (s)he is attempting to make.

On occasions, it is appropriate to put aside therapeutic focus. This is likely when a client arrives at the session in a greatly distressed state, maybe as a result of a recent incident or life event. Whilst responding sensitively and constructively to the presenting crisis, the highly skilled therapist should be able to make appropriate reference to the OCD problem (e.g. examining the effect of recent events to the person's OCD).

From time to time, 'golden moments' may occur in treatment. Perhaps a client who has struggled with the conceptualization or has been sceptical about the approach has had an experience that has changed his or her view. It is equally important in such situations that the therapist can be flexible in focus to enable him or her to work effectively with the material elicited, and to capitalize on the momentum these golden moments can engender.

Key features: *therapy maintains an appropriate level of focus on short, medium, and longer term goals. However, there is sufficient flexibility to encompass* *important issues raised during the session (e.g. therapist capitalizes on 'golden moments'). Such flexibility maintains consistency with overall goals.*

0   No focus. The therapist follows anything raised by the client, or completely ignores issues raised by him or her

1   Very little focus evident. The therapist is frequently sidetracked by clearly irrelevant digressions, and is ineffective at averting them

2   Therapist remains reasonably focussed during the session, but some problems or inconsistencies (e.g. easily sidetracked or struggles to allow appropriate attention to other issues that may arise that are outside the presenting problem)

3   Generally appropriate therapeutic focus. Some difficulties present; for example, spending too long on some agenda items, getting sidetracked by minor issues, misses some opportunities to pick up on other issues (i.e. inflexible)

4   Maintains a clear focus. Generally adept at picking up on other issues arising and making links with the presenting problem. Minor problems evident; for example, occasional difficulties at averting unproductive or irrelevant diversions. *Or* sufficient flexibility to put aside goal-orientated intervention when clinically indicated (e.g. following a bereavement), but makes insufficient links with overall goals

5   Maintains a clear focus. Skilfully picks up on other issues arising and is able to utilize them in a useful and productive manner. Identifies unproductive diversions with clear reference to goals. *Or* flexibility to put aside goal-orientated intervention when clinically indicated (e.g. following a bereavement) whilst maintaining consistency with overall goals (e.g. examining the effect this may have on the OCD)

6   Adeptly integrates issues raised during the session and negotiates a revised agenda with client. Identifies 'golden moments' and works effectively with material elicited in the session.

15 Integration of exposure into a cognitive framework
Introduction

Salkovskis (1996) suggested that interactions between cognitive and behavioural elements are involved in the maintenance of all anxiety problems, and discussed the close coordination of both cognitive and behavioural techniques. Thus behavioural experiments are an essential component of therapy for OCD. In OCD, behavioural experiments generally involve the behavioural principle of 'exposure', with the added emphasis of testing a hypothesis. However, caution should be exercised regarding the focus of the behavioural experiment. Where a client has concerns regarding contamination with HIV, the focus of the exposure is not the virus per se, but to toilet door handles, for instance, since avoidance of such a situation is one of the key components fuelling the concern. The therapist is not attempting to disprove the likelihood of contracting HIV but is reinforcing the alternative (psychological) view of the person's presenting problem as one of worry. Thus, behavioural experiments directly test appraisals, assumptions, and processes hypothesized to be involved in the patient's obsessional problems (e.g. demonstrating that attempts to suppress a thought lead to an increase in the frequency with which it occurs) (Salkovskis *et al.*, 1998).

Considering exposure in the context of behavioural experiments may therefore involve a range of strategies, including the following categories:

1. To assess the extent to which a particular process may be maintaining the client's concerns (e.g. checking the door repeatedly makes them feel *more* rather than less worried about security).

2. To elicit worrisome thoughts and underlying appraisals where avoidance is prominent (i.e. the client is unable to say why (s)he feels so driven to wash his or her hands 20 times because (s)he does so automatically without allowing the feared consequence of not doing so to enter his or her mind).

3. In typical behavioural fashion, to discover that anxiety levels eventually decrease when no neutralizing action is performed (i.e. habituation occurs). However, this is not the sole message that should be derived from the exposure task. It should be couched within a cognitive-behavioural framework, with the therapist asking questions such as, 'What have you learned from that?' rather than the more didactic, 'Your anxiety will reduce if you resist carrying out neutralizing rituals'.

Exposure or behavioural experiments should be relevant to the content of the session. For the most part, they should be devised collaboratively based on the conceptualization and the client's understanding of what appears to be maintaining his or her problem. In the initial stages of therapy, the client is likely to require more guidance on appropriate tasks. This can still be done in a way that actively engages the client in the task, perhaps by asking questions such as, 'How could you find out why you feel so afraid of touching the toilet seat?' in situations where rituals are used to prevent direct exposure. Even when the client is reluctant to make suggestions, the therapist needs to guard against being prescriptive, although it is permissible to make suggestions for the client to consider in a Socratic manner. Above all, the exposure task should be relevant to the content of the session and must have a clear rationale which is understood by the client.

As therapy progresses it is beneficial for the client to take increasing responsibility for devising his or her own exposure task. The ultimate goal would be for the client to carry out a suitable experiment of his or her own design without discussing it with the therapist beforehand. When reporting back in the following session, (s)he should do so in broad terms about how successful (s)he thought it had been and what (s)he had learned, but without divulging the actual activity, as this could be a way of subtly obtaining reassurance from the therapist (more details about reassurance-seeking are described in Section 4 of this Appendix).

Key features: *exposure is an important part in CBT for OCD. The key difference between exposure in CBT and behaviour therapy is the way in which it is set up as a behavioural experiment. Such behavioural experiments should be derived collaboratively with the client, rather than prescriptively, and have a specific hypothesis which the experiment is devised to test.*

0   Therapist fails to use exposure either in the session or as homework task

1   Therapist utilizes exposure, but in a prescriptive fashion. Rationale given was behavioural (e.g. habituation) or no rationale given

2   Therapist attempts to set up exposure task as a behavioural experiment, but numerous problems evident; for example, hypotheses unclear, no rationale given, task not arrived at collaboratively

3   Competent application of exposure as a behavioural experiment. Reasonable hypotheses. Some problems; for example, minimal collaboration, not clearly linked to session

4   Competent application of exposure as a behavioural experiment, arrived at collaboratively. Clear hypotheses. Obtains feedback to ascertain client's understanding of the task. The therapist 'got out of his/her chair', and modelled first in experiments/exposure task, where appropriate. Minor problems/inconsistencies

5   Very competent application of exposure as a behavioural experiment. Relevant to the content of the session. Therapist elicited feedback to ascertain client's understanding of the task and identified and discussed potential obstacles to the client's success with the task. Minimal problems

6   Excellent application of exposure. Client understands and can apply the cognitive model, and is able to set up his or her own behavioural experiments, or very good application in the face of difficulties.

16. **Homework setting**

Introduction

Progress is more likely to occur when clients are able to apply the concepts learned in the therapy sessions to their lives outside; homework assignments are the bridges between therapy and the real world. Homework helps transfer within-session learning to real-life settings. To facilitate the transfer, the homework material is usually based upon material discussed in the session (adapted from James *et al.*, 2001).

In Section 15 of this Appendix, the integration of exposure into a cognitive framework has been outlined. Whilst it is de facto a major component of the homework, homework may incorporate a range of other activities relevant to the content of the session. For example, the person may be asked to keep a daily diary where (s)he records situations in which obsessional concerns are triggered, appraisals of the concerns, and then a balanced view (i.e. modification of responsibility appraisals) or some reading may be suggested to further the person's understanding of some aspect of the problem.

Homework may involve discrete activities, or may involve some broader changes. For example, where OCD has become the main focus of the person's life, to the exclusion of all other activities, it is important to fill the vacuum that reducing (or eliminating) rituals would leave. To this end, homework may involve finding out about evening classes or applying for a part-time job, or a similar activity that is geared towards medium- and long-term goals.

Comments about the need for a collaborative approach in homework setting, and a task consistent with the conceptualization apply in the same way as for Section 15.

Key features: *homework tasks should be appropriate for the stage of therapy, consistent with the conceptualization, and have precise and clear goals. Later on in therapy, it is appropriate to encourage clients to take responsibility for setting their own homework. Homework should always be reviewed at the next session.*

0   Therapist fails to set homework, or sets inappropriate homework

1   Therapist did not negotiate homework. Insufficient time allotted for adequate explanation, leading to ineffectual task being set

2   Therapist negotiates homework unilaterally and in a routine fashion, without explaining the rationale for new homework

3   Therapist has set an appropriate new homework task, but some problems evident (e.g. not explained sufficiently and/or not developed jointly)

4 Appropriate new homework jointly negotiated with clear goals and rationales. However, minor problems evident

5 Appropriate homework negotiated jointly and explained well, including an exploration of potential obstacles. Minimal problems

6 Excellent homework negotiated, or highly appropriate one negotiated in the face of difficulties.

Part 3: Observations regarding the therapeutic intervention

17. Client complexity

Introduction

Whilst the initial assessment carried out prior to accepting the client for treatment will have detailed information about complexity and comorbidity, on the rating scale the rater is asked to assess how complex (s)he judges the person to be on the basis of his or her subjective judgement of the session being rated. Whilst comorbidity is not always apparent in the session, what is more important is the way in which the client presents on a specific occasion. For example, interpersonal style may vary from one session to the next, and a client who is often compliant may on occasions become quite obstructive, or a recent life event can change the complexity of the case. These factors can affect scores obtained on previous items, and this item is intended to give an indication of whether this is likely.

Key feature: *the nature of the presenting problem is not necessarily the defining feature in terms of client complexity, but involves factors such as interpersonal style, level of comprehension, 'psychological mindedness', etc.*

0 Client is straightforward in terms of diagnosis and presentation

1 Client meets diagnosis for more than one disorder, but is relatively straightforward

2 Client meets diagnosis for one or more disorders, and presents some difficulties (e.g. adverse life circumstances, irregular attendance, some non-compliance either within or between sessions, has difficulty understanding concepts, etc.)

3 Client is often difficult to work with; for example, uncommunicative, highly distractable, or chaotic in presentation, manifestation of OCD during session makes adherence to agenda difficult, etc.

4   Client is invariably difficult to work with; for example, constantly attempts to dominate the session, refuses to work collaboratively, consistently dismisses therapist's attempts at a coherent intervention.

18. Consistency with trial protocol
Introduction

This item is optional and is included because the scale was developed as a method of measuring adherence in treatment trials using CBT for OCD.

Key feature: *particular criteria need to be met for the standard of therapy to meet the requirements of treatment trials. The rating is not a question of 'Is this a good therapist?' or whether the intervention was good or effective, but whether the method and standard of delivery is consistent with the stringent requirements of a treatment trial. As such, it is important to strive for homogeneity amongst trial therapists.*

No	For the most part, the therapist works outside the remit of the trial protocol
Sub-threshold	Generally consistent with trial protocol, but some problems and/or inconsistencies
Yes	Style and content is consistent with trial protocol

© Elizabeth Forrester, IOP OCD Group, 2004.

References

Padesky, Christine A. (1993). Socratic questioning: Changing minds or guiding discovery. A keynote address delivered at the European Congress of Behavioural and Cognitive Therapies, London. Vol. 24.

Rogers, Carl. (2012). Client Centred Therapy (New Ed). Hachette, UK.

Salkovskis, Paul M., (ed.). (1996). Frontiers of cognitive therapy. Guilford Press.

Salkovskis, Paul M. (1998). Psychological approaches to the understanding of obsessional problems. Obsessive-compulsive disorder: Theory, research, and treatment, 33–50.

Index

Printed and bound by CPI Group (UK) Ltd, Croydon, CR0 4YY